## Praise for *The Scent of God*

"*The Scent of God* is a terrifying, passionate, and exalted examination of what it means to love with your whole heart. The facts of Beryl Bissell's life make this book impossible to put down. The extraordinary beauty of her writing made me wish this book would never end."

—Ann Patchett, author of *Bel Canto, The Magician's Assistant* and *Truth and Beauty*

"Vivid detail and skillful dialogue. . . . The strength of Ms. Bissell's memoir lies in the unflinching examination of her motives for entering and leaving religious life. . . . A compelling and soulful read."

—*National Catholic Reporter*

"Bissell seems to find inner joy even during life's most difficult trials, and she writes about spiritual matters with a marvelous clarity of vision." —*The Washington Post Book World*

"It is rare to read a memoir that isn't at least occasionally self-aggrandizing and narcissistic, but this one is never so. Instead, Bissell's humility and blatant honesty are refreshing, invigorating, and inspirational." —*Library Journal*

"*The Scent of God* is one of the most beautiful books I've ever read. With language so crisp and vivid you feel like you're walking beside her, Bissell tells the story of her movement into the convent and out again. Her writing is pure poetry, and poetry is probably the only way to convey the tension between her commitments to God and to her human family. Reading this story, you come to realize that the book

itself is about faith, about trusting in what we can't possibly understand, surrendering to what life gives us and recognizing that even
the most unbearable moments are gifts. Here, in Bissell's writing,
you find God's grace swirling around inside every contradiction."

—SHERI REYNOLDS, author of *Rapture of Canaan*
and *A Gracious Plenty*

"Bissell writes lyrically and frankly." —*St. Paul Pioneer Press*

"An ode to passion both spiritual and sensual. Meticulously re-
searched and skillfully written, it is the story of a woman who twice
gave up everything for love—first for God, then for a man."

—*The Star Tribune*

"Beryl Bissell's memoir is breathtakingly passionate, painful and ex-
hilarating. A mature and gifted writer answers the question most of
us don't dare to ask: Did I live the right life?"

—SANDRA SCOFIELD, author of *Occasions of Sin*

"A deeply moving tale of a woman torn between her love for God and
her love for one of his emissaries." —*Publishers Weekly*

"Accounts of genuine spiritual anguish and unspeakable loss."

—*Kirkus Reviews*

# The Scent of God

A Memoir

✖

## Beryl Singleton Bissell

COUNTERPOINT
A MEMBER OF THE PERSEUS BOOKS GROUP
NEW YORK

Copyright © 2006 by Beryl Singleton Bissell

Hardcover published in 2006 by Counterpoint
A Member of the Perseus Books Group
Paperback published in 2007 by Counterpoint

Counterpoint books are available at special discounts for bulk
purchases in the United States by corporations, institutions, and other
organizations. For more information, please contact the Special Markets
Department at the Perseus Books Group, 11 Cambridge Center,
Cambridge, MA 02142, or call (617) 252-5298 or (800) 255-1514,
or e-mail special.markets@perseusbooks.com.

Designed by Trish Wilkinson
Set in Fairfield Light

A CIP catalog record for this book is
available from the Library of Congress.
HC: ISBN-13 978-1-58243-348-6; ISBN 1-58243-348-8
PBK: ISBN-13 978-1-58243-361-5; ISBN 1-58243-361-5

10 9 8 7 6 5 4 3 2 1

*Dedicated to my son,*
*Tomás Ferdinand Bosca,*
*and in memory of*
*Vittorio Bosca Pelle and Francesca Maria Vittoria Bosca*
*You are always in my heart*

# Contents

## Dawn

## Midday

# *Dusk*

# Dawn

# Matins

"*Benedicamus Domino.*" The call moves from one cell to the next, the sacristan knocking softly on each door, reminding the sleeping nuns that it is time to rise. It is 11:45 P.M.

"*Deo gratias,*" you whisper in reply. You rise quickly and move through the dimly lighted corridors toward the choir, where the sanctuary light dances in ruby brilliance through the darkness to await the beginning of Matins, or Vigils, as it is also called: the hour of the night watch. Watch and pray, Jesus admonished his followers, and from the earliest ages Mother Church has taken his words literally, gathering her children like the virgins in the parable, to wait for the coming of the bridegroom.

Rising for prayer in the darkness of the night reveals the essence of monastic life: the penitence that casts off sleep, the praise that soars toward God. Your role as a cloistered nun is thus defined: you are set apart to render unceasing thanks to the Creator, to become the voice of the Church while the rest of the world sleeps. Your entire life reflects the mystery that is the Church, the body where each member fulfills a specific role; yours is to remain open to the moment, to listen for the still soft voice of the divine, to become a light shining in the darkness.

You prostrate yourself in reverence before the altar and move toward your stall, where you lift your breviary, the book containing the prayers of liturgical worship known as the Divine Office, and kiss it, as ritual demands. As the sacristan lights the candles on the altar, you prepare the pages of the three nocturns of Matins, so that you'll be ready when their opening versicle is intoned: *"Domine, labia mea aperies"*—O Lord, open my lips—to which you respond, *"Et os meum annuntiabit laudem tuam."* And my mouth shall proclaim your praise.

A bird soaring into flight, the exultant opening of Psalm 94, *"Venite, exsultémus Domino,"* rises into the darkness. Come let us praise the Lord with joy!

# 1

## God in 1947

God didn't often visit our house, but when he did, he was most likely to come on a Friday.

"Mom," God would say, speaking through my brother Stephen, "did you forget that it's Friday. It's a mortal sin to eat meat on Friday."

My mother didn't need God, or Steve, for that matter, to remind her that she had forgotten it was Friday. "Of course I forgot it was Friday. Do you think I fixed this meal so you could sin by eating it?" she asked.

We repeated this conversation several times a year, perhaps even several times a month. Mom's usual response was to bring up the starving children in Europe who would certainly not be fussing about meat on Friday. She'd remind us that she knew more about hunger than we ever would, having spent her childhood starving in London during World War I.

"All we had to eat was suet pudding," she said, pointing to our bowls brimming with stew. "The Salvation Army fed us. God knows, it's a greater sin to waste food than it is to eat meat on Friday."

I wanted to believe my mother, but at Sunday school Sister Mary Alice told us that eating meat on Friday was a mortal sin, and she was a nun. Probably even a saint. Besides, we knew the meat wouldn't be wasted if we didn't eat it. Mom could put it in the refrigerator, as she did with other leftovers. We didn't remind her of this, though, because there was always the possibility that instead of fixing the small red potatoes mashed with pot cheese and sour cream that she sometimes served on Fridays, she'd open a can of the fish cakes that we hated. A whole case of them lurked in the basement pantry, waiting for just such an opportunity to intrude into a Friday meal. Frying those fish cakes and smothering them with catsup did little to make them palatable.

We had boxes of food in our basement, samples sent by businessmen seeking loans from my father's bank: pimiento-stuffed olives on little plastic trees, cashew butter, sardines packed in oil. Even the slimy canned chicken à la king tasted better than those fish cakes. As I bent over my plate, secretly glad to be eating stew, I added this meal to the growing list of mortal sins I'd lugged around ever since Sister Mary Alice first introduced me to them. Mortal sins were much worse than venial sins such as lying about doing my chores or pinching my younger sister, Judi. Mortal sins could send me to hell.

My list of mortal sins also contained several Sundays of missed Masses. Sunday was the day when dress parades were held at Kings Point, New York, where my oldest brother Greg was attending the U.S. Merchant Marine Academy. On dress-parade Sundays we'd leave the house early, not to go to Mass but to have time to eat dinner at the Kings Arms, a fancy restaurant near the academy, where waiters in black suits and bow ties served us roast beef and French-cut green beans before we went to the parade grounds.

"But what about Mass?" Steve would ask.

"God will understand," my father answered. "Family takes precedence in such matters."

My father's voice sounded unusually jolly when he said this, as if by sounding jolly he could charm God by saying to him: "Surely, when it comes to family, you are bound to understand." Even though

I thought my father sounded convincing, I wasn't sure how God felt. Just in case my father was wrong about this family precedence thing, I added missing Mass to my growing list of mortal sins.

God visited us in other ways as well. One day he sent word through Sister Mary Alice, who taught my catechism class, asking why I wasn't going to Sunday school. Sister didn't ask me herself—she couldn't because I wasn't there. Instead she sent Sue Brown, who was in first grade with me at Airmont Elementary. Sue never missed Sunday school.

I was in the bathroom when she found me. "Sister Mary Alice wants to know when you are coming back," she said.

I pretended not to hear her and shut the stall door behind me.

"Beryl? Sister wants to knoooooow." Sue's voice followed me inside.

I fussed with the toilet paper, covering the seat as my mother taught me to do in public bathrooms.

"Beryl-l-l-l."

I clasped my feet around the toilet bowl, hoping Sue would think I'd disappeared. If I was quiet enough, maybe she'd forget she saw me going in, would think the door was closed because someone had played a trick and locked it from the inside. I waited. On the other side of the bathroom stall, Sue's saddle shoes and neat white anklets also waited. When the bell rang for class, I waited for the shoes and socks to leave. They didn't. I wiped myself carefully from front to back as my mother had taught me and flushed the toilet.

"Well?" Sue asked as I left the stall.

"I have to ask my daddy," I mumbled. I had no answer for God, who spoke in Sister's words through Susan Brown. I couldn't get to Sunday school if my parents didn't take me.

We called our comfortable Tudor-style home Twin Oaks, in deference to my English mother, who insisted that the property have a name. Built on a lovely spring-fed lake in Saddle River, New Jersey, Twin Oaks was a perfect home in which to grow up. We swam and

fished and boated and skated on the lake; had miles of country roads
on which to bike, hills from which to launch sleds and toboggans,
woods and fields to tramp through, abandoned farm houses to investigate, and creeks and waterfalls to explore.

Our family looked as perfect as our home: beautiful mother
whose English accent was as charming as she was lovely, a handsome and successful banker father, two smart, good-looking boys,
two lively little girls. This perfect family gave no outward sign that all
was not well within. My father was not abusive or violent when he
drank to excess, he was actually rather sweet and funny; it was my
mother who assumed those attributes. When my father drank, my
Snow White mother turned into the evil queen. Their fights terrified
us as children. The pounding on the doors at night, the screaming
arguments, the bottles of milk that shattered around us as we cow-
ered at the breakfast table. Mom would flail at Daddy with her
hands and fists and we would scream and sob, begging her to stop.
Although Daddy's drinking triggered my mother's wild grief, the way
he sat there—never raising a hand to defend himself—broke my
heart. I loved them both, and wanted desperately to protect them
from whatever it was that caused my father to drink and my mother
to rage.

When my father was gone for days at a time ("bingeing," as my
mother called it) we children received the brunt of Mom's anger.
Even dandruff was enough to set her off; my twelve-year-old brother
Stephen, who had the most, used to cower behind the old grand-
father chair when Mom went after him with the hairbrush, whacking it against his head as if he deliberately cultivated the flaky white
stuff. But Mom's anger, even when directed at us, was not nearly as
frightening as her flights from the house to "look for Daddy."

One day I found a note tucked under the radio next to my bed. "I
am dying of a broken heart," it read. I was seven years old and just
learning to read, but with the insight of the very young I knew what
my mother meant. I'd seen her run to the car, her nightgown billow-

ing behind her; had heard the tires spitting gravel, the screech as the car hurtled from the driveway onto Oratam Road and into the night. From then on, when Daddy was late coming home, I tried to distract my mother by setting back the clock, hoping to fool her into thinking it wasn't as late as it really was, terrified at what she might do because of Daddy's drinking.

When Daddy wasn't drinking, I plunged into life on the lake with a child's fervor, seeking comfort in nature from the turmoil that inevitably lay ahead. In search of security and a safe place to grow, I turned inward, finding within myself the stability I couldn't seem to find in my family. I didn't realize it then, but I had already begun my search for God. At that time, however, God was a scary being whom I knew only through what I'd learned of sin.

I was in the sixth grade when my parents took me out of Airmont Elementary and enrolled me as a day student at the School of the Holy Child, in Suffern, New York. Housed in a Victorian mansion on a hill above the town, Holy Child was home to around fifty boarding students and thirty day students, all girls. Its grand staircase rose like an ascending angel toward the classrooms on the second floor and the dormitories on the third; and on the first landing, where the angel's wings flared toward the east and west, a statue of the child Jesus opened its arms in welcome.

I loved the tranquillity of school days suffused with prayer and presided over by soft-spoken and learned nuns: being one of a small class of seven, wearing a uniform, curtseying to Reverend Mother, making quick visits to chapel. The God I learned about at Holy Child was not the judgmental God of Sister Mary Alice's catechism class but a loving and accepting deity who had sent his only son to show us what divine love meant. I yearned for this kind of love, stable and secure and certain. I related the love the nuns shared with us students to their lives dedicated to a God of love. Everything the nuns fed me about this loving God I consumed. My appetite for faith was insatiable. Love's message replaced that of retribution and my child's heart opened wide to embrace it.

Once, as my mother drove me home from school, she mused about the need that would drive a woman to seek such a life. "What reward do the nuns have but a crust of dark bread and a hard bed to sleep on at night?" she asked.

"But they have everything," I responded indignantly, amazed that she didn't already understand. It was so simple. They had God, didn't they?

## 2

## *Island Living*

In the summer of 1953, when I was thirteen, we moved to Puerto Rico, one family among a small contingent of Americans arriving to take advantage of the island's new status as a commonwealth of the United States and the exemption from state and federal taxes that it offered to new industry. My mother hated leaving our Saddle River home and blamed the move on my father's drinking. She wanted us children to have the happy childhood she'd never had, and he had put that dream at risk. Drinking had cost him his job as vice president of a New York bank.

My father had a different rationale for our move. A member of the bank's board, Don Rafael Carrión Pacheco, had personally invited him to Puerto Rico to develop a credit information and review division for Banco Popular, a small but growing island bank. The truth probably lies somewhere between—a combination of loss and opportunity.

Although we were excited about moving to a tropical island, insecurity pervaded our transition. Earlier that year we'd become boarding students at Holy Child so that Mom could join Daddy in Puerto Rico and prepare a home for us there. She returned in less than a month. Despite his promises, my father had started drinking again.

One Sunday, Mom brought us home to Saddle River for a visit. Twin Oaks was empty; all of our belongings were in storage awaiting shipment to Puerto Rico. We sat on the floor in that empty house and listened as she told us that she planned to divorce Daddy. She was leaving for England and while she was there she would look up a British Navy captain who'd been in love with her for years.

We didn't cry or wonder what would happen to us. Mom had threatened to divorce Daddy before, but when she brought us back to Holy Child later that afternoon, the school was more a sanctuary than ever, a place of shelter from the uncertainty and turmoil of our home.

When Mom returned from England a month later, we heard no more about the British Navy captain. Long after my mother's death, I came across a letter my father had written to her at that time. Penned in his exquisite writing, it contained the brief but powerful plea that might have brought her back home.

"Please come back to me, my beautiful Violet, for even the skies have not stopped weeping since you left."

Our first home in Puerto Rico was a garden apartment next to the Condado Lagoon in Santurce, a suburb of San Juan. It had highly polished black and white terrazzo floors, jalousie windows, and a bidet in the apartment's one bathroom. Instead of the plush comfy furniture that made our New Jersey home cozy and warm, we had woven leather chairs slung on curved teak frames, bamboo and ebony tables, and huge pottery lamps. On the terrace, rattan furniture with bright yellow cushions melded with huge pots of red hibiscus, and fuchsia and bougainvillea tumbled over the wall that separated us from the hotel pool next door. We headed to that pool every day to swim.

"You were flirting!" Judi's voice was stiff with accusation. We'd spent the morning swimming at the hotel pool and were on our way home for lunch when she hurled this accusation at me. Her flip-flops made scuffing noises as we walked. Flirting, flirting, flirting, they repeated.

Flirting? What did she mean, flirting? I hadn't been flirting. I'd been having fun with two boys who reminded me of Greg and Steve. I missed my older brothers. Greg was a captain aboard a ship in the Azores Islands. Steve was still at Dartmouth.

"You're mad because I didn't pay enough attention to you," I challenged. "How many times do I have to watch you practice a back flip anyway?"

"You were flirting," she repeated, so adamant that I began to wonder whether she was right. If Judi thought I was flirting, maybe those boys thought so, too; maybe I was acting like girls who wore too much makeup, smoked, and hung out with boys. Cheap, my mother called them. I didn't want to be cheap. Next time the boys came around I ignored them.

The episode with the boys at the pool marked a turning point in my relationship with Judi. Until then, she had been my favorite companion. Her tears could pull me from any friend who didn't want my baby sister tagging along. In Puerto Rico, Judi did not return the favor. She made friends of her own—boys and girls—and spent most of every day in their company, disappearing with them and not returning until it was time for supper. Lonely and awkward in my thirteen-year-old body with its budding breasts and swelling hips, I felt lost and out of place. I'd watch Judi head off into her new exciting world and wonder how she made friends so easily when I couldn't seem to find any of my own.

*"Mani, plátanos, guineos,"* chanted the voice in an off-key timbre outside the apartment on Barranquitas Street. The rumble of cartwheels on pavement and this strangely dissonant song pervaded an early morning already filled with bright sunshine. I pulled on some clothes and ran out the door to investigate. A small man, his leathery skin pulled tight over his bulging arms, his entire body straining, pushed a rickety cart on which were heaped raw peanuts, green plantains, tiny golden finger bananas, oranges, and pineapples. Hairy

gourds, fat green breadfruits, and pear-shaped melons were tucked among them.

*"Tiene quenepas?"* I asked in my hesitant Spanish.

I'd been jealous the day before when Judi came home sweaty and jubilant. "What have you been doing?" I asked.

"Walking on walls and eating *quenepas*," she said with a smirk. I didn't even know what a *quenepa* was.

The man grinned, an amazing toothless smile that crinkled his whole face, as he pointed to some twigs to which marble-sized green fruits clung.

*"Diez centavos."* Ten cents.

I ran back into the apartment to get my beaded coin purse. Judi was still sleeping. I felt a surge of delight whip through me. Now I'd know her secret.

I sat on the tiled steps leading to the foyer and tried to peel the fruit's nubbly skin, but it was tough and refused to give. My fingernails weren't long enough to pierce it. Meanwhile, Judi awakened and came in search of me. Finding me outside, she opened the door and squatted down next to me, yawning. She smelled warm and salty. Her soft curly hair brushed my face.

"That's not how you do it, stupid." She said, grabbing one and placing it between her teeth. "You break it with your teeth."

I bit into one as she did, amazed when it opened with a popping sound and the fruit practically leaped out of the shell. My tongue curled and jaw tightened as the slimy pellet skittered against the roof of my mouth. I sucked at its sweet-sour flesh and the thin membrane slowly dissolved, leaving only threadlike fibers clinging to the pit. I held the pit and pulled the fibers off with my teeth until none were left and the pit was as smooth as a polished wooden ball. I tried to pull another *quenepa* off its twig, but it refused to budge. I put my teeth around it with the stem still attached and shivered as the thin shell split with a crisp pop. This time the fruit stayed inside. It sat like a transparent egg yolk inside a tiny olive shell. I squished the pod and the fruit leaped again into my mouth. I turned to Judi grinning and for a moment we shared the delight of discovery. Then she jumped up and dashed into the house. Nancy and Iris were expecting her at the pool. Once again, I was alone.

That summer Daddy stayed sober. He was home every night in time for supper, played *generala* (similar to poker dice) with us, took us for evening walks, treated us to coconut-flavored ice and fried plantain chips, and turned every Sunday into an excursion. Daddy planned these jaunts like a tour guide. He'd make a show of consulting the monthly tourist magazine *Que Pasa en Puerto Rico* for special events, and would get suggestions of "places not to miss" from his business associates. We'd visit the most beautiful and historic towns, native restaurants renowned for traditional island foods, archaeological sites, beaches, and rain forests. Daddy drove hunched over the wheel, trying to safely negotiate the narrow roads that snaked through the mountain highlands. We'd pass through clusters of corrugated-tin huts that teetered on long skinny poles over mountain edges, and women carrying large rectangular water containers on their heads with half-naked children running alongside—the little boys wearing shirts but no pants, the toddler girls wearing panties but no shirts. Sometimes we'd encounter children by the roadside selling tiny bananas so sweet and tangy that they tasted as though they'd been squeezed with lemon. There was a scent in the Puerto Rican countryside of ripening fruit and wood smoke, the aroma of roasting pig and freshly baked crusty bread. The landscape was on fire with color. There were hibiscus bushes as big as trees and heavy with scarlet, fuchsia, and canary-colored blooms; *flamboyán* trees looking like flaming parasols over the valleys; mountains resembling upside-down, pistachio-encrusted ice-cream cones.

"They might be dirt-poor, but what a view these *jíbaros* have," Daddy would say expansively, as if a view made poverty acceptable. *Jíbaros* are what the mountain people call themselves, and they say it with pride. It reflects their strong enduring spirit—wise, honest, brave, self-sufficient. When Americans use that term, it sounds patronizing.

I was bothered by the discrepancies between our life and the lives of those we saw on our drives. During the short time we'd been on the island, I'd seen the swampy slums that the urban poor lived in, the rickety tin huts on the mountainsides, the crippled children, the street urchins selling shoe shines for a dime. Yet these people had a dignity and a grace that impressed me. Take Mary, for example, the lovely dark woman who cleaned our house for two dollars a day. Mary brought us *pasteles* cooked in plantain leaves, and *sancocho*—a beef stew redolent with native herbs—so we could taste native cooking, and shyly invited us to her wedding at San Jorge. We did go, standing in the back of the church as the priest blessed Mary's union with a thin young man dressed in a clean but too-large suit.

I thought of Mary one Saturday as I waited with my parents for the queen of the casino to parade down Avenida Ashford. I wondered whether Mary, too, was crushed among the onlookers, craning her neck to catch the first glimpse of the horse-drawn carriages, listening to sound of hooves on pavement, laughing at tails lifted occasionally to emit a steaming pile of dung. Did she envy the young girls in these coaches, and the queen riding in the final carriage—a white one adorned with flowers—wearing a gown so heavily weighted with gold thread and seed pearls that it was rumored she would have to change to a lighter gown in order to dance? What would Mary think of such a gown? I was filled with confusion. I was impressed by the panoply of this parade but felt shamed by my pleasure in its lavish display. Torn by my mixed feelings about poverty and privilege, I asked Daddy how such excess could be justified when there were myriad poor without enough to eat.

"Things will get better soon," my father told me, "That's why we're here. American industry will provide jobs for these people. They will have opportunities they never dreamed of."

I wondered whether this bounty would also come to people like Mary who worked for two dollars a day, to the crippled children, to the little boys with *brillo* boxes selling shoe shines.

# 3

## Puerto Rican Adolescence

When school began that fall, Judi and I followed the patterns we'd begun when we first arrived on the island. Judi immediately made friends and got involved in extracurricular activities, while I hurried home as soon as school was over. I was invited to join the glee club and to play volleyball after school, but demurred, saying my mother needed me at home. This was a lie, of course. My mother didn't need me; I needed her. My mother and my home were my only refuge, apart from the one other place I found comfort—any church into which I could slip to pray. More than ever, I found myself seeking in God the friendship and love most teens seek in one another. I rose early every morning so that I could get to Mass before school began. I felt safe and beloved in God's presence.

Mom couldn't understand my behavior. She wanted me to be popular, to have an active social life. The fact that I didn't, that I preferred staying at home, troubled her. That summer, she'd packed me off with my brother Steve, who'd just returned from Dartmouth, to a *quinceañera*, a fifteenth birthday party for the daughter of one of my father's banking acquaintances. It was the perfect way to make friends, she said. When we arrived, my brother was ushered to the dance floor, where good-looking boys were always in demand, while I was guided to a chair and given a plate of small sandwiches, mints, and petit fours to keep me company. Dressed in my good organdy dress, ankle socks, and patent leather shoes, I sat by myself trying to look happy, watching the beautiful Puerto Rican girls in cocktail dresses who shimmered when they walked and danced as if the music lived inside them. I felt terribly lonely, even when I closed my eyes and remembered that God was with me.

Until we moved to Puerto Rico, I'd thought I was Mom's favorite child. As a toddler I'd once solemnly advised her that she needed to hug Judi more so that she'd feel special, too. I no longer felt this way. Mom appeared to be either displeased with or ashamed of me. I was gaining weight and she was quite vocal about the added pounds. When she was angry she'd sometimes call me a fat pig or a clumsy ox. These remarks devastated me, especially when made in front of others. I dreaded being compared with my thinner, more popular classmates—girls like Vicky, over whom the boys went gaga.

Besides being thin, Vicky was athletic. She loved to play volleyball and tennis, she water-skied, and she tried fancy dives off the high board. "You'd be thin like Vicky if you weren't always sitting around on your backside, reading," my mother told me, with Vicky standing there listening, which certainly didn't make going to the beach any easier.

Vicky had come to live with our family while her parents were in the Virgin Islands opening a new hotel. She arrived with only a small suitcase that held her school uniforms, a bathing suit, some play clothes, and one good dress. Her little bag of clothes contained few things with which a teenager could make a strange place more homelike. There were no stuffed animals, no photos of family and friends, no favorite books.

"Best not to have a lot of things to lug around," she said as she shook out her pleated skirt before hanging it up. "Start feeling at home and, wham, they pawn you off on someone else: Seems like I've spent part of every year living with someone else."

"You've lived with other people before?" I asked, trying to imagine what it was like to be sent from home to home.

"Well, it's not so bad. It's almost as comfortable living with strangers as it is with my folks: they're loud and they drink like fish."

Mom worried about Vicky. One night, I overheard her say that Vicky was too beautiful and that a girl like that, without a real home, might end up as a photographer's model. I wondered what my mother meant by "photographer's model," because her voice dropped when she said it, as if being such a model were something shameful. Her remark troubled me for days. Earlier, as a child of ten, I'd seen the word "prostitute" in a newspaper article and had asked her what it meant. "A woman who allows a man to do anything he wants with her body," she responded. As I pondered my mother's words about Vicky, I wondered whether being a photographer's model had anything to do with letting a man do anything he wanted with one's body.

I was even more troubled when, not long after the photographer's model comment, I overheard Mom worry about me in much the same way. "I wonder what will happen to Beryl," she said. "She's so good."

I don't remember if my father ever responded to these queries, or if they were the only questions that drifted down the hallway at night. They are, nevertheless, the two that stand out in my mind. The way Mom phrased her worry—"I wonder what will happen to Beryl, she's so good"—made it seem as if being good was just as dangerous as being beautiful, as if both goodness and beauty led toward some implacably hostile future. Why, then, were beauty and goodness attributes I believed my mother wanted to see in me?

At Academia Perpetuo Socorro, the private parochial school where I was a freshman, I continued to avoid the boys and was careful not to flirt. I must have presented a rather formidable front to the boys at school, because they began singing "Stormy Weather" whenever I was around. In the spring of that year, however, seemingly undeterred by my disdain, a high school senior invited me to the senior prom.

For this, my first real date, I twisted my auburn hair into a French knot and adorned it with tiny white flowers. My gown was an ankle-length light-green tulle that matched my eyes. While dancing, I stepped on his toes. He stepped on mine. "Excuse me." "Excuse me." I closed my eyes to concentrate. A crowd of dancers circled around us, cheering and laughing.

That invitation was a first step in severing my apron-string mentality. A more powerful catalyst was something that happened on the last day of school: my classmates arrived bearing gaily wrapped packages for a birthday party that no one had told me about.

With the same determination that was to erupt at other times in my life, I decided I would never be overlooked again; I'd become the popular girl my mother longed for. The best way to do this was to join every extracurricular activity the school offered. That way I'd be certain to make friends.

When school began again that fall, I joined the glee club, the newspaper, the debating club, the student council, and the Thespians. I even helped to form a cheerleading squad for the school volleyball team and danced and leaped and bounced to the cheers a classmate from Texas taught us. My efforts to stand out must have worked, because later that fall I was voted Academia Perpetuo Socorro's Ideal Girl. Talk about joy! I hadn't even known that I was in the running. I could hardly wait to get home to tell my parents. As I climbed the stairs back to my homeroom after the announcement had been piped throughout the school by loudspeakers, I overheard a classmate say that the election had been unfair. There were senior girls more deserving than a sophomore newcomer. My face burning, I pretended not to hear, but I knew she was right. My happiness crumbled. Embarrassed by the truth of what I had overheard, I did not tell my parents about the honor that had been given me that day. They learned of my new title only when the principal called to invite them to the award ceremony.

"Why didn't you tell us?" they asked.

"Because I don't deserve that title!"

"Of course you deserve it; don't be so foolish," said Mom.

"Of course you deserve it; you're my daughter aren't you?" said Dad.

From then on they insisted on telling everyone that not only had their daughter been voted "most popular girl at school"—a misperception that I kept trying to clarify and that they just as diligently ignored—but this popular daughter had "forgotten" to tell them about her title!

Meanwhile, despite his promises, my father had begun drinking again. Just as she'd done at Twin Oaks, my mother went berserk. As a teen, I blamed Daddy for not caring enough to stop drinking, for not heeding Mom's anguished "If you loved me you'd stop drinking" accusation I'd heard her hurl at him so often. When he didn't come home at night, and Mom ran out of the house in a frenzy and disappeared into the unknown tropical night, I'd put on a calm front for Judi's sake, telling her, as my brothers had once told me, that Mommy had gone to look for Daddy. Then I'd crawl into bed and curl into a fetal position and shake with fear and rage. If anything happened to Mommy, I thought, I'd kill my father. I'd feel a strange surge of elation then, would sometimes find my hand clenching an invisible knife, jabbing it over and over again into his chest—grinding my teeth and hating him with all my heart.

# 4

## Transitions

*I* was fifteen and a sophomore in high school when a series of events occurred that had a profound influence on the direction my life would take from then on. I think of such happenings as messages from God. The people who enter my life, the events that transpire, all have something to teach me if I look hard enough. These incidents can be as simple as a dream, as ordinary as a clash with a loved one, as traumatic as death.

It was the kind of November day when someone was bound to run from the hotel to warn us about the undertow. Older people, usually, the skin on their arms wobbling as they motioned to us, their legs stick-thin like the posts holding signs that warned swimmers of the strong undertow. Vicky and I would pretend we didn't hear them. We'd watch them shout against the roar of the sea for a few minutes before they'd give up and go back to the pool shaking their heads. Maybe if they'd been younger we'd have listened. We were so sure of our strength then, so certain that nothing serious would ever happen to us. Older people worried too much, we thought. They didn't realize that we were invincible.

That afternoon, heat shimmered from the beach. We ran fast, the sand searing our feet, straight toward the ocean, leaping like porpoises into the foaming wall of water that came roaring at us. We loved flinging ourselves into that wild embrace. The best part of swimming in the ocean was fighting the suction that vied against us, riding the waves, crashing with them onto the beach, clawing against the undertow as it surged back out. That day the surf was especially strong. Water and sand burned its way into our noses and down our throats as we scrambled to rise before the next wave hit us. Wave after wave surged upon us. They hurled us onto our backs and sucked us under. We decided to dive under them to the other side of the breakers where the water was calmer. I loved that plunge into the quiet hazy-green world that exists under the turbulence of the surface. When we surfaced again, we had breached the waves and entered the rolling waters on the other side. We floated on our backs with the sun beating down on our faces and the water so cool around us—rising and falling on the belly of the breathing sea. I could hear the muffled drone of its waves washing around my ears. Lulled by this music, I became drowsy, and my thoughts drifted. Time lost its boundaries and the present became all encompassing.

My reverie was interrupted when I heard Vicky calling me. "We've floated too far to the east, Beryl." The urgency in Vicky's voice startled me. The waves were sweeping us toward the coral reefs in front of the hotel. We turned and began swimming back to where we started. It was then that we noticed the dark shape rolling near us over the swells. It looked like a log but I couldn't really tell because I'm nearsighted, and although Vicky had perfect vision the sun's glare on the water made it difficult to see. Sometimes in winter, the barracudas and sharks come close to shore to mate, and we'd seen enough people without hands and feet to feed our imaginations. One of us mentioned "shark," and we both torpedoed back toward shore.

Almost as scary as the threat of a possible shark was the group of men standing on the beach and pointing toward us. We were fourteen, and self-conscious about our new womanly shapes—uncomfortable in the presence of older men who liked to ogle us, sometimes pressing against us in the buses and whispering things we didn't understand. When two men broke from the group and started swimming in our direction, we dove underwater and swam toward the shore. Getting out of that water, though, was a nightmare. Our legs couldn't move fast enough and the undertow kept trying to suck us back in. When we finally reached the wet-packed sand, we realized that the men didn't care about us. They still faced the ocean, a strange silence encircling them, making them impervious to anything except the two swimmers who were struggling back toward shore pulling something between them.

"What are they doing?" I asked Vicky. She just shook her head because she could see what I couldn't. They weren't pulling a log. They were pulling a body.

Drawn by curiosity, we moved toward the edge of the circle. The boy on the beach could not have been more than fifteen and he was beautiful, his dark wet hair curling tightly around his golden face, his body frosted with salt and sand, water glistening like tears on his lashes, the longest lashes I'd ever seen. Near him on the beach a man knelt with his face in his hands, rocking in the same rhythm that the sea had rocked the body of the boy. I noticed him because one of the bystanders pointed toward him and said how sad it was that he should lose *another* son to the sea.

I sat down on the beach, because suddenly I couldn't stand anymore. My legs had gone all shaky. As I was out there floating on those waves, listening to their muffled roar and musing on the infinite number of times they must have rolled upon one beach or another, trying to compare their never-ending repetitions to the days of eternity, a boy my age had ridden those waves straight into forever. Eternity was on the beach and this boy had been taken and I had been spared. The voices murmuring around me faded. My hands and feet dissolved. I remained like this until Vicky leaned over to shake me.

"Beryl, what's up? Didn't you hear me? I'm hungry. Let's go get a hamburger."

The memory of that death haunted me for weeks. I was no longer simply a teenager; I was a teenager who could die. Though I did not doubt the reality of eternity, thoughts of living forever did not make death palatable. What if, instead of happiness, a person had experienced misery while alive? How then did one approach death? I became preoccupied with wondering if the people I encountered were happy. Did happiness dwell in the house from which emanated the spicy scent of native cooking? Was the lady selling lottery tickets on the street corner happy? What about those tourists lounging around the hotel pool? Did the beauty of the island, which Mom so appreciated, ease the pain of Daddy's drinking? Was my father's joy in his work recompense enough for my mother's rage when he drank too much? When it came time for them to die, would they wish they'd lived their lives differently?

What about me? How would I go about living so that I could yield to death in peace, knowing that I had done all that I could, the best that I could, and had known happiness?

While I pondered life and death, my mother worried about my emerging sexuality.

Boys, boys, boys! Mom warned me about them all the time. Don't let them kiss you. Don't let them know you like them. Certainly, never let them know you love them. Boys want only one thing and once they've gotten what they want, they'll walk all over you.

My mother's messages and warnings about boys confused me. On the one hand, she was telling me to beware of boys, on the other, that I should be popular and go out with as many young men as possible. The impression I got was that I was to be some sort of ice princess whom men would desire but never possess. I was aware that my mother was probably trying, to the best of her ability, to protect me from making mistakes that might hurt me. But her messages were contradictory. When it came to sex, my mother pushed me toward and pulled me back from it, time and again.

In 1954, when I was fifteen, we moved from the Barranquitas apartment to one on Condado Avenue in Santurce, and I met the dark-eyed and dimpled collegiate son of the couple who owned the building. Jose, nicknamed Gogui, walked with a bit of a swagger and had a way of tossing his head that I found positively sexy. Having exchanged my wallflower persona for that of a vivacious brunette with hazel eyes, I found Puerto Rican boys terribly attractive anyway—with their dark hair and eyes, their sinuous, muscled bodies, their charming accents and seductive ways. Boys now often looked my way, and when Gogui started showing up whenever I left the house, I realized that more than coincidence was at work.

At a Christmas party for which we both already had dates, I caught him watching me. I smiled at him and he smiled back. For the rest of the evening, we gazed soulfully into each other's eyes from across our partners' shoulders. The following afternoon, as I left the apartment for the beach, he offered to drive me. He opened the passenger door and bowed. He was so good-naturedly gallant. Once in the car, however, I felt awkward. I didn't know what to say, or how to act, and my thumping heart was making it difficult to even breathe. I gazed out the side window and tried to act nonchalant.

Into the silence flowed a question. "Why are you so beautiful?" Gogui asked.

I'd never been asked such a question before and wasn't sure of the right answer.

"Because God made me that way," I answered. It was the best I could do. I knew I was pretty. I also knew that being pretty was God's doing, not mine.

Gogui laughed, and I wondered whether my answer pleased or offended him.

"So, has your summer been good?"

"Yes, I suppose so."

"You looked happy the other night . . . at the party. I envied the boy you were dancing with."

"He's only a friend." I assured him. "I don't have a boyfriend, at least not a steady one."

"That's not what Steve told me. He said you have several boyfriends."

"Steve said that? Why would he tell you such a thing?"

"Because I asked, I needed to know before I asked you something. I'm leaving for Lehigh tomorrow. If I wrote to you, would you answer?"

"Of course," I said in as demure a voice as I could muster.

I awaited Gogui's first letter with ardor, imagining love notes filled with longing and desire, messages into which he'd pour the fullness of his love for me and write the lovely tender things he couldn't put into spoken words. Disappointing is hardly the word for his first letter's opening salvo. "How are you?" Several paragraphs of school news and studies later, I realized there would be no declaration of love in Gogui's letters. Nevertheless, I answered them immediately and tucked them carefully into my handkerchief drawer. Save them, wrap them in pink ribbon—that's what other girls did.

One day while I was writing to Gogui, Mom asked me whether I always answered his letters so promptly. When I said yes, she shook her head. "Don't you know how to play hard to get? Men only appreciate what they have to work for. Let Gogui write several letters for every one you answer."

Mom was beautiful; men flocked around her wherever she went. They kissed her hand, told her how lovely she was; they followed her with their eyes. I believed her. Men didn't get passionate about women who fell like ripe fruit into their open hands. I wanted Gogui to feel passion for me. With an aching heart I tore what I'd written into small pieces and threw them into the wastepaper basket. Then I began the long wait for a letter that Gogui would never write.

When Gogui next returned home he wasted no time in asking me why I hadn't written. "Were my letters that boring?"

I couldn't tell him that my mother had told me to play hard to get, so I asked him why *he'd* stopped writing.

"I have my pride."

His simple words revealed how unfair it is to play games with re-lationships. How could this hard-to-get ploy lead to love when it cre-ated imbalance, when it generated a petitioner and a benefactor mentality?

"I'm sorry, Gogui!" I said, and like a fountain from which a stop-per has been removed, the reason I hadn't written gushed from my lips. Rather than looking disturbed, Gogui laughed and gave me a quick hug.

"Have you been to the rooftop?" he asked, still smiling. He turned toward the new apartment building. "The view up there is great."

We took the elevator to the penthouse where we could see the entire Condado shoreline, its white beaches and palm trees and lovely homes, stretching all the way from Isla Verde on the east to Miramar on the west. It was more beautiful than I had dreamed, the perspective so wide and sweeping and freeing. We leaned on the bal-cony wall, our arms barely touching, the breeze rumpling our hair, the sun hot on our backs.

"It's beautiful, Gogui. You must love it up here."

"When I am here, Beryl, where I can see so far, I feel almost as if I could fly; but it is different in reality. I was born with a hole in my heart that the doctors have not been able to fix. Up here, though, I don't worry about my heart, I think of the future and what it will hold for me."

He stopped. I tried to absorb his message. Gogui was ill? What was he trying to tell me? As if intuiting my confusion, Gogui said softly, "I've made up my mind that when I find the right girl, I'm go-ing to hold her close and never let her go."

He didn't need to say more. I was certain he was talking to me, that I was the girl he meant, that it didn't matter if he had a heart defect.

The future looked so incredibly sweet at that moment—a tender young man to love and to be loved by—that I practically danced my way home and burst into the apartment shouting, "Mommy, I'm so happy. I think Gogui loves me."

When Gogui called the next morning to tell me that his uncle had died during the night, our plans to date one another had to be abandoned. Rather than the fraternity dance, the movies, the walks and beach dates, Gogui and I made do with holding hands and talking while sitting in full view of our parents on the wall separating our two buildings. A number of teens hung out there. Camilla, who lived in the duplex behind our apartment, sometimes joined us.

Camilla had an unsavory reputation. She hung out at the naval base, a place where no *nice* girl went, even if she did claim to be engaged to a sailor. One day, as I puttered around my room, rearranging the furniture and tidying my drawers, my mother flung open the door to tell me she'd just seen Gogui offer "that hussy Camilla" a ride in his car.

"So what; can't he offer her a ride? She's probably going to the grocery store."

"There's only one reason to pick up a girl like Camilla," Mom said, sounding more triumphant than outraged. "Now you know what kind of a boy he is!"

It came back to me then—Gogui's first words to me in his car— "Why are you so beautiful?" What if he was saying those same words to Camilla at that very moment?

"I don't believe it," I shouted at Mom, but when she'd left my room I fell sobbing onto my bed.

Gogui waited for me the following afternoon, swinging his legs and knocking his heels against the cement wall. When he greeted me I ignored him. I walked right past him without responding. If he was innocent, he'd demand to know why I was snubbing him. If he didn't, he was guilty.

"Aren't you even going to say hello?" he asked. Had he phrased it differently—had said "Why are you ignoring me?"—I would have responded. Instead, he said "Aren't you even going to say hello," as if he knew why I'd flouted him. I never gave him a chance to defend himself, to explain his reason for giving Camilla that ride. Instead, Gogui and I never spoke again. He flew back to Lehigh University and I went back to school. Though I tried to put Gogui out of my mind, he never really left. Thoughts of Gogui became synonymous with betrayal and heartbreak. If this was human love, there had to be something better. I didn't know it at the time but that "something better" was only a few weeks away.

In the spring of 1955, my sophomore year, Perpetuo Socorro's student body made a one-day "mission"—a spiritual retreat meant to turn us away from frivolous preoccupations with popularity and worldly success and back toward God. From my seat near the front of the auditorium, I watched intently as a lanky priest moved from one end of the stage to the other, his sweat running in rivulets down his face, his cassock making a flapping noise like the wings of a gull.

"Discover who you are," he advised us in rapid Spanish. "Go deep into your heart and claim the self you find there. Take that self out into the world with you. You have a mission. You are God's messengers."

Though my Spanish was not good, I understood enough to be moved by his message. That night, while attempting this "going deep into the heart" business and not realizing that it would initiate a lifetime of effort, I knelt next to my bed and closed my eyes and tried to imagine moving within my heart. Instead I felt like I was lifting boulders. After an hour of fruitless searching and emptiness, I grew tired and discouraged.

Folklore and myth are rife with dreams. Scripture, too, is full of dreams: Abraham's dream of his seed multiplying in a promised land, Jacob wrestling with the angel, the dream that commanded Joseph to take Mary of Nazareth to wife.

I have always been a dreamer. Dreams have warned me of impending deaths and given me insight into the future. As a child I learned to fly to escape from the swirling knots of snakes that inhabited so many of my dreams—flying with ease from danger until a friend told me that dreaming of flying was sexual.

The night of the retreat, I did not dream of flying. Instead I dreamed of an unseen but powerful hand that reached for mine—a presence so real and encompassing that I could barely contain the pain of it. Rapture poured from that hand and engulfed me, pulling me toward it with overwhelming tenderness. I was loved. Oh, how I was loved . . . loved and accepted just as I was, because I was. Nothing was hidden from this love; all my shortcomings were known, acknowledged, and accepted. It didn't matter if I was popular or shy, smart or slow, fat or thin. I, Beryl, was beloved. Inflamed by such love, I became a bird beating its wings against too strong a wind, a string on a violin stretched to an ever-higher pitch, an ember leaping toward the source of all heat. Muscles pulled from tendons, tendons from joints, joints from bones. To hold such love I knew I must die. With all my heart, I wanted to die.

For weeks, dazed by the power of this dream, I walked half in and half out of this world. Gone was the overwhelming need to please that, until then, had driven my behavior and efforts. I still worked hard in school, because I loved learning, but I no longer cared whether or not I was first in my class. I still went to parties and dances, but I felt separate and detached. I didn't change much outwardly. Inwardly, however, I lived in the awareness of God's overwhelming and unconditional love.

In early June 1955 Mom and Dad flew with us to New York so we could fulfill Mom's longtime dream of taking her family to England. We planned to take a boat from New York, but in one of those serendipitous happenings that sometimes answer even unspoken payers—miracles of grace, perhaps—a maritime dock strike took shape on the very day we were due to sail. Our trip canceled, we stayed in the city and visited relatives and friends. We even went to see the nuns at Holy Child. The return to that lovely school elicited wonderful memories of peace and safety and prayerfulness. Judi and I pleaded to be allowed to attend that school again, but Daddy was firm. My parents could not afford it.

I turned to God. "You know I want to love you. You know I can't do this very well in Puerto Rico. My days are too superficial there. I want to live a more meaningful life."

After two weeks in the city, we gave up the idea of a trip to England and returned to Puerto Rico. Not long after our arrival home, we received a momentous phone call from Mother Columba.

"A full board and tuition scholarship has just become available. Would Beryl like to receive it?" Judi and I hugged each other and laughed. With a full scholarship to cover my final two years of high school, my parents could afford to send Judi back to Holy Child as well.

When school began that fall, Judi and I returned to Holy Child without a moment's regret at leaving Puerto Rico. Giddy with joy, I carried my suitcase into the dormitory assigned to high school juniors. It faced east and had a lovely round alcove where my bed was located. The alcove windows provided a glorious view of the rising sun and overlooked the lawns, tennis court, and a small pond leading to the hockey field. I unpacked quickly, hung my uniforms in the closet, arranged my underwear and pajamas in the white dresser drawers, and then hurried off to the beautiful chapel with its Chagall-inspired stained-glass windows and ochre-colored marble altar to give thanks.

Soon after I arrived back at Holy Child, I began to find small cards at my place in chapel. We called them holy cards, as they usually featured an inspiring picture of a saint or Jesus on the front and a prayer on the back. The ones left for me were specific, and they were all similar—a photo of Jesus knocking on a door, bending his head as if waiting for an answer. Printed in delicate black script on the back was a prayer for religious vocations. I didn't want those cards. They threw me into turmoil every time they appeared. I wanted to belong to God, but I wanted to love my way. I didn't want a vocation, which in Catholic parlance meant becoming a nun. I was dating Fernando, a boy I had met in Puerto Rico after breaking with Gogui. Fernando made my insides slide when he held me close as we danced. He taught me how to kiss and was fun and smart and comfortable to be with.

Now, another holy card had been left at my place in chapel. I shoved the card toward Sweeney Boyle, who knelt next to me. Sweeney grinned and stuck it in her missal. Clouds of incense drifted round us, mingling with the light streaming through the stained glass windows and filling the air with a dense, cloying aroma. The headache that had begun that afternoon while I was playing field hockey tightened into a band that circled my head, every heart-beat ramming it deeper and forcing tears, unbidden, to stream from my eyes. The pain grew worse as the sweet voices of the children filled the chapel with the "Tantum Ergo," the famous hymn composed by Thomas Aquinas in honor of the blessed sacrament. Its refrains merged with the incense and throbbed in muffled cadence until I thought I would faint from the thick scent and sound. White-faced and sweating, I hurried from the chapel. I needed air.

"Are you all right, dear?" Mother Louis asked as she hurried after me from chapel. She looked at my flushed face, placed a cool hand on my burning forehead, and took me to the infirmary. On learning that I couldn't remember the last time I'd moved my bowels, she gasped. One week, two weeks? She gave me two tablespoons of mineral oil and put me to bed in the infirmary, where I collapsed into the cool sheets and closed my eyes. Within minutes I had fallen into a deep sleep. For five days I burned with fever, aware only of the bells that signaled changes in class periods and student processions past the infirmary to the chapel for prayer.

While I was ill, my parents came to visit. I felt better the day they arrived, and stood on the bed to show them how thin I'd gotten. When they left, I crawled back under the sheets, exhausted. That night the fever spiked to 104.6 degrees. I looked at the nurse's size 10 shoes and thought she was a man. When she leaned over to kiss me good-night, I was certain the nurse, a simple farm woman who had gone to nursing school after her children left home, was a man. This man-woman creature frightened me. "Don't touch me!" I screamed, pushing her away with my hands. The nurse rushed from the infirmary to get Mother Columba, who called Doctor Hussey, an old family physician who still made house calls. I vaguely remember him standing next to my bed. Everything about him seemed to shake—his head, his hands, his voice talking about jaundice and possible liver damage. Too ill to listen and dizzied by his shaking, I closed my eyes.

I'd read enough lives of the saints to believe that illness was sometimes the trigger that turned them from lives of frivolity to holiness. Was I ill because I was fighting my vocation? Did God want me to be a nun?

"Give me a sign, God," I prayed. "If I get better I'll become a nun."

My parents later told me that on that very night, in their hotel room, my mother woke from sleep screaming. "Beryl is going to die! God is going to take my child!" That night, in the Holy Child infirmary, I woke from sleep bathed in sweat. I did not die. Instead, I gave myself to God.

# 5

## Following My Vocation

When I was twelve, I heard Francis Thompson's *Hound of Heaven* performed in choral recitation at Holy Child. Coached by a wondrous white-haired British gentleman who'd once been a member of the Old Vic company in London, the choral group brought to the poem all the drama of a Shakespearean performance. Each time the senior class practiced this poem for their graduation ceremony, Thompson's words shuddered through me: beckoning, terrifying, thrilling. "Ah, fondest, blindest, weakest, / I am He Whom thou seekest!" Though still a child, I recognized the power of such longing. At sixteen, pushed by the need to possess and be possessed by the one whose persistent love Thompson limns so well, I believed that only as a nun could I focus my attention on so great a love.

I didn't know how to tell my parents that I wanted to become a nun. Our family had no history of religious vocations. I knew, instinctively, that my mother would fight my desire to become a nun, so I kept it secret. At Holy Child, far from my parents' concerned scrutiny, I could pursue holiness without interference and consider the various options that would make such a life reality.

Having read and reread *The Autobiography of a Soul,* by Saint Thérèse of Lisieux, my favorite saint, I thought of becoming a Carmelite, like her. The cloistered life would allow me to devote myself to love in a way that a teaching or nursing order could not. Then, one Saturday night, an event happened that drew my consideration to another order of cloistered nuns.

We were noisy that night, screaming with laughter at the impromptu performance Judi and another classmate produced, retelling their forbidden excursion into the heart of the convent, an off-limits section of the school where the nuns lived. Mother Columba, who had been trying to pray in the chapel above us, accused us of unseemly hilarity. Didn't we know, she demanded, that Poor Clare nuns were at that very moment enduring cold and hunger and sleeping on straw for our salvation? In her hands she held a copy of *A Right to Be Merry*. Those nuns knew true happiness, she said. If we thought joy consisted in unbridled laughter we had much to learn. Mother's words struck me with surprising force. I was intrigued by a happiness found in deprivation.

In 1956, *A Right to Be Merry* swept onto the nation's best-seller lists, written by a nun in a Poor Clare Monastery in Roswell, New Mexico. I was enraptured by Mother Mary Francis's portrayal of cloistered living in the tradition of the great saints of Assisi—Francis, the little poor man, and Clare, the beautiful young woman who followed him into poverty and established her own order of nuns. My idealistic antennae positively bristled with the certainty that this was the life for me, especially when I won a copy of the book at a game of chance while attending a fund-raising fair at Marymount College in Tarrytown with Sweeney Boyle.

"If I win that book," I thought to myself, "it will be a sign that I'm meant to become a Poor Clare." I tendered my dime and selected a number. The attendant spun the wheel, and voilà, I won.

I no longer dreaded becoming a nun. *A Right to Be Merry* erased any doubts that remained. I longed to become a Poor Clare, like the book's author. The idea of living in rapturous contemplation and embracing hardship willingly in reparation for the sins of the world intoxicated me. Reveling in my new sense of purpose, I often took the gravel path that led through the gardens toward the nuns' cemetery. There I could sit quietly and rest in the awareness that God was with me and within me. I sat on the stump of an old cedar and looked up at the sky through gossamer shawls of mauve and silver-green leaves. I ran my hand across the tiny blades of grass that pushed through the earth. The chirping of the warblers filled me with music of my own. I drifted into the beauty that surrounded me. I leaned inward toward the bright secret of my love.

Meanwhile, I'd begun writing to several Poor Clare monasteries on the East Coast, looking for the one where I'd feel most comfortable. The response I received from Mother Charitas in Bordentown, New Jersey, made me feel at home almost at once. I felt a surge of inner certainty that this was the monastery I was meant to enter. It had the additional advantage of being located near Trenton, little more than an hour from New York City and even closer to Newark Airport, which we used to fly to and from Puerto Rico; it would be a convenient place for family to visit.

During my final year at Holy Child, I was chosen as president of the Sodality of the Children of Mary, a select group of students who took the Mother of God as their model. As Sodality president I wore a blue sash fringed with gold and knelt in the first pew on the aisle on Our Lady's side of the chapel. Sweeney Boyle, the president of the student council, also wore a gold-fringed blue sash and knelt across from me on Saint Joseph's side. I no longer shoved holy cards with prayers for religious vocations onto her. As Sodality president I wrote spiritual columns for the school paper, *The Columbine*. One column was on the young Italian peasant, Maria Goretti, who was canonized by Pope Pius XII. Maria had died rather than lose her virginity. She was a martyr to purity. I chose Goretti because purity was on my mind.

Over the summer holidays in Puerto Rico, despite my longing to become a nun, my body had turned to fire. It seethed in response to physical stimulation, especially while dancing with Fernando, the boy I'd met after losing Gogui and whom I continued to date. Though I was rarely in a compromised position because of the presence of chaperones, I once had to ask him to stop kissing my neck even though my body craved those kisses. The surprising thing was that the fear of disappointing my parents was almost as strong a force in keeping me chaste as was my love for God. The desire to please my parents, a source of strength when I was tempted to sin, became an obstacle in the battle for my religious vocation.

One day in early spring of 1957, my senior year, my mother called to say that she was in New York and wanted me to meet her in the city so she could help me select a dress for the prom. I found this a strange request, as I couldn't imagine my mother flying to the States to buy me a gown. Although my father was a highly respected banker and we'd always had lovely homes, we never seemed to have an excess of money. My father drove a car that was literally falling apart—the fender once fell off on a busy San Juan street—and took perverse pride in driving this car to work. It proved he was an honest banker, he'd say, grinning. Boarding school had put an additional strain on our parents' budget, even with one full scholarship. The small monthly check my father sent us from Puerto Rico provided Judi and me with barely enough funds to buy necessities like paper and pencils, soap and shampoo.

Greg had left the merchant marines by this time and was living and working in New York. On "boarders' weekends" and holidays, Judi and I often stayed with him at his sixteenth-floor apartment on West Twenty-third Street, in Chelsea, as did Mom and Dad when they were in the city. As soon as classes ended that Friday, I took the bus from Suffern to the city. Mom arrived at Greg's apartment shortly after I did, her arms filled with packages, which she dumped onto the couch in order to hug me.

"Oh, Beryl," she cried, "I've the most wonderful news. We have a new home: a condominium. It's big and bright and has a view of the ocean from three sides. You have your own room, and, best of all, you can swim whenever you feel like it. It's right on the beach." She ripped open a package to show me her purchases: peach-colored sheets with my name embroidered on them, even on the pillowcases, and matching initialed towels. My heart sank. I felt like the omniscient narrator who, while the family plans the wedding, knows all along that the bride is going to elope. My mother's plans did not include losing a daughter to God. They did include going to Loehmann's, in Brooklyn, a fashion discount store, to get my gown.

The next day, we left Greg's and went to the station to catch a subway train to Brooklyn. "Hurry," Mom said, dashing toward a platform where our train was about to pull out. I ran ahead of her and jumped on the train just as the door slammed shut. Mom didn't make it. Stunned, I watched my mother's small figure disappear as the subway train screeched and rocked its way down the tracks. I had no idea how to get to Loehmann's. By the time I decided to get off, thirty or more city blocks separated me from where I'd last seen my mother. A check of my pockets revealed a half piece of gum, several scrunched Kleenex, and one dime (not enough for return fare). I got off in the Village and headed toward Fifth Avenue, and then began the long walk uptown to Twenty-third Street in a gray drizzle on a cold March day. I arrived back at Greg's sodden and irritable, but not nearly as upset as my mother, who'd expected me to get off at the next stop and wait for her. Worry made her voice shrill. It was now too late to go shopping and tomorrow was Sunday. The stores would be closed.

"That's okay, Mommy," I said. "I don't need a gown. I don't even want to go to the prom."

"Not want to go to the prom?" Mom's voice sounded incredulous. "It's your graduation, isn't it? How can you not want to go to the prom?"

Greg winked at me from the door that separated the living room from his tiny kitchen, and said in too loud a voice, "Maybe you don't care about proms because you want to become a nun."

How I hated him at that moment. I should have known he'd be suspicious. On the weekends that Judi and I spent with him at his apartment, I'd gone to daily Mass, kept the *Imitation of Christ,* by a fourteenth-century monk, Thomas à Kempis, next to my bed, and carried a rosary in my purse. On Thanksgiving, while we waited, hungry, for Greg's turkey to finish cooking because he insisted we save our appetites, I told Judi we could offer our hunger for the poor souls in Purgatory.

"Did I hear you say *offer it up,* little sister?" Greg had said, darting out of the kitchen and waving a spatula at me. "You sound just like Mother Gabriel at Holy Child. God knows I love the dear woman, buckteeth and all, but her philosophy is bloody awful. You're not thinking of becoming a nunny-bunny, are you?" Before I could respond, the sausages he'd been frying to pacify our hunger went up in flames and he rushed back into the smoke-filled kitchen to put the fire out.

Hoping my mother hadn't heard his remark about my wanting to be a nun, I stayed silent, but this time Greg wouldn't let the subject drop. "Well, you do, don't you?" he asked, giving me one of his toothy grins.

"Well, now that you mention it, I do," I said, lifting my chin defiantly.

"Do what?" The blood had drained from my mother's face, and the little line between her eyes deepened until it was a black furrow. I didn't want to look at her. When she was angry, her eyes looked right through the person who displeased her. It was as though that person slid off the earth and became like the ghosts in movies who keep trying to interact with humans because they don't know they're dead.

"Become a nun," I stammered.

"A nun? What do you mean, a nun?" My mother reached out to grip the dining-room table. I flinched, thinking she was going to slap me.

"I want to give my life to God." My voice was trembling now, and I could feel tears starting to burn behind my eyes. I'd never been good at arguing things that were precious to me, especially when my wishes collided with my mother's.

"You don't know what you're talking about," she said harshly.

I knew then that I'd lost her. She'd gone into what I've always thought of as her pulling-down-the-shades mode. With each sentence she snapped down another set of mental blinds, refusing to listen, asking questions to which she wanted no answers.

"Who in their right mind wants to bury themselves alive?" *Snap.*

"What are you afraid of?" *Snap.*

"After all we've done for you." *Snap.*

She turned her back and began banging soup bowls down on the table.

"I'm not burying myself alive, Mommy. And I'm not afraid. It's a hard life." I gingerly put spoons and knives next to the abused bowls.

"It's a waste. That's what it is," she said and snapped down the final set of shades. We ate our soup in silence. Each mouthful stuck in my throat.

In *Enduring Grace,* Carol Lee Flinders's beautiful book on women mystics, she writes, "To be idealistic and impulsively generous at that age—to think it completely reasonable that another reality should exist that is a real improvement over the one we can see and touch and smell—these almost define a particular kind of teenager we have all known or even been." My mother could not understand such reasoning. She thought that the love of a man and security were ideals all young girls treasured and that living for God was an unrealistic option that anyone with the least bit of common sense would drop once she'd experienced life. She believed she could change my mind, but the more she pressured me to change course the more obstinate I became.

During one of the ongoing arguments my mother and I had in Puerto Rico the summer after I graduated from Holy Child, I told her that I wasn't interested in the things the world offered.

"But what about marriage? Children?" she'd asked.

"Marriage? You think I'd be happier married? *Is* there such a thing as a happy marriage? What I've seen is a lot of anguish. I don't want to marry and submit my life to a man. I don't want to be betrayed by someone who might fall out of love with me. Look at Daddy. He loves his job and his drink more than he loves you." The words were out before I could stop them.

"What can you know of love?" My mother shot back, and abruptly left the room.

Resisting my parents was new to me, but I experienced a love more wondrous than any I would find with a man. God's presence was everywhere. In the apricot-tinged sun that dipped toward the horizon at sunset, in the almond-tinged faces of the children at play in the parks. I heard God's voice in the rustle of the palm trees, felt God in the evening breeze, found God in the fragrance of the night. Into every moment of every day I carried my search for God. The certainty that no one would ever love me as God loved me made me strong.

My parents did not give up easily. They continued to pressure me to go to college before entering a convent. If I had a true vocation, it would endure through college. Besides, God wouldn't want me to waste the scholarships I'd won. I knew differently. Mother Columba, my adviser at Holy Child, had warned me that college was the "graveyard of religious vocations." My choice of a cloistered life made my decision especially difficult for my parents to understand. Why would their bright young daughter want to lock herself away from the world when the best in life could be hers? If I insisted on sacrifice, why wasn't I choosing a religious order where I could at least be of service? It was self-centered to choose a cloister when there was so much need in the world.

This last argument was the most difficult to refute. It only made sense if one believed, as I did, in the power of prayer. I was convinced that becoming a contemplative nun was the most important and powerful choice that I could make, the one that could do more for the world than ministering to a necessarily limited number of humans. For those around me, however, this was not a powerful enough argument. Though love was an acceptable reason to marry, it was not a good enough motive to enter a cloister. I couldn't prove that in giving myself totally to God, in making contact with the divine source of all life, I could do more for the world than I could ever accomplish in the world.

I relied on the letters Mother Charitas sent me to stay optimistic. They were warm and chatty and filled with encouragement.

"It is terribly difficult for some parents to accept their daughter's desire to enter a cloister. Most often their desire for her happiness eventually convinces them to let her go. Don't get discouraged, Beryl. Your sisters here are praying for you and look forward to the day you will join them at our Bordentown monastery."

That summer, at a party to which my parents invited every boyfriend I'd ever had, with Latin music pulsing through the living room and a table laden with fat shrimp, sliced mango, and spiked punch, I skulked around talking about nothing but God, making it clear that I was not interested in superficial things like parties and relationships. Besides boyfriends, the house was full of family friends, banking acquaintances, and old school chums, all of them apparently marshaled to break my resolve. Don Rafael Carrión Pacheco, the man who had built Banco Popular from a tiny bank to one of the island's major financial institutions and who'd invited my father to join him in Puerto Rico, cornered me. He was an imposing figure despite the slight stroke that had folded one of his eyes and crumpled that side of his mouth. Dressed impeccably in a white business suit, his thick white hair cropped very short, Don Rafael began a relentless barrage of questions. Why did I want to do this foolish thing—hurt my parents like this? He even offered to take me to Europe when he and his wife went the following summer. "Let us show you how wonderful this world is. You have no idea what you are leaving. You are just a child."

I had no language other than spiritual yearning with which to convince him, and so with my beliefs under assault, I responded as I had since I was a child: I burst into tears and ran sobbing from the house.

My parents made one final effort to change my mind. They appealed to my love for them. "You can enter the monastery," they told me one morning in late August, "but you will break our hearts."

"Oh, thank you, thank you," I cried, hugging them tightly. "You won't be sorry. I'm going to become a saint."

# Lauds

In the monastery, Lauds follows Matins. At 1 A.M. dawn is hours away, yet you are already celebrating its arrival. Lauds leads you from darkness to light, celebrates the new day and the rebirth hidden within each moment.

The psalms of this hour swell with gratitude for the gifts of morning, for the opportunity to begin again, which, considering our propensity for false starts, is no small blessing.

Lauds possesses a spirit that springs from life itself, the cycle of birth, death, and rebirth reflected in all living things. It rises with the sun, is found in the new blade of grass, the butterfly, the baby. It exists within every moment, even those charged with fear or sadness.

With Lauds touching the barest edge of morning, you give thanks for God's beneficence. After the final blessing, you return to bed, where sometimes you lie awake for hours, too cold in winter to fall back to sleep, too hot in summer to rest easily, waiting for the sacristan to summon you back to chapel at 5 A.M.

# 6

## Entering the Monastery

Greg, my cool bachelor brother, the heartthrob of students and nuns at Holy Child and the surrogate father Judi and I stayed with on occasional weekends, had his own way of getting attention—a madras jacket. A riotous plaid of reds, oranges, blues, greens, pinks, lavenders, and yellows, this jacket was his favorite, the good-luck charm he wore to blind dates and family gatherings. Greg was to wear this jacket on his first date with his future wife, Griselda. When Griselda saw him standing at the foot of the stairs dressed in this jacket her heart stopped. What would Papa think? Then she looked into his shining face, and in that instant fell in love, making it a very lucky jacket indeed.

On October 11, 1957, one day after my eighteenth birthday and the day I was to enter the Monastery of Saint Clare in Bordentown, New Jersey, Greg insisted on wearing this jacket.

Mom said, "Not on your life," but I didn't care what Greg wore. I just wanted to get going. I was ready. My trunk was packed with the articles of clothing we'd purchased at the Ave Maria Shop in downtown Manhattan that, along with four hundred dollars, made up the dowry I would bring to the monastery: one dozen long-sleeved undershirts, three black flannel slips, three black cotton slips, six yards of bird's-eye (a dimpled cotton the nuns used for sanitary napkins), one dozen towels and facecloths (enough to last a lifetime), one pair of black oxfords (to be exchanged in six months for the heavy black sandals of the novice), and one dozen white handkerchiefs. I sat on this trunk filled with my material things in the hallway of my brother's apartment, waiting for my mother and my brother to come to terms about appearances, as I moved toward a life where appearances meant nothing.

Daddy sat in the living room, buried behind the newspaper. A steady vapor of smoke rose from the cigarette he was smoking. Another cigarette still burned, forgotten, in the ashtray on the small table next to him.

He folded the paper and looked at me hunched on my trunk. "Come sit in the living room, Beryl. You're making me nervous sitting next to the door like that."

"Yeah," Judi said. "You're making me nervous too. You can take my place." She looked up from the game of *generala* she and Steve were playing.

"No, I'd rather wait here," I said. "This jacket stuff should be over soon."

Greg riffled among his clothes, returning again and again to the offending jacket, which he finally yanked from the closet. The empty hanger rocked on the supporting bar and clanked onto the wooden floor. "It's a damn good jacket," he muttered under his breath but loudly enough to be heard.

Mom sat down on the bed and folded her arms. I could tell she wasn't going to relent. "Greg. You can't wear that to the monastery. It's not in good taste."

"I'll have you know this jacket was handmade by a fine tailor." He turned his back so that Mom wouldn't see him grinning: he loved these conflicts. He was so different from Steve in this respect. Steve had seen enough of Mom and Dad's fights to want to lay off arguing forever. Greg, however, thrived on disputes. He especially delighted in shocking and angering Mom.

"Well, it looks cheap!" She waited. When Greg didn't respond she added, "What will the nuns think?"

"Who the hell cares what the nuns think? I'm not entering the bloody monastery."

Mom gasped. Warming to his topic—he had Mom's total attention now—Greg continued, "I like this jacket. It makes me feel good. My little sister is becoming a nunny-bunny, and I need something to help me feel good about that."

Greg shrugged into the jacket and beamed at me from across the room. I grinned back. His audacity was amazing. My parents were still suffering from my decision to enter the monastery, yet Greg—the brother who helped me break the news to them in the first place—was making an already difficult step even thornier for them. It's no wonder that toward the end of his life, he took the name Brother Thorn when he joined the third order Franciscans. This time, as usual, he succeeded in totally rattling my mother and doing what he wanted. We drove toward the monastery with Greg's madras jacket sending shock waves from the front seat of the car.

Fernando, who'd gone to high school at the Bordentown Military Academy, had warned me that the monastery looked like an asylum; my first glimpse of the building shook me nonetheless. Not only was it on one of the busiest streets in Bordentown and next to a major highway, it looked nothing like the cloister for which I'd hoped: all soaring arches and pillared porticoes. Its brick façade was the color of dried blood, its shape institutionally rectangular. Greg whistled and said that the leaves drifting from the maple on the front lawn looked positively festive in comparison.

He looked around and spotted a sign in the front yard, "Monastery of Saint Clare," printed in yellow on a brown background. "That's what we need," he said, "a photo of all of you in front of that sign. We need to record the day my sister became a nunny-bunny for posterity."

I sighed. Another delay! The nuns had expected us at three that afternoon, and though it had taken little more than an hour to drive from New York City to Bordentown, not far from Trenton, it was already four-thirty. Only when we arrived at the monastery had I learned that my mother had set the clock back to delay my entrance. We hadn't left Greg's apartment at one-thirty as I thought, but at two-thirty. Delaying us even more, we had stopped for ice-cream sundaes on the way.

"Greg," I pressed, "we're already late."

"The nuns can wait," Daddy said. "They will have you for the rest of your life. We have you only for a few more minutes."

Judi reached out and hugged me and stifled a sob. "I'll miss you so much, Beryl. It won't be the same without you." I squeezed her back. She'd do fine. She'd never really needed me.

The picture taking finally over, I walked quickly toward the front door of the monastery and my family hurried after me. We climbed the steps and entered the vestibule, which was dark and silent. "At least it smells like a monastery should," I thought to myself. The scent of wax and lemon oil settled lightly about us, transforming the entryway into a narthex. Facing us were two large wooden doors resembling sentries and, to the left, a turnstile over which a small typed notice urged us to "Please Ring." I did. When a soft voice from behind the turnstile intoned, "Praised be Jesus Christ," my knees quavered.

"It's Beryl, the postulant," I stammered, shaken by the disembodied voice.

"Dear child!" The voice swelled in timbre. "We wondered what had happened to you. You're so late. I'll call Reverend Mother. Take your family to the second parlor. It's down the hall to the left."

Inside the parlor, a heavy double wire grating behind which hung a heavy black drape separated one half of the room from the other. Hard-backed chairs arranged in a semicircle implied that we were meant to sit down. I didn't dare look at my mother. I knew she was thinking that the next time she visited I'd be on the other side of those gratings. The idea thrilled me as much as it pained her; those gratings were the symbol of my total separation from the world, a separation for which I longed and which she dreaded. The sound of a door closing forced me toward the edge of my seat. We held our breath as the curtain was pulled back, revealing two nuns, one tiny and fat, who I thought must be Mother Charitas, the abbess. With her round glasses and inquisitive blue eyes, she reminded me of a jolly elf disguised as a nun. The lovely slender nun with the dark eyes was Mother Consolata, mistress of novices—in charge of all postulants and novice nuns. Noting my parents' somber demeanor, Mother Charitas turned to them and asked whether we'd had a pleasant journey; it was a beautiful day, wasn't it? My relief at the ensuing conversation was short-lived because Mother Consolata addressed my parents, saying, "I understand how hard giving your daughter to God must be."

"How can you understand how we feel, when you have never lost a daughter?" my mother retorted, taking an instant dislike to the woman whom, in my mind, I'd already begun calling "Mother." I lowered my eyes, embarrassed by Mom's outburst.

"Your pain is natural, Mrs. Bissell," Mother Charitas interjected. "Just remember: God is not to be outdone in generosity. You've given Him your daughter. He will bless you in return." She quickly diverted the conversation, asking whether we'd had trouble finding the monastery. My father smiled at this, knowing she was referring to our late arrival.

I piped up then, explaining that my mother had set the car clock back an hour to delay our arrival, and we'd stopped for butterscotch sundaes, "the last one I'll ever have," I said, beaming proudly.

"I wouldn't be so sure about that," Mother Charitas said, smiling mischievously. "We occasionally have ice cream. As a matter of fact, every summer we have a picnic and sundaes are part of the menu."

My parents brightened at this bit of news, but I was taken aback. Mother Charitas laughed at my puzzlement. "You will eat well here, Beryl. We grow our own vegetables and process our own milk. And we have a very productive chicken yard, lots of good eggs."

Knowing that I was not going to starve (a strange concern considering the way she'd nagged me about my weight in Puerto Rico), my mother started to relax. When a bell interrupted our conversation, Mother Charitas said it was time to say good-bye. My mother gasped and turned pale.

I jumped up from my chair in the parlor and hurried down the hallway toward the entryway without waiting for my family. I longed for the moment when I would walk through the cloister doors to give myself to God.

"Wait, Beryl," Daddy called after me. He was holding Mom's arm. She looked as if she were about to fall. I stopped midflight, stunned at the sight of her anguish.

I must have hugged Judi and Steve good-bye, but all I remember of that parting are my parents and Greg: my parents because of their grief, Greg because of his outrageousness.

Daddy put his arms around me. "It's not too late, Beryl. You can still change your mind." He smiled but his lips trembled.

"Kiss your lovely novice mistress on the nose for me," Greg said and gave my shoulder a squeeze.

I reached toward Mom, who stood trembling next to Daddy. Frightened by the vehemence of her feelings, I embraced her quickly, then turned toward the open doors.

"I'll never be able to touch you again," she cried.

Filled with a sudden longing of my own, I turned around for one last glimpse of my family. All I could see was Greg's madras jacket, the only bright object amidst the gloom of that entryway.

# 7

## Within the Walls

"May God grant you peace and holy perseverance." Soft cheeks pressed against mine as the community of nuns embraced me and whispered this greeting. *Oh, yes, I will persevere*, I thought. I had no doubts that I would spend the rest of my life in this monastery. Mother Consolata, the novice mistress, walked behind me, cutting short any effusive greetings. She said each nun's name as I moved into her embrace: Mother Madalena, Sister Mary Paschal, Pacifica, Jacoba, Philippa, Benigna . . . foreign-sounding names that I could not attach to a face because the nuns' veils were lowered and I could see nothing above the tips of their noses; only the postulants Kathleen and Marilyn showed their faces. Their veils did not have a flap to conceal their eyes. When I reached the end of the line, the abbess clapped her hands and the nuns turned, tucking their hands into their sleeves and bowing their heads to walk in procession toward the chapel.

"*Magníficat ánima mea Dóminum, Et exsultávit spiritus meus in Deo Salvatóre meo.*" My soul magnifies the Lord and my spirit rejoices in God my savior—sang the nuns. My spirit soaring with those words, I floated along in their wake, following my new family into the heart of the monastery.

I had waltzed around Greg's apartment in the long black skirt, blouse, cape, stockings, and oxfords of a postulant. Now, on the day of my entrance, I donned these clothes in a cloister dormitory where muslin curtains separated small cubicles containing only a wash-stand, stool, and mattress supported by three boards on trestles.

"Leave your secular clothes on the bed, Sister," Mother Conso-lata said as she placed a towel and facecloth on the washstand. "I'll return in a few minutes to help you with your veil." She lifted the trunk and started to leave the cubicle.

"Where are you taking my things, Mother?" I asked. She was tak-ing the trunk away and we hadn't finished unpacking yet. I still needed to remove the small album of family photos my mother had prepared, the notepaper and pen she had tucked in with the towels.

"Your things? What do you mean *your* things, dear?" Mother Con-solata raised her perfectly arched eyebrows. "Poor Clares don't have things of their own, Sister. You do want to be a Poor Clare, don't you?"

I turned away so she wouldn't see the tears that sprang into my eyes. My mother had helped me to pack those things. I had wanted to touch them one last time.

That night, I discovered I was to be spoon-fed bits of monastic life. I was sent back to bed for Matins. I was disappointed. I'd been looking forward to getting up at midnight. Like other idealistic teens, I wanted to be challenged and getting up at midnight to pray would be especially hard. Deflated, I listened as the others donned their habits in the dark and rustled out the door toward the choir. Soon the soft cadence of midnight prayer pushed through the darkness to my cubicle. I fell asleep thinking of the new life that lay ahead of me. When the wooden clapper woke us at 5 A.M., I leapt out of bed and fell with a crash onto the floor. My leg had fallen asleep. Sister Marilyn, the postulant who slept next to me, scratched on my cur-tain. "Are you all right?" she whispered.

*How embarrassing*, I thought. *My first day and I'm already upsetting the routine.* I was still tying my oxfords when Mother Consolata told me to come to the Novitiate, where the rest of the sisters were waiting to form a procession to choir for the morning hours of Prime and Tierce.

Breakfast, which followed 7 A.M. Mass, was spare: hot coffee with milk and peanut butter on a slice of bread, eaten standing and facing the wall. I hadn't eaten peanut butter since Mrs. Mitchell showed us second-graders that a little elf with a pointy beard and tiny cap lived inside each peanut, and I didn't want it now. As I returned to my place at the table, with my dry bread and cup of coffee, Mother Consolata took me by the arm and led me back to the serving board, smeared a thick wad of peanut butter on my bread, and smiled. That smile clearly meant: eat it.

From the second floor came the hiss of the stoves in the altar-bread room where the Communion wafers were made, the *thump, thump, thump* of the cutters—the scent of hot wheat dough wafting down the stairs into the kitchen, where Sister Mary Rose bustled around with Sisters Agnes and Ellen Clare in tow, peeling potatoes, grating cheese, and sautéing onions for dinner.

I worked with Sister Mary George in the laundry room. Sister had been up since four, soaking dirty tunics and underwear in large tubs along one wall. A turbine-shaped washing machine chugged noisily, while next to it, Sister Marilyn spun the washed clothes dry in an extractor. Sister Kathleen and I carried the heavy baskets of freshly laundered clothing outside to dry. As we hung the wet tunics up to dry in the cold morning air, my hands grew red and began to ache. The weather had turned chill the week after I entered, and the morning was bright with frost. The cold ached through my arms and into my chest. I felt as though I was holding ice in both hands. This pain filled me with a leaping sense of joy. I was suffering for love, just like the saints, experiencing in a small way what Christ had suffered as the nails were hammered into his wrists during the crucifixion. Two white pines towered over the laundry lines and I looked into that blue, blue morning sky through their wondrous lacy needles, knowing I was exactly where I wanted to be: On my way toward becoming a saint!

We'd almost finished hanging the laundry when Mother Consolata appeared wearing a blue checked apron and carrying a large basket. She settled near the kitchen steps and began shoving mounds of dried corn husks into a large rectangle of striped ticking. I watched as she prodded and packed, her face becoming ruddier and shinier with each handful.

"Can I help?" I asked. I needed another chore. The laundry work was finished.

"This is your bed, dear, and no, you can't help. Besides, I want to make sure this tick is as uncomfortable as possible and that it lasts a long time."

Her words thrilled me. I'd only been a postulant for a few days and already Mother Consulata thought I was ready for penance! That night I would sleep on a lumpy tick propped on trusses like those that the other novices used. Mother Consolata caught me grinning and frowned slightly, waving me toward the garden where Sister Kathleen was picking the remnants of the lima bean crop.

For the rest of the morning Sister Kathleen and I worked in the long rows of plants with their shriveled bean pods, standing up straight occasionally to ease our backs and to drag the wagon heaped with baskets of picked pods to the next row. The plants were dry and covered with dust. Every time we yanked at a pod, the stems and leaves sent a shudder of powder into my nose. I sneezed all day. I sneezed through Vespers, meditation, collation, Compline, and the rosary. When I climbed onto my cornhusk mattress that night, I was still sneezing, and under me—crackling with every move I made—the cornhusk mattress inhaled and exhaled, its breath filled with whatever pollens clung to that filling. On and off the bulging mound I climbed all night, groping my way to the bathroom for tissue, convinced that this was the end of my vocation. I was allergic to religious life.

# 8

## Becoming a Novice

My six months as a postulant passed quickly. Save for my ongoing bouts of hay fever, religious life suited me. I settled easily into a schedule built around prayer and silence, the simple manual labor of the fields, laundry, and kitchen that allowed me to focus my attention on the God to whom I was dedicating my life. We lived in silence, a stillness broken only by the tolling of the chapel bells, the nuns' voices chanting, and an occasional instruction issued in a soft voice. I thrived in that glorious quiet and grew to love the simple, routine tasks that left my mind free to focus on God's presence. I learned to build a quiet place within me that nothing could disturb. There I would imagine myself sitting with the Christ of the Gospel of John, the one who encouraged Mary to keep him company while her sister Martha bustled about serving her guests.

Wonderful, too, and immensely freeing, was the belief that in the monastery it didn't matter if I was fat or thin. Unused to a diet with so much starch (some meals were so heavy in carbohydrates—lima beans, potatoes, macaroni, and bread—that a novice once quipped it was a wonder we could bend our legs after such a repast), I grew fat without concern.

I didn't realize what problems this weight gain would cause at a time when all my energies were focused on becoming a bride of Christ (a term then used for nuns that has since fallen out of favor). Postulants were dressed as brides on the day of their investiture as novices to signify their commitment to Christ, even though they would not make their first vows until two years had passed, and it would be another three years before they made their final vows. On the day I was to receive the clothing of a Poor Clare novice—the coarse woolen tunic, the rope cincture worn as a belt, and the white veil—I, too, would first be dressed as a bride. This tradition of dressing the postulant as a bride on the day she received the holy habit was to throw my spiritual life into a tailspin.

The monastery had two wedding gowns with which to clothe the brides of Christ. Two weeks before my investiture with the religious habit, I tried those gowns on. Mother Consolata selected one, and zipped it up—it was a snug but successful fit. She washed and pressed it, and the following week invited the abbess, Mother Charitas, and the vicaress, Mother Madalena, a woman whose girth appeared to equal her height, to the final fitting. This time the gown did not close. The zipper halted midway between my waist and shoulder blades.

"Too heavy for a young girl," said the vicaress officiously.

That this huge nun should say I was too heavy hurt more than my mother's calling me a clumsy ox or comparing me with my thinner, more graceful friends. "Too heavy for a young girl" burned like caustic salt rubbed into an already irritated wound. Was it possible that in the monastery my weight would continue to plague me as it had when I was at home?

Even in boarding school, Mother Stella, my art teacher at Holy Child, another portly nun, had used my weight to prod me. After Mass one morning, she stopped me on the stairs to ask whether I was enjoying my return to Holy Child.

"I love it, Mother," I responded. "It feels like home."

"I'm glad to hear that," she replied, her fat Buddha face wreathed in smiles. "And what are you doing besides enjoying school and getting fat?" She then glided away, her black veil and habit billowing behind her like a pirate galleon at full sail.

The afternoon I tried on the wedding gown, I silently promised myself that never again would anyone, *ever*, call me fat! I'd show them, I vowed; I'd get so thin they would beg me to eat. I imagined the vicaress and other nuns encouraging me to eat more of the day-old donuts the local bakery donated, to take a second helping of potatoes, to put more butter on my bread. It made me feel better.

The ceremony of clothing, which was to take place on April 19, required an eight-day retreat of preparation. I asked the novice mistress if I could incorporate fasting into the regime of prayer and silence. She agreed and remarked that I just might lose some weight in the process. Mother Consolata's statement sealed my resolve. If I'd had a pen filled with blackest ink, I'd have etched "never again" into my hand. Instead I wrote it on my soul.

And so it was that I made my first real acquaintance with hunger. By the end of the week I had made such strides in fasting that I could feel the difference in the way my postulant's garb fit. On the day before the ceremony of investiture I ate nothing at all, and knew that the wedding gown would zip up with ease. I washed my long hair and then sat on my bed in the dark trying to roll its silky weight on rags. I wanted to look beautiful one last time.

That night I dreamed I was walking on a beach. It was dark and my feet ached with cold. A strong wind pushed me toward an object lying half in, half out of the water. It looked like a Medusa's head; seaweed swirled about it like snakes in the tide. I fought the wind. I didn't want to go near that object or the terrible stench that emanated from it. The body of a dead dog in Puerto Rico had smelled like that, its bloated body buzzing with flies and crawling with maggots, and I was terrified. As the wind pushed me relentlessly forward, the monstrous form assumed the shape of a trunk like the one I'd brought with me to the monastery, and tumbling from it was a pile of rotted and reeking clothes. I knew those clothes belonged to Gogui.

In the year of Our Lord 1212, a young noblewoman of Assisi left her life of privilege to follow an outrageous mendicant in his journey toward Christ. In the darkness of a night lit only by stars, Clare met Francis in the woods outside the city; there he cut off her long blond hair and clothed her in the rough robe of a beggar. In those days, beautiful young women did not live with pious mendicants, not even to serve Christ, so Clare founded an order of nuns and fought till her dying day for approval of their right to live without possessions, or as she and Francis called it, "the Privilege of Most Holy Poverty."

How anxiously I had waited for the day when, like Saint Clare, I would don the clothing of a Poor Clare novice. It was not the resplendent wedding of which my mother had dreamed, but no bride felt more radiant than I.

When the bishop asked, "Dearly beloved daughter, what is your request?" I repeated the words I had repeated so often—loving the sound of them, yearning for what they offered—words that still reverberate clearly and unforgotten more than forty years later.

"Reverend Father, I ask you for the love of God, of the Most Blessed Virgin Mary, of our holy father, St. Francis, of our holy mother, St. Clare, and of all the saints, that you would deign to admit me to the habit of the Second Seraphic Order; to do penance, to amend my life, and to serve God faithfully until death."

"Thanks be to God," responded the bishop. He sprinkled holy water onto the basket of clothes I handed him and prayed that, as I would be clothed with them exteriorly, I might put on Christ interiorly. He then handed the basket back to me and I returned to the cloister altar, where, out of sight of the bishop and congregation, the novice mistress and the abbess waited.

In the visitors' chapel where the bishop presided knelt my family and friends. They had seen me dressed as a bride as I stood in the cloister chapel at the open grate before the ceremony began. I had smiled at them then, and they had taken photos of me dressed as a bride. I could hear them sniffling as the bishop handed the basket of clothing back to me and I left their sight to return to the cloister altar, where the novice mistress and abbess waited.

Perhaps it was just as well that my parents could not watch as Mother Consolata removed my bridal veil and the abbess cut great chunks of my hair; that they did not see the bridal gown slip to my feet as the rough gray wool of the habit was draped over my shoulders. They wept hard enough as it was when I next stood before them, clothed as a Poor Clare, my head covered with the white veil of a novice.

I kissed the hand-carved crucifix my parents had brought back from a trip to Germany and prayed to remain hidden within Christ's wounds. I wanted nothing more than to die to self in order to live in God. To symbolize rebirth in Christ I received a new name that the abbess had kept secret until this moment. No longer would I be called Beryl, the name my mother had bestowed on me at my birth. I was to be known as Sister Mary Beatrix of the Holy Child Jesus. Mother Charitas wrote the date, my new name and its meaning, "bearer of happiness," on a small holy card and gave it to my mother. She kept it among her things until the day she died. I found it in her box of mementoes, along with a lock of my hair that had been cut off during the ceremony, still rich and shining after so many years.

Looking back as a mother, I have a better understanding of my parents' sense of loss when I became a nun. On the day of my investiture, while I was being swept into the bosom of my new family, my parents were left alone to host a gathering of friends in the outside basement for a wedding banquet without a bride—to cut and serve a bridal cake that the bride never saw, and to pretend they were happy when their hearts were really breaking.

Later in the day, my parents did get to see me. We met in the monastery parlor, where, after the sharing of emotions generated by the ceremony, I blurted the story of my dream. I had to know what it meant. Had anything happened to Gogui? My mother looked at Daddy and asked, "Should we tell her, Ferd?" He nodded.

"We didn't want to ruin your day, Beryl." Tears filled Mom's eyes. "Gogui is dead. He died earlier this week while undergoing surgery to close the hole he's had in his heart since birth."

# 9

## Getting Thin for God

As Sister Mary Beatrix I began to fast in earnest. At first, abstaining from food was freeing. As my body grew lighter, so did my spirit. I was breaking the bond that connected my body with my soul. Light-headed with hunger, I became euphoric with prayer. I found myself spiraling to a place where the boundaries between me and the universe dissolved, an experience seared with color and white as light. Coming back was difficult. I returned feeling filled yet strangely empty.

While fasting improved my prayer life, it did nothing to curb my appetite. My body begged to be fed. I chose to starve it. At first, it took an extreme act of the will not to eat, but I liked being in control. I even began to enjoy, if one could describe it as such, the pangs of hunger that made me weak and dizzy and cramped my belly at night. *Look at you, Beatrix*, I'd think, inordinately pleased with this new me. *You're getting so strong.* The pain I inflicted on my body by starving entered other areas of my life as well. I refused to use my shawl when it was bitterly cold and rejoiced when my hands and feet bled from chilblains. I knelt on the floor during prayers until my knees grew puffy and bruised. I whipped myself with a small-knotted cord called the discipline until I drew blood. Medieval theological teaching that the body was evil and needed to be purged had infiltrated my spiritual life even as a child; my belief in bodily penance came from outdated books on asceticism and ancient lives of the saints. I had the example of St. Clare herself, who, although she insisted that her sisters be moderate in practicing austerity, destroyed her own health by excessive fasting and penitence.

In the beginning I wanted my mother and the power-figure nuns in the monastery to notice how thin I'd gotten. I did not try to hide the fact that I was not eating, as other anorectics do. I *wanted* to be noticed, to stand out as an ascetic. This was an almost impossible task when "custody of the eyes" kept everyone's eyes on their own plates at meals. It didn't take long for fasting to assume a new, more insidious persona. It became my shadow, my tormentor. Fasting walked with me through the monastery halls, accompanied me to chapel, sat with me at table, lay down with me at night. Together we thought constantly of food, discussed its flavors, and yearned for its textures. On feast days, when the general fast was lifted, fasting and I trembled with the desire to eat. And always, even as we sighed and wept, we kept our mouths clenched and our hands tight-fisted.

Soon I was eating almost nothing: a bit of lettuce, a sliver of egg, a cup of tea. Eventually I got the attention I craved. It came not from the novice mistress nor the vicaress but from another novice, who said, "You must be very happy because you'll be with Jesus soon. You look like you're dying."

When my parents came to visit in the fall of 1958, they were stunned at my appearance. I looked like an old woman, my mother said, her voice shaking with suppressed anger. I had lines running from my nose to my lips and my temples were as concave as a skull. I'd wanted to surprise my parents with my new svelte body. I didn't know that I looked old. I was nineteen. Did I really look like this, I wondered. There were no mirrors in the monastery.

"What is wrong with my daughter?" Mom demanded when Mother Charitas stepped into the parlor to say hello. "She looks like she's dying."

Mother Charitas insisted that as far as she knew I was in excellent health and that I certainly couldn't be starving. After all, we had plenty to eat. To reassure my mother she offered to get the novice mistress.

As she had on the day I entered, Mother Consolata managed to enrage my mother. "My dear Mrs. Bissell," she said softly, "have you forgotten that your daughter came here to die?"

Years later, when Consolata was dying of bone cancer, my mother had no empathy. She never forgave Consolata for what she perceived as thoughtless cruelty. She had no sympathy for a nun who would allow a child to starve herself to death, a nun so devoid of compassion that she'd justify such a death to a mother.

The psychological compulsion to avoid eating may have been as common in the late fifties as it became decades later, but "anorexia" was not a common word at that time. At the age of nineteen, I had never heard of this condition and consequently was not aware of the dangers inherent in such a disorder. I only knew that I'd been overtaken by an obsession that frightened me almost as much as it bewitched me. By this time, not only did I not want to eat but I was also having trouble digesting even the minuscule amounts I did consume.

After my Mom's visit, Mother Consolata put me on a weight-gain diet that included meat and extra food. At first I was pleased: I had accomplished my goal (actually I wanted to be begged to eat, but, hey, this was close). But then, when I still didn't eat enough, Mother Consolata ordered me to eat. Being ordered to eat was a different matter. Authority figures were encroaching on my turf—my body—and I did not welcome their intrusion.

Because the other nuns abstained from meat, Mother Consolata sent me to the kitchen, where meat was prepared for the infirm nuns as well as the extern nuns, who lived in the exterior part of the monastery and took care of visitors. Sister Mary Rose lifted an entire chicken leg from a Dutch oven and put it on a plate for me. I hadn't eaten chicken for a year. It was tender and dripping with juices.

Starving, I crammed it into my mouth, loving every wonderful bite. When I returned to the refectory to finish eating with the other nuns, my stomach became queasy. Throughout the rest of the day it cramped and roiled and grew round with gas.

When ordered to drink three cups of whole creamy milk a day, I balked. I was not interested in the rationale that it was the quickest way to get nutrients into my starving body. I did not want nourishment. I wanted to starve. I did not want to eat meat or drink milk. I resorted to deception and outright lying.

Alone in the kitchen, I found it easy to return my portion of meat to the pot of food prepared for the extern nuns and the infirm without being noticed. Getting rid of the milk was more difficult, as the cup was put at my assigned seat at the novitiate table in the refectory before each meal. Mother Consolata watched what I ate in the refectory so I needed to dispose of the milk while pretending to drink it. The propensity of cream to rise to the top provided me with the perfect ruse. While working in the kitchen, I would slip into the refectory, pour the milk into the milk pitcher, which stood on a serving table, and replace the milk in my cup with water. By the time the community arrived for meals, the creamy top disguised the water beneath.

I grew proficient in the art of pretense. If the kale was passed first, I'd pile it into my bowl, then toss a bit of potato on top so it looked like a lot. Cabbage provided a good way to fill a bowl without adding calories. I ate lots of cabbage. I agonized over this deceptiveness but was determined to have my own way. I no longer felt powerful and strong. I was a prisoner— the desire to starve, my jailer. I had by then grown so weak that even climbing the stairs to the novitiate, where we lived before we made vows, was difficult, making it necessary for me to cling to the banister to pull myself up. I fell asleep during meditation and prayer; I sometimes even fell asleep while standing in the refectory during the extended before-meal grace. Daily activities lost clarity, and one day blended into the next without distinction, everything overcast by my terrible preoccupation with food.

Compulsions showed up elsewhere as well. The nun who took care of the refectory would leave treats at my place as enticements to eating and gaining weight—pudding and fruit the nuns had not eaten, sometimes leftover desserts. I began to arrange and rearrange these treats. I'd eat a piece of cake or candy over the course of several days, cutting a tiny sliver into cubes and rectangles, and every cut edge had to be perfect and without crumbs or bumps. My rituals were floodlights. I watched myself become compulsively organized, ritualistically tidy. I knew I was sick and that this sickness was destroying my spiritual as well as my bodily life, but I had no power to rid myself of it. Gone was the soaring confidence of total acceptance that I'd once known, the experience of a God who loved me just as I was. God had not withdrawn from me, but I, in my guilt, was withdrawing from God. I prayed for forgiveness but hid my face in shame, knowing I did not want to change. What would happen, I wondered, if I died in the midst of all this deceit? Would God, loving though he was, forgive me for the abuse of his gifts, for the waste of my monastic life? I was in torment because I could see no way out of my dilemma. I yearned for the relief that obedience offered, but I was unwilling to obey.

"Help me. Dearest Jesus, help me," I prayed, not really wanting the help for which I so ardently asked.

The novitiate was filled with aspirants to religious life, among them one who was to become a lifelong friend. Mary, who entered the monastery a year after I did, was a mature twenty-five-year-old woman who had been the manager of the X-ray department of a large hospital in Albany. Although "particular friendships" were banned in the monastery, ours managed to grow. It was an odd friendship because we were so different. Fresh out of boarding school, I found monastic life easy, whereas Mary had a difficult time adjusting. She rolled her eyes and sighed during the reading, before meals, from the *Roman Martyrology*, a book I loved, containing edifying but mostly legendary tales of the saints and martyrs. We sat next to each other in

the tiny classroom off the novitiate dormitory where Mother Consolata taught us how to pray the liturgy and to practice the rule of Saint
Clare. We listened carefully and took notes, knowing that we would
be tested, not on our knowledge of asceticism, or prayer, or the rule,
but on how we lived as nuns. Mary would sometimes run from the
classroom in tears, appalled at what was expected of her: the unquestioning obedience to one's superior, the humility to place oneself at
the service of everyone, the detachment from family and friends in
the world, while I dreamed of even greater challenges (excepting, of
course, obediently eating as I'd been ordered).

One of the most difficult physical challenges for Mary was the
routine shaving of our hair every few months. While I found it convenient and comfortable to be hairless under our head covers and
veils, especially in the heat of summer, Mary vomited the first time
her head was shaved. Mary's enjoyment of earthly things surprised
and delighted me. While hanging laundry outside, she'd break into a
little dance because of clear blue skies and the scent of clean, wet
linen. At recreation, the hour after lunch when we gathered to talk
and to sew, she'd describe in detail what her family wore on their visits, the scent of her sister-in-law's perfume, the meal they'd shared
on the way to the monastery, and she would have to be reminded
that our conversation ought to be on spiritual topics. Although Mary
wasn't able to save me from my self-destructive fasting, her presence
brought humor into my efforts to be a nun.

One afternoon, as we labored in the fields collecting the summer
squash that overnight had grown to monstrous proportions, and the
ripe tomatoes that seemed to proliferate even as we picked them,
the bell for Vespers sounded. Rather than leave the wagon in the
fields and head for the choir as was expected, we took off at a gallop
across the fields, the wagon flying behind us. Mary pulled while I
tried to keep the teetering baskets upright among the tumbling
squash. Screeching with laughter, we flew toward the kitchen porch
until the wagon toppled, splattering tomatoes and squash everywhere.

Standing on the porch above us, Mother Consolata had observed the whole fiasco.

"After Vespers, you will return to this mess, and retrieve the damaged tomatoes and eat them for meals until they are gone," she said.

My heart plummeted. Hands trembling, I removed my apron and hurried up the steps.

"Thank goodness she didn't say 'squash,'" Mary muttered behind me. I turned and caught her miming a sleuth in search of clues as she tiptoed up the porch steps in Mother Consolata's wake.

Every August 12, we celebrated the anniversary of Saint Clare's death in 1253. An important event in the monastic year, her feast day was almost as significant as Christmas and Easter. On feasts of such stature, the fast was lifted and holiday fare was served at meals, including wheatmeats, an early version of mock duck, dipped in flour and fried in oil; mashed potatoes; pound cake with lemon icing; and ice cream. Benefactors provided the assorted chocolates and mixed nuts we'd find at our places in the refectory.

By 1959, I had become more anorectic than ever, and my stomach churned in dread and anticipation as I helped to prepare the festive meals for Saint Clare's feast day that year. Would I be able to avoid eating, I wondered? At dinner, I was able to slip from the kitchen into the refectory to dispose of my milk; at the same time I tossed a few pieces of candy onto Bonaventure and Rafael's plates. I was not as lucky at collation, a light supper that took place after Vespers, because the nun in charge of the refectory had not yet put the cup of milk at my place. In a replay of the tactics I had used on such occasions, I asked permission to leave Vespers and hurried toward the refectory on legs weak with fear. When I arrived, the milk was at my place, but the pitcher into which I generally poured it was not on the serving table, where it was usually kept. My hands began to shake and my heart thudded in my chest. Hurry! Hurry! What would I do with the milk? The pantry sink! That was it. I dumped most of it in the sink and had begun filling the cup with water when a movement near the pantry door distracted me.

I looked up and into the eyes of Mother Consolata. She had seen the whole thing.

The experience of getting caught filled me, a typical "good girl," with the same terror that must fill a child who has been caught shoplifting.

"Go to your cell, Sister," Mother Consolata hissed.

I doubled over as if hit in the stomach by an invisible fist. Terrified of the consequences, I scurried from the pantry toward the stairs. My legs grew leaden as I climbed. I fell on the final flight and, too weak to stand, crawled toward my cell. While my sister novices chanted Vespers, ate collation, and celebrated the feast of Saint Clare, I lay on my bed unable to move. When they returned to the dormitory after night prayers, I was still lying there, eyes open but unseeing, waiting for Mother Consolata to confront me. When, at lights out, Mother Consolata still had not appeared, I believed the worst. I would not be admonished or punished; instead, I would be sent home. I had destroyed the vocation for which I'd fought so hard, for which I still yearned. I could not imagine going home. I could not bear the thought of leaving the monastery. Despite my preoccupation with food, I loved being a nun. I loved my sisters, the manual labor that tired the body but left the spirit free (if focusing on food could be called free), the rituals, ceremonies, and prayer. I could see no future for myself in the world. Marriage and children had no appeal when all I knew of them were what I'd seen in my own family: the alcohol, arguments, and unhappiness. Careers and success were not what moved me. No! What I wanted only God could offer, and I was certain God could be found only within religious life.

Morning dawned gray and dreary. Raindrops pattered against the windows and drummed away the minutes and still Mother Consolata did not summon me. Prime and Tierce came and went, Mass, breakfast. Still, I waited. By then I had resigned myself to whatever would happen. I felt chilled despite the summer heat. My hands lay flaccid on my chest; I could not move them nor did I want to. Finally, I heard footsteps.

Every morning after breakfast and before we began work, the novices and postulants would gather in the novitiate recreation room for a monastic ritual known as the "chapter of faults," a ceremony that we would continue to practice, weekly, as professed nuns in vows. Usually the chapter of faults was a lovely if slightly routine affair, in which each nun would ask the community to forgive her for public infractions of the rule. Starting with the most senior, each sister would move to the center of the room, prostrate herself before the altar and accuse herself of whatever small offenses she might have committed, such as not keeping custody of the eyes, or answering a sister's request for help in an irritable or uncharitable manner. Sometimes, these events were even humorous, as when a nun would appear with a broken plate or toilet seat hanging from her cord, asking for forgiveness for having damaged community property.

This morning, however, the chapter of faults held the aura of a trial. Kneeling in a circle before the little altar in the novitiate, veils pulled over their faces, the novices waited for Mother Consolata to intone the Veni Creator, asking the Holy Spirit for enlightenment. I begged the Holy Spirit for the strength and wisdom to survive what lay ahead. When my turn to ask for forgiveness came, I accused myself of ongoing disobedience and of disedifying my sisters by my deceitful behavior. Outside the novitiate window, the rain stopped and a cardinal began its liquid trill. Inside the novitiate nothing moved. I waited, still folded into the position of penitence, the others circled round me on their knees. When Mother Consolata began to speak, her voice was soft as a dragon-fly's flutter; but with each word the wings beat faster and louder, scattering sparks that threatened to ignite the rug on which I knelt.

"You dare to ask for forgiveness, Sister? Have you so totally forgotten that what drew you to the monastery was the love of God? Yet here, in the very home he has provided for you, you betray him."

Sister Mary Amata began to cry. Mother Consolata turned toward her. "Sister Mary Beatrix has fallen into the clutches of the devil. She has become Satan's plaything. Vanity has destroyed her."

She paused while Sister Mary Amata snuffled into her big white handkerchief, and then redirected her words to me.

"Sister Mary Beatrix, you are not worthy to live among us. You have given great scandal to all of these children gathered here. Now, kiss their feet and ask forgiveness. Perhaps God will listen to their prayers."

I had never seen this type of a penance exacted before and was not even sure how to do it. I crawled from one nun to the next, kissing each one's feet, asking to be forgiven. With a strange sense of detachment, I could almost see myself groveling. Finally I was able to return to my place in the circle. Mother gave the blessing and the novices left for their chores. I returned to my cell wondering how long it would take Mother Consolata to make arrangements to send me home. When she came for me, I braced myself for her message; instead she told me to follow her. We walked in heavy silence toward the abbess's office.

Hope, thin as a spider's web, began to weave its way back into my consciousness. I focused all the strength of my will on the thought that Mother Charitas, the abbess who had brought me into the monastery, would not send me home. *Caritas* meant love, compassionate love, and Mother Charitas, true to her name, opened her arms to me. She did not ask me why I had disobeyed or acted deceitfully. She knew I was sorry. I fell to my knees in front of her. Gently placing her hands on my head, she blessed me. Then she lifted me to my feet.

# *Prime*

Waves of chant flow from one side of the choir to the other, the nuns' voices as soft and fragile as the morning light just beginning to seep through the windows. It is the hour of Prime and you are ready for the new day: the work you will perform, the prayers you will offer, all you will be and do this day cupped in the chalice of this hour.

As you recite the psalms of Prime, families in the surrounding towns begin to gear up for another day: mothers waking children who want to dawdle in their beds, husbands bolting a quick cup of coffee before racing out the door, the dog begging to be walked, the cat meowing for food. Soon the highways will be filled with vehicles, their lights piercing the gloom of the still dark morning. As the rooster begins his lusty paean to morning, farmers begin the milking, bakers pull crusty bread from ovens, and the night shift at the hospital longs for replacement. For everyone—the sick, the healthy, the jobless, the working—you offer this morning prayer to God.

You are one with them, and they with you: all humanity bound together in an interdependency often forgotten or ignored. You know what they might not understand . . . that no action is ever performed in a void, that everything thought or said or done touches the lives of others everywhere—the past impacting the present and the present aligning the future. You are still sleepy, but this thought lifts you to wakefulness.

# 10

## Lost in a World of Sisters

Not long after I entered the monastery, my parents abandoned their haphazard practice of the faith and became exemplary Catholics. Perhaps in an effort to understand my vocation, or because they felt they needed to reflect their new status as parents of a cloistered nun, they added Mass, Communion, and the rosary to their days. They even became members of a parish, something we'd never done as a family. My father led the efforts to renovate the termite-ridden interior of San Jorge, a Catholic church in Santurce, began a Catholic men's discussion group, and joined the Serra Club, an association encouraging vocations to the priesthood. My mother reached out to assist several convents of nuns, transporting them to doctors' appointments, providing them with necessities, making sure they were well treated by the priests. Once so vehemently opposed to my vocation, my parents were now openly supportive. By entering the monastery, I'd finally achieved what I'd longed for as a child: my parents' full approval. My mother even carried my letters—dreadful things filled with religious platitudes—in her purse, ready to spring them on anyone unfortunate enough to ask how I was doing.

Meanwhile, Judi had begun corresponding with Mother Consolata about her own possible vocation as a Poor Clare.

Before I entered the monastery, Judi had been the baby—the cut-up, the adorable sassy youngest, the child with the curls and the sixteen-inch waist. We had studied ballet together. "Judi is such a lovely dancer. Beryl, well, she tries hard." We had studied piano together. "Judi has such talent. Beryl, well . . ." My entering the monastery had changed that dynamic.

After she entered the monastery Judi told me, "It was Beryl this, Beryl that. Mom and Dad didn't appear to notice me at all. It was so hard, Beryl. I hated you at times." The only time my parents mentioned her was to regale friends with the story of her retort to a Holy Child nun who offered to pray for her: "No Sister! Don't do that. Someone prayed for Beryl and look what happened to her!"

Judi was determined to step out from my shadow. Hoping that her musical talent might win our parents' notice, she convinced Roberto Eyzaguirre, who had studied under the Chilean pianist Claudio Arrau and who gave private lessons at Holy Child, to give her a scholarship so that she could study piano with him. He heard the inherent talent in her touch and agreed to a partial scholarship. Judi went on to become his star pupil at Holy Child and was the featured piano soloist at school performances during her senior year.

Though I was aware of how immensely proud of her accomplishments my parents were, Judi still felt lost. "What is it about religious life that lifts Beryl to the realm of special?" she wondered. "If I were to become a Holy Child nun, a teacher at the school—would that make me special in my own right?" But Judi didn't want to be a Holy Child nun. Teaching held no appeal to her. She felt drawn to the contemplative life, but she wanted more than pious platitudes to get at the truth of the monastic experience.

"What is the monastery *really* like?" she wrote me. Mother Consolata intercepted that letter and answered it herself. Thus it was that neither my parents nor I knew that Judi had also begun to consider the contemplative life as her preferred vocation.

Judi did not encounter the resistance I ran into when she told Mom and Dad that she wanted to enter the monastery. Though their hearts ached to give up their "baby," they had by then achieved a better understanding of the desire to live for God that motivated her. I think they were even proud that they would be the parents of not just one but two cloistered nuns. Also mitigating the sting of losing their last daughter to the Church was the fact that Greg and Steve had both married beautiful Puerto Rican women and were expecting their first children. They would be grandparents; they would have grandchildren to cherish after all.

On the day Judi entered, I waited for her at the enclosure entry with the rest of the nuns, my heart pounding in anticipation. When she walked through the doors, I saw before me a Judi grown beautiful, her blond hair fluffed around her face, her cheeks glowing. This was the Judi who'd emerged during the years we'd been apart, whose letters had been filled with news about beaus (they loved her and she loved them), chocolate (she and her friend Kelly could eat a whole box of frozen brownies in one sitting), and dares such as eating chocolate-covered ants with braces on and grossing everyone out when she grinned. My joy at Judi's arrival was tempered by Mother Consolata's warning that we would be watched, that the walls themselves would develop eyes. Judi and I were to forget we were sisters, she said; we were to be no closer to each other than we were to any other nun. Stricken by my near expulsion from the monastery, and convinced that Judi's entrance was the real reason I'd been given another chance (had I left, Judi might not have entered), I was determined to follow Mother Consolata's orders, even if it meant keeping my distance from my little sister.

Judi, spontaneous and independent as ever, had no intention of observing such restrictions. She saw no problem in writing me notes which she'd squirrel into my breviary or leave at my place in the refectory. The demure black postulant's garb she wore did little to contain her effervescent spirit. During her first week in the monastery, she tossed a worm at Mother Consolata and hooted with laughter at Mother's shriek. When a bat dove over our heads in chapel, Judi's screams and laughter ricocheted through the hallways, even after Mother Consolata issued a stern reprimand. On December 28, the day the Church honors the Holy Innocents, the boy babies of Bethlehem slaughtered by King Herod in an effort to destroy the child the wise men sought, the novitiate was given charge of the monastery. This meant that we planned, prepared, and served the meals, and Judi, as the newest postulant, was made honorary abbess for the day.

"Really?" she said incredulously. "You mean all you sisters have to obey me?"

Assured that we would, she promptly ordered the entire community, including the real abbess, to get down on their knees and kiss the floor. I gasped and looked in surprise at Mary, who was grinning. Though taken aback, the community burst into laughter. As a body they knelt and kissed the floor.

My delight in Judi's audacity was tempered by what I saw of her suffering. Judi struggled through religious life. Every morning she resolved to stick it out another day. Silence, obedience, and renunciation did not come easily. Nor was she allowed the comfort of playing the piano. When, years later she was appointed the choir organist, her fingers had lost their flexibility. I once saw her slam the cover on the keyboard in frustration and run from the room in tears. Nonetheless, Judi persevered.

I thought of Consolata as my nemesis. I never thought of her as an advocate, but perhaps, after all, that's what she was. She'd been a nurse before entering the Poor Clares, and most likely knew about eating disorders. Perhaps she was practicing effective intervention when she so successfully terrorized me into eating. When, after the crisis with the milk, she no longer sent me to the kitchen to eat meat or ordered me to drink whole milk, was this, too, an intervention? Did she realize that forcing an anorectic to eat could backfire?

I was lucky. Many anorectics never recover, even with intensive therapy or hospitalization. Eating more than I had been doing (in case Mother Consolata was watching) but still exercising tight control over my actual consumption, I gradually weaned myself from full-blown anorexia. I maintained tight control over what I would and would not eat until I left the monastery twelve years later, but I never fully reverted to the mad obsession to destroy my body. Only while I was writing these chapters on anorexia more than forty years after the fact, while tucked away at a writing retreat, did the urge to starve myself recur. I lost fifteen pounds that month but resumed normal eating patterns on my return home.

Because I escaped this destructive disorder without counseling or hospitalization, I've sometimes wondered whether I was truly anorectic. Without a medical diagnosis I can't be absolutely sure, but I had all the standard symptoms for diagnosing anorexia nervosa: the cessation of menses; loss of more than 25 percent of my body weight; a distorted, implacable attitude toward eating that overrides hunger; and unusual handling or hoarding of food. I wanted to gain a control over my life and my body that I'd never really possessed but didn't consciously know I lacked.

We were in procession, on our way to chapel, when I felt Mary demanding my attention. Though she had not spoken, I could almost hear her telling me to look up. Mary sent nonverbal signals whenever she saw something of interest. She didn't need words; she just sort of vibrated. Sending silent messages was a useful gift in a life of silence, and it was one she used to advantage. I stole a glance at her and she raised an eyebrow, nodding her head ever so slightly toward Sister Mary Isabel, who was mischievously attaching a small bell to Sister Ellen Clare's veil. Mission completed, Sister Mary Isabel walked on, head bent, hands tucked back into her sleeves. A slight jingle now accompanied us. *"De Profundis clamavi ad te Domino,"* the nuns chanted softly. Psalm 129—Out of the depths we cry to Thee,

O Lord. A snort of laughter escaped me. Sister Mary Isabel's mien of total innocence, Sister Ellen Clare's ignorance of the bell now attached to her veil, and the ridiculous tinkle of a bell during the recitation of the De Profundis was more than I could bear. Mary shook with repressed mirth but uttered no noise. Judi heard us and joined in. With Mary shaking beside me, Judi gurgling behind me, and Ellen Clare jingling in front, I was quite undone. Pretending a sudden emergency, I flew to the bathroom where I collapsed in howls of laughter.

The next morning, at chapter of faults, I knelt with my cord around my neck, prostrated myself before the altar, and accused myself of undue levity while in procession to chapel.

"Why did you do that, Beatrix?" Mary whispered later. "Just stop it. Stop trying to be so perfect."

Mary didn't understand. I *had* to be perfect. My vocation depended on it.

It was the novice mistress, Mother Consolata, who trained us and lived with us constantly, who determined if and when we would be allowed to join the community. After the episode with the milk, I worked extra hard to convince Mother Consolata that I was worthy to make my vows. I needed to earn back her trust, to win her approval. Everything I did, whether it was eating, praying, or performing my duties, was now tainted by the desire to please her. Did she notice that I knelt during meditation instead of sitting? Had she seen how diligently I swept and dusted? Would the sisters I worked with tell her what a great help I was? With each passing day, I focused more intently on pleasing the novice mistress. The purity of intention with which I wanted to serve God had once again become compromised. The harder I worked to win Consolata's approval, the more I focused on winning that approval. She was strong and beautiful, like the women in Scripture, yet lithe and tawny as a jungle cat. Though an ascetic, she exuded sexuality. Like a fly enmeshed in a spider's sticky threads, I became almost as obsessed with Mother Consolata as I'd been with fasting. My devotion to her had all the attributes of the crushes I'd had on nuns and older girls when I was in the sixth grade at Holy Child: the attempt to gain attention, the effort to stay near the object of that crush. Having crushes on other females was common in an all-girls' school, especially before boys changed from toads to princes, but I was twenty now, old enough to be done with adolescent behavior. With other novices seemingly as infatuated as I was, the potential for abuse was astounding. We were young, vulnerable, wanting desperately to please, obedient, and docile. As I write, waves of previously hidden child molestation scandals break around the Catholic church, making me deeply grateful that Consolata focused her attention on molding us into perfect nuns (or rather, into *her* image of the perfect nun).

I wanted to love God, but Consolata had pushed God into second place.

# 11
❦

# A Mother's Scars

From the day I entered the monastery I had both loved and dreaded Mom and Dad's visits. There was the inevitable pain of not being able to embrace; the distorted vision caused by the staggered wires of the double grates and the pounding headaches this brought on; the stilted conversations engendered by the presence of a nun sitting hidden behind a screen. But when Greg was along, the conversation was never dull. Greg didn't care about the nun behind the screen.

During one visit, as I gushed over finally having found my "true home" and the wonderful "mother" I'd acquired in the novice mistress, Greg, in an unusually protective move, put an end to the conversation. I'd hurt Mom enough.

"You think you love your novice mistress?" he said, looking very serious and eyeing the screen, knowing full well that Mother Consolata sat behind it, listening. "Well I know just how you feel." He paused, looked slightly grieved, and then sighed. "I love my mistress too. Every night, she dips her breasts in wine." Greg was not there the day my parents paid an unexpected visit.

In the drying room of the basement, a room that in winter was usually full of freshly washed laundry, we novices worked feverishly to clean and freeze several crates of freshly caught codfish donated by benefactors whose annual deep-sea fishing excursions brought protein to our meatless diet. It was itchy, smelly work, and the scales flew everywhere. They hung from our eyebrows, cheeks, veils, and arms. Benny, a handyman who had come to the monastery as a young boy of sixteen and lived in a small apartment off the garage, laughed at our disgust. He cleaved the cleaned fish into steaks, neatly severing the spinal bones with a huge knife, and passed them to Mother Consolata, who packed them into large plastic containers to be frozen for feast-day fare throughout the year. We were deep into the process when the portress arrived to say that Sister Mary Edward (Judi's name in religion) and I were wanted in the parlor.

Normally we were allowed only four visits a year, so Mom and Dad's arrival at this time was particularly welcome. Judi and I rushed from the basement, tore up the stairs to the novitiate, and cleaned ourselves as best we could. Then we dashed back down the stairs and into the parlor, where we chatted happily for over an hour. Only when Daddy broached the real reason for their visit—"your mother has something she wants to share with you"—did we notice how haggard Mom looked. Knowing she was in the mainland United States to have a hysterectomy, a shudder of fear passed through me.

As a child, I'd loved my mother so totally that I often used to pray that I'd die before she did; I couldn't bear the thought of losing her. My hand pauses as I write this because I know what it is to lose a child and cannot bear to think I ever wished my mother to suffer such anguish. Those whose children actually die before they do know that this desire to die before one's parents springs from ignorance rather than love—yet it is not an uncommon sentiment among children.

Mom leaned toward us, her hands clasping a handkerchief that she twisted nervously.

"Remember, darlings, how when you asked how I got to America I told you that I'd saved my money, and when I was sixteen had enough to buy passage?" She paused and took a shaky breath before continuing. "Well, I didn't come by myself. I came with a man."

Like her siblings in England, who refused to talk about their terrible childhood even to their own children, Mom kept her past secret from us as we were growing up. Other than the reminders about the suet pudding that had kept her from starvation and the journey to America aboard a tramp steamer, we knew next to nothing about her childhood. It wasn't until we began packing my trunk for the monastery that she told me what her childhood had been like, stories that made me weep with compassion—the drunken father who slammed the piano lid on her little fingers; the stepmother who kept her home to care for the babies and beat her if the truant officer found her; the cold and airless room where she slept on springs with seven siblings; the doll she'd made from a clothespin and dressed with scraps of cloth; the rich woman who invited her home when she was nine, then kept her as a servant and let her sleep in the bathtub. That afternoon the monastery parlor became privy to the darkest secret of my mother's life.

It was August 5, 1922. Her sister Julie was getting married, and sixteen-year-old Violet was atremble with excitement. Her hair had been rolled on rags for curls, and she had a new frock for the occasion. Best yet, they were going to have sandwiches and punch after the ceremony! Sandwiches! All the children were happy, save their father. He'd gotten drunk the night before and was in a foul mood. An early-morning foray to the pub had done little to soothe his temper. Sick of my mother's happy chattering, he flew into a rage and lifted his heavy hand to box her ears. She was able to fight him off with a chair before fleeing the house and disappearing into the alleys of London's Marylebone district.

When my mother was nine, she was not so fortunate. One of her father's brutal blows had caused a massive infection within the mastoid bone in her left ear. While she was en route to the hospital—on the train by herself with a rag tied round her head—the infection burst.

When she arrived at the hospital she was rushed to the operation room for the mastoidectomy that saved her life.

A photo of my mother taken around the age of sixteen shows an exquisitely beautiful young girl, her short dark curls framing an oval face with wide-set, hauntingly sad eyes, her skin looking as creamy and translucent as alabaster. No wonder she drew the attention of an older man who fled with her to Canada—a bigamist who, according to a news clipping sent by her sister, committed suicide rather than return to England to face charges. She'd eventually escaped from him and somehow made her way to New York City, where she met my father while working in his father's beauty salon.

This visit remains an enigma. I don't know why Mom felt such a strong need to tell us of her past at that time. Perhaps she felt safe sharing this part of her life with us because we were nuns. Perhaps, aware of the mixed messages she had given us about men, she was concerned that those messages might have influenced our decisions to enter the monastery. Perhaps she was worried about her hysterectomy and wanted us to know the truth in case she should die. Mom appeared to shrivel as she told her story. I wanted the tale to end as quickly as possible. I didn't like seeing my mother's vulnerability, nor did I know what to do with the information she shared with us—how to comfort her. I didn't ask the many questions I now have and would love to ask. How was she smuggled into Canada? What was the bigamist's name? How did she escape from him and enter the United States? When did he commit suicide? What happened to the news report about his death?

A sexual predator had victimized my mother. I'm only beginning to understand the trauma this had caused her.

# 12

❧

## *Solemn Vows*

You lie prostrate before the altar—your arms spread cruciform, the pall of the dead draped over your body. *"Kyrie, eléison,"* chant the priests. *"Christe, eléison,"* respond the nuns. Have mercy, have mercy, Lord, Christ. God the Father of heaven, Redeemer of the world, Holy Spirit.

Back and forth the chanting flows, from priestly ministers to cloistered nuns, a sea of petition that washes over you in waves, receding and returning, again and again.

It is dark under the pall, but you feel bathed in light. The shroud that covers you symbolizes your death to everything save God. When the shroud is lifted, you move toward the cloister grate, your voice lifting in a song of supplication and gratitude. Your heart is full, your voice clear and strong. "Receive me, O Lord, according to Thy word, and I shall live!" Kneeling before the abbess you place your hands in hers and make your vows, promising to "live during the whole time of my life under the rule of the Poor Sisters of Saint Clare . . . in obedience, without property, in chastity and in enclosure."

Gone is the quaver from your voice, the self-consciousness with which you began the ceremony. You belong to Christ and to his body, the Church. Your life is no longer your own. You will follow in the footsteps of the great saints of Assisi who have shown you the way. Faithful to the rule of Saint Clare and its tenets of joyful poverty and service—you will run in the ways of God.

# 13

*Finding My Way Back*

Six months before I took my final vows, in 1963, Mother Consolata left the Bordentown Monastery to open a new foundation—a monastery funded and staffed by an already well-established community—in Coroico, Bolivia. Four other nuns from the novitiate went with her. When the abbess looked for volunteers to help start this new monastery I held back. I wanted Consolata to leave. I wanted to be freed of my obsession with her. I'd lived too long with my face partially averted from God . . . longing for God but unable to see God. I'd entered the monastery determined to become a saint, and what had happened? Five and a half years of religious life consumed with anorexia and with pleasing Consolata. I wanted to find God again, not to lose him in obsessions. My longing for God still seared me. I was in torment over my weaknesses, convinced that true love would never have taken the detours I had. I was weak, weak, weak and I longed for strength. I had lost sight of the love that knew and accepted me with all my faults, with a God besotted with love for me even as I sinned.

The pain of losing sight of God is wonderfully portrayed in the visions of the fourteenth-century mystic Julian of Norwich. She speaks of a servant who loves his master and runs joyfully and with "great speed" to do his will. On the way he falls and is terribly injured. Yet the greatest of all his hurts is not his pain or helplessness but the anguish he experiences because "he could not turn his face to look on his loving lord."

*For he could not turn his face to look on his loving lord.* I find these words comforting as I work my way through guilt and back to the forgiveness that has always been mine. I believe the Church has done a great disservice in not placing its greatest emphasis on God's unconditional love, for if we realized how God loves us, we would recuperate from our falls much more quickly. How many turn away from God because of guilt, because their sense of unworthiness convinces them they cannot change? Wasn't the sinful tax collector Zaccheus a prime example of the power of love to save? Jesus invited himself to the house of the sinner for dinner and Zaccheus responded with such joy that it changed his life.

Preparations for the new foundation had been going on since 1961. Sisters Mary Rafael, Michael, and Agnes had volunteered and been chosen to accompany Mother Consolata. When the small group of four nuns went to Mexico during the summer of 1962 for a six-week Spanish immersion program at Cuernavaca, I adapted easily to their absence, knowing they would be back soon. The actual departure for Bolivia, on November 6, 1962, made me sick with loss. I understood what my mother once tried to tell me about the feelings of depression that had seized her each time Judi and I left Puerto Rico to return to Holy Child for school. As she watched the plane lift off, she'd be seized with an overwhelming sense of desolation. What did she have to go back to? Her girls were gone. With Mother Consolata's departure, I felt something akin to my mother's loss. It is so much easier to leave than to be left. Leaving means change. To be left means loss.

I sat on the novitiate stairway and watched the little band of nuns walk through the cloister doors, my chest tight with pain. The bonds that lashed me to Mother Consolata were being severed; like blood flowing into limbs long bound, a searing flood of pain mixed with ex-citement informed me that I was being set free. When the doors closed, I fled down the hallway toward the chapel and fell to my knees. I was bereft, but it was an exultant grief.

The year Mother Consolata left I was put in charge of the altar-bread room. We made the Communion wafers for the diocese of Tren-ton, and this was our primary source of income. One of my duties was to rise at 4 A.M. every morning, an hour before the other nuns, to mix the batter for baking the breads. In the narrow green pantry on the second floor, I lifted twenty-pound bags of flour, dumped the flour into the industrial-sized mixer along with several quarts of water, ran the machine until the batter was the consistency of thick cream, then poured it into baking bowls, to be refrigerated until 9 A.M., when work began for the day. The next chore was to put the altar breads that we'd baked the day before into the humidifier. Moistening them was a deli-cate task. Too much moisture and their surface, shiny and thin as em-bossed parchment, became marred. Not enough moisture and the breads shattered when cut. These breads, which we mailed to par-ishes throughout New Jersey, would become the body of Christ when the priest said the words of consecration over them at Mass. The fin-ished wafers must be perfect—without flake, chip, or blemish.

I loved those early-morning hours with only the shlumping of the batter in the mixer and the warm breath of the humidifier to keep me company. The other nuns slept while I caught the first rose-colored threads of dawn and the morning chatter of the sparrows who nested in the eaves of the pantry roof. A sense of joy and won-der would fill me then, as if I were the only person in the entire monastery, perhaps the only person in the world. And slowly, alone there with the dawn, I began my journey back toward the peace and purpose of monastic life.

Mother Paschal had taken Mother Charitas place as abbess when Mother Charitas left in 1960 to open a new foundation in Del Ray

Beach, Florida. In appointing me infirmarian and sending me off to Saint Francis Hospital in Trenton for a crash course in nursing in early 1967, Mother Paschal unwittingly became something of a prophet. Neither she nor I realized how often I would need to use those nursing skills in the future. At the time, the monastery's infirmary held three elderly nuns: Sister Mary Pacifica, a poet whose book *The Divine Weaver*, floated somewhere in the monastery library, forgotten by most everyone save its author; Sister Mary Margaret, whose ruddy cheeks shone almost as brightly as her wit and who had tottered through the hallways and down the stairs to prayers until Parkinson's disease felled her permanently; and Sister Mary Brigidae, who had entered the monastery fresh off the boat from Ireland in the early 1900s and who had wandered away in her mind at the age of eighty-six to return as that same Irish lassie.

I loved being infirmarian because I loved the nuns to whom I ministered. I bathed and fed them, changed their bedding, entertained them, gave them their medicines, emptied and cleaned their catheter bags (and even inserted new ones when necessary), and pushed them in their wheelchairs to prayers and recreation. Mostly, I just loved them.

When Mother Paschal asked me to give Sister Mary Jacoba a bath and to wash "especially her hair," I had no idea that the experience would be so traumatic nor that it would force me to encounter another dark side of my personality.

Jacoba didn't live in the infirmary because she could walk. Most of us didn't know her well because she kept to herself, a dark figure that lurched through the hallways doubled under the weight of a great pile of black shawls to protect her from the drafts she was certain had caused her stroke forty years earlier. The day I was to give her a bath was Christmas Eve. The monastery had put on its festive garb. Sprigs of evergreen appeared on window sills, small nativity scenes—the work of nuns who raided every box of scraps for material with which to decorate—emerged on stairwells, the aroma of freshly baked gingerbread and sugar cookies seeped tantalizingly from the kitchen.

I collected Sister Mary Jacoba's good habit and clean head gear from the linen room and walked innocently toward her room, expecting her to greet the idea of a bath with pleasure. I couldn't have been more wrong. Sister Mary Jacoba was not at all happy about a bath, and I was not at all happy to be in her room. It was dark. She had taped wool blankets to her window and tacked scraps of cardboard over every square inch of outer wall to keep out the chill.

Jacoba's eyes brightened when she saw her good habit; she wanted to put it on right away. I told her she could, but not until she'd taken a bath.

"Are you deaf, child? I said I don't need a bath." She smiled, revealing a set of false teeth that appeared too big for her already oversized face. "It's too cold for a bath."

Sister Mary Jacoba's voice had a wheezy sound, like Marlon Brando's voice in *The Godfather*.

"Look, Sister," I said. "Tomorrow is Christmas. Think how good you'll feel, all clean and warm." I heard the whine in my voice and disliked it. I was upset that I hadn't been taught how to deal with difficult patients. I wondered what Sister Mary would do in this situation. She was so good with people. But thinking of Mary's success didn't help me; it just made me feel more inadequate.

"Have *you* had a stroke, child? Do you have any idea what this cold feels like?" I wasn't sure if I knew what the cold felt like for her, but I was well acquainted with cold. Snow and wind crept through the window panes in my cell and painful chilblains cracked my knuckles and the backs of my ankles. I'd been so cold in the monastery that it took me hours to fall asleep at night. Finally, Sister Mary Jacoba agreed to a sponge bath. Dreading my return to that claustrophobic room, I took my time in the bathroom as I prepared the water for her sponge bath. I warmed my cold hands in the hot water that gushed from the faucet and swirled the bar of Ivory soap into soft, iridescent bubbles. I walked slowly back to Jacoba's cell. She took one look at the basin filled with bubbles and told me to take it back. Soap made her skin itch.

No soap? She didn't want soap? I went back to the bathroom and filled the basin again, this time with the hottest water the sink would produce. If she didn't want soap, I'd scald the germs away. Sister Mary Thomas, who was hurrying through the hallway on her way to chapel, put her finger to her lips. I was making too much noise clomping around like that.

I didn't know I'd been assigned a task no one had been able to accomplish. If getting her washed was difficult, attempting to wash her hair was sheer madness. Sister refused to let me touch her head. I couldn't force her. I'd done all I could. Mother Paschal had given me an obedience—a task—I couldn't fulfill.

I asked Jacoba, "How can you disobey your superior's orders?"

She replied, "That's your problem! Mother didn't tell *me* to wash my hair. She told *you* to wash it."

I turned toward the door without helping her with her veil. She could cover her own greasy hair; I wasn't going to fight that battle. But Sister Mary Jacoba wasn't done with me. Simpering and smiling, she told me that she might die at any moment; that if I left, I'd be responsible for letting her die alone.

"Sister, I have three other nuns to care for and they will probably die before you," I said. "Sister Mary Brigidae needs a bath too."

"Sister Mary Brigidae!" Jacoba's voice quivered with indignation. "Why, she's just an extern. I'm a cloistered nun. Cloistered nuns take priority."

It took me a minute to digest what she had just said; I couldn't believe that a caste system existed in a place dedicated to love. As far as I knew Jacoba had done little for anyone; that she should place herself above Brigidae—who had spent her life serving visitors, cleaning floors on her hands and knees, and even begging for the cloistered nuns when times were hard—enraged me.

"Oh really," I said, wrath etching each word with contempt. "In whose book of rules does it say that, Sister?" I paused, trying to gain control of my fury. "If a cloistered nun is what you are, then I'm sick to call myself one." I groped through my mind for something loathsome to compare her to, but could find nothing adequate.

"Keep crying wolf, Sister, and you will die alone," I said. I turned and ran from her cell, afraid of the rage that surged through me. I wanted to kick her, to beat her with my fists. I collapsed in the hallway outside her cell as the implications of my wrath barreled down on me. I, Sister Mary Beatrix, was capable of a violence that could kill.

It has been said that wise men make mistakes, but only fools repeat them. Although I'd like to think I'm no fool, not long after this occurrence I would lash out in a similar fashion against one I loved.

## 14

# Your Mother Needs You

On a chill but brilliant November morning in 1969, I rose with the rest of the community, attended Mass, ate and worked and prayed at the prescribed intervals—fully expecting to return to bed that night knowing that tomorrow would thread today's smooth groove. Life in a monastery is after all meant to be tranquil. Like a river, it flows through the liturgical year with prayer coloring its spectrum and silence marking its rhythm. For twelve years I had ridden this river as one of a family of thirty-five women ranging in age from eighteen to eighty-six. Within this family I had prayed and worked, suffered and laughed. Together, we negotiated the difficulties of communal life; together, we journeyed toward the God for whom we yearned. What I did not expect in such a life was for this river to flood, to sweep me up and over its banks and to deposit me in a place where anything could happen.

A few days before Thanksgiving, I had just finished tucking Sister Mary Brigidae into bed, when Sister Mary Rose burst into the infirmary, panting. When Rose hurried, the monastery floors shook in protest. Bridgie, as we fondly called Brigidae, peered over her wire-rimmed glasses and viewed Rose with some consternation.

"Sister, you're much too fat to be hustlin' fair to shake your bones and it's no good for your heart either." She wagged her head as she admonished the rotund nun.

"And you should mind your manners, Bridgie; it's not nice to call your sisters fat." Rose's good-natured face crinkled in a smile as she hugged the ancient nun.

Then, still wheezing and wiping her face with her blue-checked apron, she told me that Mother Paschal wanted to see me in her office. As she spoke the smile she had bestowed on Bridgie gave way to a frown. Her words triggered an alarm within me. I'd been called to the abbess's office only a handful of times, the last time, in early October, to be told that my father had suffered a massive stroke. I removed my apron with trembling hands and hung it behind the dispensary door. Hurry, Sister! Hurry! The late-afternoon sun danced across the polished floors as I hastened through the hallways and down the stairs toward the abbess's office.

I knocked, and in response to Mother Paschal's "Come in, dear," stepped inside her office, keeping my head lowered out of respect.

"Sit down, Sister Mary Beatrix," Mother Paschal said.

Though her office was sparsely furnished, containing only a heavy wooden desk and two glass-fronted bookcases stuffed with books, the only chair other than hers was filled with papers and unopened mail. She helped me clear it off and smiled apologetically. Mother Paschal was a small, birdlike woman with quick jumpy ways who suffered from multiple allergies and a nervous stomach and seemed always to be either clearing her throat or belching. I sat down and waited for her to resume speaking.

"Would have been a mercy if God had taken your father before this," she said without preamble. "I know this sounds cruel, but strokes are terrible things and can drag on forever. Your dear mother hasn't had a good night's sleep since your father came back from the hospital. She's worn to a frazzle and doesn't know where to turn."

This was news to me. Although I knew my father was paralyzed on his right side and unable to speak, I hadn't realized how bad the situation was. My mother's last letter had sounded optimistic. She was confident that God would listen to our prayers and cure Daddy completely.

"I've prayed hard to discern God's will," Mother Paschal said, clearing her throat repeatedly. "And it's been terrible, just terrible, trying to decide how best to help—what with our vows of enclosure and all. But it seems to me, Sister, that it's God's will that you go to Puerto Rico to help your parents. I've consulted with the bishop, and he agrees that you should go."

She withdrew a handkerchief from her pocket and blew her nose forcefully before continuing.

"Your brother Greg will pick you up tomorrow to take you to the airport. I know this is rather sudden, but it's best this way. I don't want the others to know, not even your sister. I will tell the community myself after you've left."

My stomach clenched as the implications of her words sank in. When nuns "left" the cloister, it was always kept secret. One moment they were there, and the next they were gone. Was I being told to leave the monastery for good?

"Of course, you won't be bound by enclosure while you are gone, but I expect you to keep your vows as perfectly there as you do here," Mother Paschal continued.

What a relief the words "while you are gone" were. "While you are gone" meant I would be returning. Mother paused. There was a moment of silence during which I tried to formulate, in words, the multitude of questions I had: How long would I be gone? Why me, and not Judi? Before I could phrase them, Mother told me we'd be late for Vespers, so I'd best kneel for her blessing. Moving automatically, I slid off the chair and onto my knees. She made a fluttery little movement over my head with her hand, and then motioned me toward the door.

That evening, Sister Mary stood just inside the door of my cell and watched me pack the suitcase Mother Paschal had left in my cell.

"What a relief!" Mary said, her eyes crinkling with laughter. "When I saw you coming out of Mother's office, I thought your father had died! Don't you worry, Beatrix; you'll do just fine in Puerto Rico. You're such a wonderful nun. You will share God's love with those around you."

Mary had an uncomfortable way of discarding rules when she felt there was good reason. We were breaking two rules at that moment: silence and undue familiarity.

"Shush, they'll hear you," I cautioned. Even though I was leaving, I wanted to retain my image as the perfect nun, yet here was Mary in my cell. We were forbidden to enter one another's rooms, but that had not deterred Mary. She'd come to comfort me and on learning I was going home to help, could barely contain her excitement.

"Who would have thought it? Mother Paschal, of all people. Do you know what this means, Beatrix?"

I shook my head uncertainly. The implications of this step were huge. Never in our experience had a cloistered nun been sent home to help care for a parent; we were not even allowed to attend our parents' funerals. Cloistered nuns made a fourth vow, that of enclosure— the solemn promise to stay within a monastery's walls for the rest of their lives.

Mother Paschal was not exactly an innovator. As abbess, she took great care to ensure that we followed the spirit of Saint Clare's rule. She had bowed to the liberal changes of Vatican II by having a chapel erected that allowed us to see Mass, and had followed through with the recommendation to introduce the vernacular into the liturgy, but she wanted nothing to do with other more suspect changes such as the reexamination of ancient tradition and theology. Her attitude toward the new theology that emerged from Vatican II had caused a rift between my father and the monastery. Worried that my mind was turning to mush in the monastery (my letters had become an insipid mess of half-baked pieties), he'd sent me books by theologians such as Karl Rahner, Edward Schillebeeckx, and Hans Küng, which he hoped would energize my intellect. Without saying a word to me about their arrival, Mother Paschal had intercepted these books and sent them back out the door with the priests who came to say Mass. When Daddy asked me what I thought of the books he'd sent, I had no idea what he was talking about.

I went to Mother Paschal and asked if we'd ever gotten those books.

"Tell your father that we have better things to do than to waste our time on suspect theologies," Mother Paschal replied.

My father was furious when he heard this and immediately stopped making financial gifts to the monastery. Mom took up where he left off, saving every penny she could from household funds to send donations, overtly asking for the nuns' prayers but surreptitiously trying to ensure that her daughters were well taken care of.

Mary's delight in Mother Paschal's decision to bend monastic rules made me feel better. I trusted Mary. She was everything I'd hoped to become as a nun—warm, caring, womanly, wise. Her gift was more total than was mine; when she made her vow of obedience, she gave up the self-determination she'd practiced as a working adult, whereas I simply moved from childhood docility to monastic obedience. She knew that her vow of chastity involved a daily recommitment to life without husband or children, whereas I'd been relieved to be freed of the betrayals and hostilities I'd seen at home.

In Puerto Rico as a teen, I'd had to struggle to remain chaste; entering the monastery had freed me from that most powerful catalyst: sexy young males. When my menses stopped soon after I entered (probably due to the anorexia), I thought it a blessing, relieving me as it did of desire, as well as the monthly intrusion of cramps and messy sanitary napkins. Chastity was a breeze. All this ended in 1967, when it was discovered that I had an underactive thyroid.

Mother Paschal had become worried when Dr. Posta, a tall, sallow man who came to the monastery once a year to give the nuns check-ups, discovered that my red blood cell count was abnormally low. When the count kept plummeting despite daily injections of iron, he thought I might be suffering from pernicious anemia and suggested that I be sent to see a specialist who was coming to Saint Francis

Hospital in Trenton to give a seminar on diseases of the blood. This specialist diagnosed my problem as an underactive thyroid, a condition for which I'd already been tested but which had not been detected by blood work, radio-active iodine, or basal metabolism testing. A quick tap on the back of my ankles with a reflex hammer—resulting in a quick jerk upward and slower descent—was demonstrated before a gaggle of nurses and doctors as an almost foolproof method of detecting hypothyroidism.

Thyroxin for an underactive thyroid boosted my red blood cell level. It also stimulated my dormant sexuality. First to respond were my breasts, which grew hard and painful. I was sent to the hospital for diagnosis, where large masses were found in both breasts. Cancer! The nuns fell to their knees to pray. I greeted the news with joy. Today, the word chills me, but then, with the indomitable confidence of youth, I had no fear of death. My body was the only barrier separating me from God. I would die young, like Saint Thérèse of Lisieux, an illusion that dissipated when we learned I did not have cancer but fibrocystic breasts.

Along with swelling breasts came physical response. One lovely summer night, lulled by the swish of passing cars under my cell window, I was jolted awake by the local drum and bugle corps as it marched up Crosswicks Street almost directly under my cell window. Primitive, rhythmical, throbbing, the beat of those drums penetrated my sleep with startling heat. Unable to stop my body's response, I checked my hands to make sure they were folded on my chest. Finding them there and not between my legs, I thanked God that at least I was innocent of deliberate arousal.

Religious life was not rich in ecstatic moments. God did not often pierce our hearts, drawing us toward him in a blaze of light because we'd chosen to live our lives for him. The sense of God's presence had been remarkably absent for several years, but it had not troubled me. I knew that emptiness was an important part of the journey toward union. With the return of sexual feelings, I felt this absence more keenly. I remembered being held in Fernando's arms while dancing, the warmth of his body and the thrill of such closeness. I found it difficult to dislodge the longing those memories elicited.

As I prepared to leave the monastery for my journey home, I knew that Mother Paschal's order would put my vows to the test. I wondered why God was sending me to Puerto Rico, especially as he was omniscient and privy to my thoughts. My vocation was at risk— both God and I knew this, but neither of us let Mother Paschal in on that secret.

# Midday

# *Terce*

Terce follows Prime and begins with a hymn to the Holy Spirit. Morning has dawned and light eases through the windows, marking its bright passage across the choir stalls by bathing the thin pages of your breviary in amber. You can feel its warmth through your veil. You are finally awake, and with your senses more fully engaged you prepare to open yourself to the gifts of the Holy Spirit.

From its opening hymn through its final antiphon, Terce sings with the love and trusting hope that is the spirit's signature.

"Let flesh, and heart, and lips, and mind, sound forth our witness to mankind; and love light up our mortal frame, till others catch the living flame."

Terce reminds you that your life as a contemplative is to be lived with the fullness of the spirit. Your thoughts, words, and actions; your senses and your body, are to bear witness to the love that fills you. Through you, this love will flow to others, a river of life that passes from the monastery to the neighbor down the street, to families across the world, and back again. You are living the mystery of the body of Christ, the spirit of God the life force that connects you to others, to all of creation: the sparrow that makes its nest in the eaves above the kitchen, the carrots and beans that simmer in heavy pots on the stove, the teenager walking past the chapel with his arms around a girl, the woman who eases her aching body under a bridge to find shelter from the cold.

# 15

## The Return

It was easy to feel confident in New Jersey, surrounded by my brothers, their wives, and their leaping, hugging, beautiful children; but on arriving in Puerto Rico, I felt frightened. As I stepped off the plane onto the hot tarmac of the airport, the muggy night air assaulted me, draping itself like a heavy blanket over me, making it difficult to breathe, and separating me from those who milled about the gate greeting loved ones. I looked for my mother's face among those waiting and saw only strangers. I waited there at the arrivals gate until it was almost empty, but still my mother didn't show. As the last passengers disappeared toward the baggage claim area, I hurried after them to fetch my luggage.

My mother was not at the baggage claim area either. What could have happened to her, I wondered, and began to worry about what I should do. How long should I stay there waiting? I needed to make a decision of some sort. Telephoning home was logical, but I had no money and didn't even know our phone number. Did I need a dime to contact the operator? Filled with apprehension I dialed "O." Much to my relief, an operator answered. Certainly I could call collect. She'd even help me find the phone number, she said.

"Hello, Mommy?" I blurted on hearing my mother's voice quaver over the phone—the same slight break in its tones, the same faint British accent.

"Beryl, where are you, darling? You should have been here an hour ago!" She sounded puzzled.

What did she mean, *where are you*? Where would I be but at the airport—waiting. Had she expected me to get home on my own? If so, why hadn't I been warned?

"I'm at the airport. No one came to pick me up." I tried to sound matter of fact but a querulous note crept into my voice. The worry in her voice embarrassed me. I was thirty-years old yet I was acting as if I were still in the cloister, dependent on a mother superior to tell me what to do.

"Can't you take a taxi?" she asked.

"I have no money, Mommy. Did you think I'd have money?"

"No money?" Mom paused as if to digest this information; then, suddenly cheerful with resolution, she suggested I take a taxi anyway. She'd pay the driver when I arrived.

Several drivers slouched against their vehicles smoking: sexy, swarthy men, dressed in button-down shirts and looking slightly sinister in the airport lights. I tried to assess which one looked safest. Before I could decide, a slightly built middle-aged man with a thin mustache swaggered toward me. His was the first taxi in line.

"*A dónde, Hermana?*" he asked—Where to, Sister?—tossing my battered leather suitcase into the trunk and opening the passenger door for me.

"*Park Terrace, por favor.*"

"*Park Terrace?*" he interrupted. What is this Park Terrace?

When I told him it was the condominium on Ashford Avenue, he snorted with impatience. There were many condominiums on Ashford Avenue. He needed an address. His remark surprised me. When I left Puerto Rico, Park Terrace was the *only* condominium in the Condado area. I searched my memory for an address, but all I could summon up was a description of the casino next door. The casino he knew, so off we sped in a screech of tires, careening from the airport exit toward Avenida Isla Verde. Suddenly, the driver swerved to the left, launching us above the once-familiar street below. I didn't remember this highway; it hadn't been here when I left Puerto Rico to enter the monastery. This couldn't be right, I thought. Nothing looked familiar. Perhaps this taxi driver hated Americans and I was being kidnapped for ransom. Mom's letters had mentioned unrest on the island fomented by the *Independentista* movement, whose members wanted Puerto Rico freed of American domination. Trying to sound matter-of-fact, as if people took taxis all the time without money to pay for the ride, I told him that my mother would pay him when we arrived at the apartment.

Rather than upsetting him, the fact that I had no money appeared to soften him. He began asking questions: What brought me to Puerto Rico; why was I staying at an apartment instead of a convent; where was my convent?

Struggling to speak in Spanish, a language I hadn't used in years and had never spoken well, I told him about my father's stroke, that I was going to help care for him, and that I hadn't been home in twelve years. As we talked, I peered anxiously from the window, looking for some familiar landmark that would guarantee we were going the right way. When I saw the sign for Avenida de Diego and the driver flashed his directional to the right, I sank back into my seat, relieved. The taxi sped down the almost-empty street toward the twelve-story building with "Park Terrace" written in large script across the stone façade—the condominium where I'd spent only one summer before leaving for the monastery, the home my mother had filled with such dreams.

My mother was waiting for me in the entry way. It was twelve years since I'd touched her. How soft and frail she'd become. I could feel the bones in her shoulders, the slight tremble in her arms as we embraced. My father's sickness had turned my beautiful mother into an old woman in a house dress. I held her close and forgot that the driver was still waiting to be paid. When I remembered, he was already climbing back into his taxi. I ran toward him, shouting at him to wait so I could pay him.

As he turned toward my voice, I saw tears in his eyes. "Don't worry, Sister. Just pray for me," he said. Then off he roared, pulling away with the same screeching of tires as at the airport, a man whose courtliness made a farce of my earlier fears, who asked only prayers as payment for bringing me home.

I turned toward Mom and followed her into the lobby. As we entered the elevator I asked her how Daddy was doing.

"Come and see," she said.

The elevator rocked slightly, humming as it carried us toward the eighth floor, my mother reminding me which neighbors lived on each floor. When the door finally opened, the memories came flooding back. Poor man's orchid, fuchsia, and spider plants hung in front of the window that separated our apartment from the Horns's, the same plants my mother had cultivated when we first moved to the island. I could hear the water splashing onto the terrazzo floor as she gave them their morning ablutions, knew how quickly the puddles would dry with the morning sun and ocean breeze.

The front door's wrought-iron gate let out an awful squeal as we opened it, protesting the corrosive salt air eating its joints. As we entered the living room, I almost forgot to breathe. Before me, like a jeweled necklace of lights, the Condado shoreline shimmered toward Isla Verde. The lights had been scattered and random when I last saw this view. I took a long look, and then followed my mother toward the bedroom where my father waited fettered by the paralysis that had destroyed his future and precipitated my journey home after twelve years' absence.

I heard my father before I saw him. He was moaning in concert with the wind that cried through the open windows of his room. My parents' bedroom suite had been pushed out of the way, and a hospital bed filled the center of the room. Daddy lay staring at the ceiling, a shriveled version of the handsome man he'd once been.

"She's here, Ferd! Beryl's here," my mother announced—her voice breaking as she said my name. Daddy turned his head toward me.

What was it in his cry that still haunts me? Relief? Welcome? Longing? His eyes scored me with petition, seared me with anguish. My father: my brilliant, handsome, wounded father.

"We were saying the rosary, Beryl," Mom said, placing her hand on Daddy's head. "Every day we pray for a miracle."

My father's face twisted. "No, no, no, no, no!" he cried. The rosary he held in his left hand flew through the air and landed under the bureau. Only the tip of the crucifix remained visible. My mother reached down to retrieve it and tried to put it back in Daddy's hand. Daddy held that hand toward me as if to ask why prayer hadn't helped him.

"Oh, Daddy! I'm so sorry; so terribly, terribly sorry." I bent over the bars of his bed to take his hand and started to cry.

# 16

## Waking Up

When I think again of those days, of the excitement that spiraled continuously within me, I feel the hot sun beating down, the raindrop rustle of the palm trees, the whispered flattery of the men. But most of all, I remember the freedom.

I woke that first morning to the sound of waves crashing on the beach below, the pink and gold of the rising sun playing across my face. Despite my father's condition and my mother's frailty, I felt a wild surge of happiness. Eight floors below my window, a receding wave shimmered back toward an oncoming breaker, leaving a froth of bubbles to mark the edges of its ride. A solitary man jogged along the beach, the wet sand forming silvery halos around his footprints.

The sound of the waves and the beauty of the morning scene filled me with the urge to leave the apartment, to rush out into the morning and onto the street as I hadn't been able to do in twelve years. I smile at this memory now, for having spent many years since then walking city streets and fighting their traffic from behind the wheel of a car, I find it strange that I should have once thought streets so thrilling. But that morning—filled with the anticipation of setting off into the world after years of voluntary seclusion—I could hardly wait.

I didn't know what time Mass started but decided to go anyway. I could pray while waiting if I was early. I dressed quickly, unlocked the iron gate, and slipped into the foyer, deciding to forgo the elevator and take the stairs. I clattered down the eight flights taking great skipping leaps, my habit billowing around me. Once outside the building, I felt like the gulls soaring above me—free, free, free, they seemed to cry—and that freedom coursed through me as the familiar ocean breeze pushed me toward the street and lifted my veil. Leaving Ashford Avenue, with its towering condominiums, I turned onto the smaller streets where charming stucco homes slumbered in the dawn and red and yellow hibiscus waited for the morning sun to prod them into scalloped wheels of color.

I was not the first to arrive at the parish church of San Jorge that morning; several women were there already. They knelt close to the altar, their mantilla-covered heads bowed, their rosary beads slipping like shining fish through their fingers. I knelt behind them where their murmured prayers would be less likely to distract me and opened my breviary to recite Matins and Lauds. I lost myself in the familiar words and ancient rhythms of the psalms, allowed myself to be carried to the internal place of quiet I so loved. I was still praying when the rustle of people standing reminded me that I had come for Mass.

A priest of medium build, with a shock of hair so thick and black it looked unreal, strode to the altar with the flair of an actor. He insisted on singing an opening hymn, even though there were only a handful of old ladies and me to join in, challenging us to "sing, sing!," his ringing tenor voice showing us how and encouraging the old ladies' hesitant notes as his hands marked the time. This priest filled me with contrary feelings. I found his motions embarrassing because they were so theatrical, yet his voice enchanted me. I judged him unkempt because his cassock was frayed and his hair windblown and messy. Yet I found his presence compelling. I was drawn and repulsed simultaneously. The combination troubled me. I knew that this priest would shake up my life and I set myself against him.

"Who is that priest at San Jorge, the one with all that black hair?" I asked Mom when I returned from Mass.

"Oh, you must mean Padre Vittorio. He does have a lot of hair, doesn't he? He's actually a tenured professor at the University of Puerto Rico in Rio Piedras and teaches Humanities, I think. Ferd helped him get a mortgage."

"What do you mean 'helped him get a mortgage'? He doesn't own a home, does he?" I was feeling scandalized already. A priest owning property!

"He doesn't really belong to the parish. I don't know what his status is, but he's an awfully good man. Ferd thought a lot of him. He never forgets us. Comes every Wednesday and Friday to bring us communion."

I sighed in exasperation. It looked like I'd be seeing more of this priest than I wanted to.

I loved baking bread, the feel of the dough under my hands—warm, growing smoother and more elastic as I kneaded it, cupping, pushing, and pressing until its surface shone like silk. I liked the fragrance of baking bread even better, the way it filled the apartment and wafted into the hallway, penetrating the elevator and funneling its way down the stairs to the front lobby. I baked bread for my parents, for Padre Ramirez at Stella Maris, the parish church in Condado, for the young doctor who cared for my father at the Presbyterian Hospital—but I had no intention of baking bread for Padre Vittorio, not even when my mother suggested it.

"But he has no one to look after him. He'd love a loaf of your bread."

"No one to look after him!" I sputtered. "Why does he need looking after?" The thought of the flamboyant priest needing care set me bristling. Why were we supposed to dote on priests anyway? Let him take care of himself. Even his name irritated me. Padre *Vittorio*. Such a triumphant name! He probably chose it himself.

"He gives himself to everyone. He takes no time for himself. A saint, I think," my mother answered.

On the occasion of Padre Vittorio's visits several times a week to bring Communion to my father, I realized that even though he was nice enough, my initial antipathy toward him had not waned. I wondered why I felt so irritated every time I saw him, especially when I usually made an effort to like people. One morning, as I was escorting him back to the front door after he'd blessed my father, I decided to offer him a loaf after all. Maybe reaching out would help me conquer my dislike.

"I baked this morning, Padre. Would you like a loaf of bread?"

The priest's face brightened. "You baked bread? How wonderful. I would be honored."

While I wrapped the bread, which was still warm from the oven, Padre Vittorio waited in the living room. I noticed him wiping his hands against the sides of his cassock and wondered whether he was nervous. The thought made me smile. "Here you are, Padre," I said, holding out the bread, but instead of taking the proffered loaf, he bowed slightly and opened his hands so that I had to give it to him. He stood there cupping the bread as if it were made of gold. "Why, he thinks I've baked it just for him," I thought, already regretting my gesture; it was just a loaf of bread, yet he was behaving as if I'd just given him the Baby Jesus.

"When you come to Communion," he said, his voice quavering, "I think, what is this angel doing, taking Communion from me? Now you give me bread." I looked up and noticed for the first time that his eyes were the color of dark caramel, that his nose was chiseled like that of Michelangelo's *David*, and his lips were full and gentle. Funny, I'd not noticed that he was handsome. It is easy, in retrospect, to see this moment as a turning point in the direction my life would take. It was also a turning point in his. According to his nephew Carlo, who was living with him at the time, Vittorio went home, placed the bread on the table, and said, "She baked me bread. She baked me bread with her own hands."

## 17

*Sexy Feet*

After the initial rush of concern that typically follows a hospitalization or serious illness, visitors stopped coming to see my father. They were apologetic. It was just too painful to see my father like this: paralyzed on his right side and unable to speak. Maybe he frightened them with his crying, with the way he shouted "No" over and over again. Nothing, however, could keep Nellie away. When Nellie swept into the apartment full of vigor and voice, my father would bang his left arm up and down on the edge of his chair and shout "No, no, no, no, no," just as he did when he was angry or upset or wanted something, only now his eyes practically disappeared into his face with pleasure. Nellie could tell him that he looked like shit or ask him what he thought he was doing in a wheelchair and my father would shake his head and look as perplexed as his "Nos" implied, but it was clear from his eyes that he loved her teasing.

Nellie Carrión was the wife of Don Rafael Carrión Pacheco's son, also Rafael (called Papi), the president of my father's bank. She was one of my mother's best friends. She was also the person, I was later to learn, who had harangued and harassed by letter and by phone not only Mother Paschal but the bishop of Trenton to send me home to help my parents. One morning when I had been in Puerto Rico for about two weeks, Nellie called to ask if I'd like to take a trip with her into the mountains. Her cook wanted to spend some time with her family, and Nellie, who was driving her there, needed company on the return trip to help her stay awake. To travel through the Puerto Rican countryside meant negotiating treacherous, twisting, narrow mountain roads where trucks and buses and *publicos*, public taxis that carry many passengers, careened around corners as if they were the only vehicles on the road. One needed to stay very alert on such journeys. Anxious to revisit the spectacular mountain scenery I hadn't seen in over a decade and encouraged by my mother, I quickly silenced the inner voice that reminded me I hadn't been sent home to go sightseeing. Nellie needed me.

On our way to the small mountain *finca*, the farm where her cook lived, Nellie pressed her foot hard on the accelerator and the car leaped ahead. The narrow roads with hairpin turns did little to slow her down. I clutched the bar above the window and wished I had a set of brakes on my side of the car. Suddenly Nellie slammed on the brakes and shifted into reverse. The car screeched backward several hundred feet and stopped next to a truck heaped with pineapples. An old man trotted toward us, slapping his head in amazement when he saw a woman driving. Never in his life had he seen a woman drive in reverse like that! Delighted with his reaction, Nellie purchased several large pineapples and graciously accepted another in honor of her driving prowess. She winked at me as she sped away and began to sing, "Anything you can do, I can do better," her husky, slightly gravelly voice filling the car and making the cook and me laugh.

We were on our way back to Nellie's when she finally told me the real reason she had invited me on this trip. She needed to talk to me, woman to woman. "The old ladies at church are gossiping about you," she said.

"Really," I said, not sure what to expect. "What are they saying?"

"'That little nun had better be careful,'" Nellie responded, turning her head to look directly at me. "'She has sexy feet.'"

Sexy feet! The old ladies might as well have said I was exposing too much cleavage. How could my feet be sexy? I was covered from head to foot in layers of clothing that resembled a shapeless sack, tied in the middle with a white cord. I clumped along in heavy black sandals with soles too thick to bend. Franciscan Friars made those sandals. They made them to last, not to be sexy. I looked down at my feet and Nellie did too. Only the toes showed beyond the straps. "Better be careful, Beryl. Wear shoes. Remember the men down here."

Nellie could be blunt. She'd once told me that men didn't really want wives, that "They'd prefer three women. A maid, a prostitute, and a mother for their children." She was on target with her concern about my naïveté. I'd grown careless in Puerto Rico thinking that my religious habit kept me safe. I'd even begun to enjoy the charming metaphorical flatteries called *piropos* that had embarrassed me as a teenager. That very morning, an elegant older man had sighed, "*Que lastima! Un bombón tan rico, pero en esa envoltura!*"—What a shame, a delicious candy but in such a wrapper!—and I had smiled and said thank you.

There was something exciting in this allusion to my feet, to the hint that toes peeping from beneath a habit might arouse a man. I sucked in my breath at the dark warmth that filled me and hoped Nellie wouldn't notice my burning face.

Back at her house, Nellie plied me with food for my parents. She pulled a chilled plate covered with wax paper toward the front of the refrigerator, saying, "I made flan for your father. He loves it." Dark amber liquid shimmered on the caramel-toned custard that she placed carefully on the counter. "What else can I send? You like rice and beans?" I loved rice and beans! Soon the counter was filled with containers to take home: fried sweet bananas, fresh mangoes and limes from her garden, pastelles wrapped in plantain leaves. My mouth watered at the sight of her wonderful native cookery. I hadn't realized how much I'd missed Puerto Rican food. A clock chimed in the hallway.

"Aye, can you stay a bit? Papi will want to see you. He can take you home." Nellie pointed me toward the living room and left to phone his office. The living room hadn't changed much since Judi and I had waited there for our parents and Papi and Nellie to return from one banking event or another. Furnished in French Provincial style, the room filled with a peculiar heaviness at night as moist air pressed against me like an impassioned suitor, while outside, cicadas and *co- quís* (minuscule frogs native to Puerto Rico) sang noisily, and the scent of ripening limes and frangipani drifted through the iron grills protecting the windows. Occasionally, a centipede would appear, only to disappear under the rug carpeting the beautiful terrazzo floor. A strange restlessness used to fill me then, making my nerves crawl, as if the insect had found its way onto my body. I could never find the source of the itch, but it would follow me home and into my dreams.

While I waited for Nellie, I gazed at a painting of two women with a child taking its first steps. In a way, I was taking my first steps, too, back into the sensation-filled world that I had fled as a teenager, and that, I'd discovered since my return, I really loved. Nellie padded barefoot into the room. She carried a half-empty bottle of Asti and two long-stemmed glasses and wore a shapeless flowered robe.

"Ah," she sighed. "Now I can breathe. I had to get out of that girdle. It was killing me. Papi hates it that I've gotten fat, so I told him: 'You have six kids and see what happens!' Men, eh! But you don't have to worry about them. *Verdad?* Lucky you." She plopped down into a chair and began to pry the cork out of the bottle.

When Papi arrived he dropped his briefcase, tossed an armload of papers onto a small table in the hallway, and swept me into a strong hug. He planted a kiss, Puerto Rican style, onto both cheeks, and then, holding me at arms' length, said, "You look wonderful, Beryl. Religious life seems to agree with you, but I'm glad you've come home. Ferd and Vi really need you."

I barely heard his greeting, so shaken was I by the thrill of that hug. Papi was gorgeous, sexy, with tight curly hair, craggy features, and dark eyes. Later, as Papi drove me home, Nellie's culinary bounty on my lap, I wondered if men like him would find my feet sexy. The memory of his hug bolted through me like an electric shock. What did this mean? That I wanted to be hugged so I could feel again the same pleasure?

Want! Desire! New words in a life dedicated to abnegation. Wants were those tingling sensations that now kept me company wherever I walked, that filled me with the desire to see and to touch. Little shops heaped with cheap merchandise, children rushing past in plaid school uniforms, men in business suits driving shiny new cars, women with shopping baskets on their way to the market; everything so different from the stark white walls of the monastery, the flowing gait of the nuns in procession, the silence of our daily chores.

I'd smell the spicy sharp smells of native cooking and want to cram my mouth full of it. The sounds of the street tantalized me, the shouts of children, the clanging of construction sites, the voices behind the modest walls that separated the houses from the street.

# 18

❧

# *Seeking a Friend*

$F$or centuries, writers and historians have theorized about the relationship that bound Francis and Clare. Some have concluded that they were "in love." Certainly Clare and Francis loved one another, but were they "in love" in the romantic way we define that term? Clare's writings are full of her admiration and respect for the little Poor Man of Assisi, and Francis revered and cherished Clare. She was certainly not an infatuated young girl when she followed Francis into the service of the poor suffering Jesus. Having no wish to marry and become subject to the rule of a husband, she had already sold her dowry and given its proceeds to the poor, and would soon be mothering an entire community of women who followed her into religious life.

In our monastery, similar friendships existed between some of the nuns and their male advisers. Most often, these were women who entered the monastery later in life. Many were college graduates who'd had successful careers. Some were from other orders where the concerns of their teaching or nursing mission kept them from the union they sought with God. In the search for a more meaningful way of life, they'd sought the counsel of priests who steered them toward monastic life as practiced by the Poor Clare nuns. These women brought to religious life a greater understanding of what they were leaving than those of us who entered at a younger age. Making one's own decisions, questioning values, accepting or rejecting belief, were not options in which I had much practice. At an age when other teens were leaving home for marriage, college, or jobs, I had entered a monastery where obedience—as I understood it—precluded making such decisions. These women, however, seemed fully able to combine obedience with the traits I so admired in them: compassion, understanding, and warmth.

Not all the nuns had spiritual directors, only those who requested them. I was a novice in 1958 when I asked Bishop Ahr of Trenton if he would help me in my life of prayer. The bishop came to the monastery once a month to give a lecture on spirituality and would afterward meet with those who requested his direction. I was anxious to make great strides in mysticism and wanted to move immediately from the basics of mental prayer to full-blown contemplation. I managed to convince the bishop that I was already well grounded in prayer. Instead of reading and studying the Scriptures, I read Saint John of the Cross. This Spanish mystic, poet, and contemporary of Saint Teresa of Avila is best known for his *Dark Night of the Soul*, which relates the soul's journey toward union with God to Christ's agony and abandonment. I tried to convince myself that my aridity at prayer was really the dark night of the soul and that I was only one leap away from divine union. The reality was that I had just begun my journey toward God. Karl Rahner once wrote that the experience of God is the experience of life, and vice versa. Well, I had little experience of either God or life. What I needed was an understanding of who I was and what this "I" really believed. So often I wanted to tell the bishop that we were moving too fast, that I had not been honest with him—"Wait," I should have said, "we need to slow down. I'm not ready for mystical prayer. I don't even know how to meditate properly. We need to go back to the basics of spiritual living."

I no longer felt the upwelling of distrust I'd experienced when I first met Padre Vittorio. In fact, I'd grown to like him. When he came to visit Dad, I liked the way he asked my father how he was instead of directing that question to Mom, as others did. I enjoyed the sermons that he delivered with such sincerity and fervor. I even delighted in his scattered, absent-minded-professor way of dropping books and papers as he hurried to his car. Although I knew him only through what I'd observed and what my mother told me about him, I convinced myself that he might be the spiritual director I needed. I even began to relate the strong presentiment that he would change my life as a sign that, yes, this was indeed the man who could help me become a saint. Had I been more honest, I would have acknowledged that it wasn't just an adviser I wanted—I wanted someone to love me.

When Daddy first returned from the hospital after his stroke, my mother contacted one of the best therapeutic hospitals in the country, the Kessler Institute in West Orange, New Jersey. I think everyone believed that with good therapy, he could regain his lost skills and return to a normal life. This belief sustained us during the Christmas holidays, and in late February 1970 we received the news that Kessler had an opening for Daddy.

"You're going to get better, darling," my mother said, and my father's eyes filled with tears. He reached out with his left hand, the one that still had movement, and grasped hers. Their eyes seared the other with hope.

By this time I had been in Puerto Rico for three months, but I still had not said more than a perfunctory "Good morning" to Padre Vittorio. The morning following the phone call from the Kessler Institute, I decided to wait for Padre Vittorio outside the sacristy after Mass. He almost collided with me as he rushed out the door in his haste to get to the university. He turned crimson and apologized profusely. I countered with my own apology. Then I began fumbling for the words I'd practiced the night before. How did one begin such a relationship? Ask for a trial run?

"Would it be possible, Padre," I asked hesitantly, "to discuss my spiritual life before I return to the monastery?"

He smiled. "Sister, it is you who should teach me about prayer."

Friendship? Now that was a different matter. A friendship based on God's love—well, what could be more wonderful?

"Why," he said jubilantly, "you might also be able to help me with my English!"

And so we began as new acquaintances do, talking about what interested us, sharing bits of our life's journey, growing more enthusiastic as we realized we'd had similar experiences, our words tumbling over one another's. We'd both entered religious life early and suffered from compulsive behaviors; Vittorio had grown as inordinately attached to a Father Superior as I had to Mother Consolata. We both yearned to live for God. Earlier in his life Vittorio had even been a monk, and had left the ancient order called the Minimi only when he realized he was more interested in serving the people of God than his fellow monks. He also knew more about the Poor Clare Order than I'd suspected, having once been chaplain at a monastery of Poor Clares outside Rome.

"I used to ride my little Vespa into the hills to get there," he told me. "How I loved that Vespa, but how many times did I fall. In winter, motorcycles are not good."

A Vespa? The thought made me laugh. I recalled the weekends when my brother Greg rode all the way home to Saddle River from Iona College (before he joined the Merchant Marines) on his teensy Vespa, covered with dust, his long legs tucked practically up to his shoulders, and his hair blown about so that he looked like a dandelion gone to seed. It was easy to imagine Vittorio, robes flapping in the wind, thick black hair streaming behind him, scooting up and down Rome's hills on his way to say Mass.

# 19

## The Return to the Monastery

"Don't drink too much, Ferd," Papi quipped, putting his hand on my father's shoulder. Daddy grinned his crooked smile, and Mom and I laughed. Drinking was one thing we no longer worried about. My father ate and drank only what we gave him.

Papi had gotten all of us first-class tickets for the flight to Kessler. He was anxious for my father to regain his speech. Several weeks earlier, he and several other bank vice presidents had come to ask my father's advice on a large loan he'd been working on prior to his stroke. It had been a frustrating experience. Daddy tried to nod his head in the direction that would signify what he'd advise. "No, no, no, no, no," he said, trying to summon the words he wanted to use.

"You mean that we should not make that loan?" Papi asked.

"No, no, no, no, no," Daddy repeated, looking with distress at Papi. Papi turned to Mom. "What is Ferd trying to tell us, Vi?"

Mom began to say what she thought Daddy would advise, and my father went wild. He let out a great cry and started to sob. The bankers got up hurriedly and left, apologizing profusely. They did not return again, not even to visit.

We arrived at Newark airport in the early evening of March 13, 1970. An ambulance was waiting on the tarmac to take Daddy to Kessler. The emergency crew helped my father into a wheelchair and covered him with blankets. It was blustery out, and the sleety snow cut into our faces as we followed the wheelchair down the ramp toward the waiting ambulance. My mother's light coat was no protection against the cold. She began to shake violently.

"Get in quickly, Mom," I told her, climbing inside the ambulance to hug her good-bye.

"You're not coming with us?" She reached out to grab my arm, panic edging her voice. She looked so frail and frightened, like a bird fallen out of its nest.

"I have to go back to the monastery. You know that, Mom."

"But I thought you'd come with me." Her words filled my eyes with tears. I'd wanted to go with her, wanted to make sure she was all right, but Mother Abbess said I was to return immediately to the monastery. My parents no longer needed my help. What difference would it make to tack a few more hours onto the journey, I wondered. I felt a clench in my heart and tightening of my jaw. Obedience was becoming much more difficult, now that I'd started thinking for myself. I rubbed Mom's hands and held her close.

"You'll be fine, Mom," I crooned. "And, Daddy, you make sure to get better. We need you to get well; the bank needs you too."

Daddy nodded and made the garbled "Ah-m-m-m-m" sound that signified he understood. I climbed out of the ambulance and hurried toward the airport gate. My Puerto Rican sojourn had come to an end.

Mom rented a small apartment near Kessler during the month Daddy was there. Her descriptions of this time were so vivid that I sometimes think I must have visited my parents there. In my mind I can visualize the hallway where my mother found my father weeping the morning after he'd been admitted, unable to find his way to his therapy session. It still hurts to think of my father's humiliation and helplessness at Kessler. All his life he'd set goals for himself; had risen from messenger boy to internationally respected banker and had chaired the boards of numerous organizations. Now he couldn't even find his way to a therapy session. Distressed that my father was expected find his way around when he could no longer read a map, my mother began spending entire days with him to make sure he got to meals and was cared for properly.

The Kessler Institute was a heartbreaking and futile experience for my parents. On his first night there, Daddy's gold watch, the one he'd continued to wear even though he could no longer tell time, was stolen. At Kessler, we learned that the stroke had been too severe, that it had robbed him of the ability to relearn the skills he needed to become self-reliant. After less than a month, my mother was told to take Daddy home.

"Build a ramp and give him plenty of tender loving care," the doctor advised.

My mother did not give up easily. She returned to Puerto Rico and managed to accomplish what the Kessler Institute had not been able to achieve. She taught my father how to walk.

Returning to the monastery after three months in Puerto Rico was more difficult than I'd thought it would be. I knew the cloister might seem confining after the freedom I'd experienced in Puerto Rico, but I didn't expect it to be so lonely. I'd always loved solitude, and was grateful to be back among my sisters, whom I had missed terribly, but I had changed. Gone was the adolescent nun focused solely on eternity, her place usurped by a young woman who had seen the world as if for the first time.

I missed my parents, their beautiful spacious and bright apartment, the scent of salt air and damp concrete. I missed the people, their laughter and rapid-fire conversations, the island nuns who had shared their friendship and even their convents with me, inviting me for meals and an occasional overnight to supply what I lacked in religious companionship. I had seen such goodness in Puerto Rico, had experienced so much beauty there, that for the first time since I entered the Poor Clares I began to have doubts about the value of monastic life.

Adapting again to a rigid monastic schedule based around liturgical prayer was even more difficult. In Puerto Rico, rising on and off all night to help my father, I'd learned to sleep through any noise save the ones he made. This ability to turn off noise and reenter sleep caused me real problems when the sacristan called us for Matins. The soft tapping and whispered *"Benedicámos Domino"* often failed to wake me. In the morning I'd wake with a start at the sound of the wooden clapper and realize that once again I'd slept through Matins. Missing Matins was a sign that my commitment to religious life was waning. It troubled me greatly. For years, even when I was no longer a nun, I continued to have nightmares about missing the call for Matins. Matins had always been one of the most precious and satisfying practices of my religious life—prayer, praise, and penance rolled into one powerful expression of devotion and love. It was inconceivable that I now found it so difficult to fulfill.

Vatican II had taken longer to infiltrate the monastery than the teaching and nursing orders, but eventually even the Bordentown Clares began to initiate new practices. I returned to the monastery to find that many changes had taken place in my absence. The parlor grate had been replaced by simple wooden lattice that could open like a window; the pure wool habit had been replaced by a wool blend that was lighter and less expensive; we were allowed more frequent visits from friends as well as relatives; and although we still needed to get permission to write letters, our letters were no longer censored. When I asked for permission to write to Padre Vittorio, it was given readily. I wrote him several letters between March 1970, when I returned, and May, when I received his first reply.

"I am hesitating to write. My English, it is poor. I am just a beginning," he wrote, and went on to say that he was traveling to Italy for the summer and would be flying through Newark on the way.

"Would you be so kind as to ask your Mother Superior if I might visit?"

I did so, and Mother Abbess agreed. I was thrilled. Not only had Padre Vittorio not forgotten me, I would actually get to see him again, something I'd never dreamed possible.

Padre Vittorio arrived at the monastery wearing a black suit and Roman collar, instead of the cream-colored cassock he'd worn in Puerto Rico. In the cassock he appeared very much a priest, but in a suit he was priest and man—a good-looking Italian man at that. I began to wonder if this visit was a good idea after all. I didn't know how to have a friendship with a man; I'd never really had a male "friend." The men in my life had been family or boyfriends. In contrast to the edginess his masculinity aroused in me, Vittorio appeared very much at ease in the monastery parlor. When he spilled a cup of tea on his pants, his laughter erupted spontaneously.

"Mother Superior will think I have peed," he said.

Embarrassed, I averted my eyes as he began to dry his slacks with the napkin that had been provided with his tea. I excused myself saying I would get him a clean napkin, and hurried from the parlor. When I returned, the extern nuns, who doted on visiting priests as if they were precious if slightly recalcitrant school boys, had already provided him with a fresh tray of tea.

Still nervous because of Vittorio's natural earthiness, I steered the conversation away from Vittorio or myself to a safer topic—my parents. Vittorio responded that Mom was having a hard time caring for Daddy and looked very frail and tired.

"She's getting too thin," he said. "I suggested she get a nurse to help now that her 'angel' has returned to the cloister."

Was "angel" what Mom called me, or was Padre Vittorio still thinking of me in those terms? In my letters, I'd made no attempt to hide my faults from him, sharing the anger I sometimes found so hard to control, my tendency to be judgmental and opinionated, and my problems with Matins. I wanted him to see me as a real person. I didn't want to be any one's angel—not Mom's nor his, but, not wanting to hurt him by saying this, I again changed the subject and asked why he went to Rome every summer when such travel must be a luxury for a priest.

Vittorio didn't seem at all perturbed by my questions. "I go to see family," he said. "My brother Costantino is ill, and I have many nieces and nephews. Travel is my only cost because I stay at my sister Maria's home in Rome—can you believe, the same apartment I lived in as a boy? Also, I have many friends to visit, and I research materials for the honors classes I teach at the university. The Vatican libraries, they are very fine for such study."

"What's it like to spend a summer in Rome?" I asked. "Tell me about it!" It was such a stupid question but Vittorio smiled and shook his head.

"In August, Rome gets very hot," he answered. "Every one goes on holiday. I go to the Alps. Maria and Gianni have a summer home there." He leaned toward me and beckoned, a mischievous smile playing about his lips. "Why don't you come with me?"

His remark startled me. Go with him to Italy? What an amazing thing to say! Did he mean what I thought he implied by making such a suggestion? I think I laughed to cover my confusion.

That summer Vittorio sometimes sent me scenic postcards, sometimes short one-page letters. Finding airmail envelopes with green and red chevrons and his distinctive European handwriting in my mail cubby sent a jolt of excitement through me. His letters were mostly spiritual in tone: advice on good spiritual books to read and occasional news about his family. I wrote similar letters in reply. I probably mentioned how wonderful it must be to live in Rome where St. Peter had once walked and taught, and where so many saints had died as martyrs. (I have no letters from this period, for, in the spirit of detachment that was part of the rule of Saint Clare, I never held on to things I loved.) The thought of his being there fascinated me. I kept pondering his question, "Why don't you come with me?" and wondered whether he had already begun to think of me as more than a friend. Rather than rejecting such a possibility, I started to research Italy.

Getting books from the town library was another concession offered by Vatican II and I made good use of it. Under the pretext of learning more about the Church, I asked for and received permission to read books on Rome and Italy. Of course I couldn't go to the library, but the monastery's handyman, Benny, would fetch them for me, and soon a two-way commerce in books was trafficking between the monastery and the library. I read everything Benny brought me. One of these books was a collection of photographic essays on Italy in which a photo of Rome—its cobbled streets wet with rain and reflecting light from street lamps and neon signs; its purple sky rent with lightning—sent a disquieting premonition, like the one I'd had when I first saw Vittorio, lurching through me. One day I *would* be in Italy with him.

# Sext

When the small choir bell tolls at 11:30 A.M., you respond immediately. You have been at work all morning: pouring batter on the shining plates of the altar-bread stoves that resemble a rectangular waffle iron, cutting the sticky residue from the sides with a dinner knife, and carefully lifting the beautiful white breads bearing raised images of the Nativity, the Crucifixion, Pentecost. If you are an excellent baker, you run two or three stoves at a time. Perhaps you've stood all morning at a wooden board, cutting the breads into the large hosts priests use for consecration. They must be perfect, no chips, no flakes. You remove your apron, release the loop and wooden dowel that secure the front of your habit around your hips. The scents of dinner rise from the kitchen below: stewed tomatoes, onions, cheese, hot applesauce . . . You are hungry, but monastic life keeps your priorities straight. Before replenishing the body, you must refresh your spirit, renew your commitment to the life of prayer and service that drew you to this place. Blessed are they who dwell in your house, O Lord.

# 20

## Taking Care of Daddy

In July of 1970, shortly after my mother succeeded in teaching Daddy how to walk, he made his tottering way to the bathroom, walker clanking noisily across the floor, and fell. My mother, her back already injured while struggling with our salt-corroded garage door, tried to lift him and fell with him onto the floor.

Once again, I was called to the abbess's office.

For twelve years the belief that God's will was manifested through our superior's orders had been drilled into me. "Mother Abbess *is* God's will," a fellow novice once told me. The lives of the saints were filled with examples of unquestioning obedience, and my personal heroine, St. Thérèse of Lisieux, had written, in her spiritual autobiography, *Story of a Soul*, that good nuns made the will of their superior their only compass. "They can never feel mistaken, even if they are certain their superiors are wrong."

God's will eased my conscience. If God didn't want me to make another trip to Puerto Rico, wouldn't he have done something about it before this? Wouldn't God have inspired Mother Abbess to send Judi instead? Besides, this trip would probably be my last. When I got back to the monastery, I promised myself, I would work extra hard at renewing my commitment to religious life.

With the same excitement that was to mark each subsequent trip home, I boarded the plane at Newark Airport and watched the New York skyline disappear. I, Sister Mary Beatrix, was once again airborne; beneath me the broad expanse of the sea stretched as far as the eye could see, melding with the horizon along an invisible seam. So immense, so vast! Just like the freedom I felt expanding within me.

Having taught my father how to walk, my mother focused her formidable will on teaching him how to talk. Every morning she'd sit with him at the dining-room table to work on verbal and coordination skills. I can still see them, their heads almost touching, my father attempting to place the letter and number blocks in the appropriate squares, my mother encouraging and correcting him. For the first half-hour he worked hard, trying to match things, to repeat the words my mother carefully sounded out. "No-oh, no-oh, no-oh," he'd intone, softening his voice, trying to get the inflections just right. No new words, just the same old "No." Then, he'd shove the learning boards off the table. The little chips would scatter like flavored Chiclets—gray numbers, white vowels, red consonants—across the terrazzo floor.

On this my second sojourn in Puerto Rico, my brother Greg, knowing that I was skilled enough to take care of Daddy by myself, arrived with his family and swept Mom into their car with them, absconding with her for a two-week tour of the island. It was a wonderful, hilarious time that helped her recuperate from the stress of unremitting caretaking.

While Mom was gone, I found my father relatively easy to work with. He didn't put the pressures on me that he put on my mother and we were able to develop our own methods of communication. I knew that even though he could not speak, his mind was intact, an understanding that was brought home several weeks before Mom left, when I asked her for envelopes. Daddy immediately began banging his hand on his chair and saying "No," but with an inflection that drew my attention. He lifted his cane and pointed toward the hallway. Thinking that he wanted to go to the bathroom, I helped him out of his chair and walked him there. He shook his head and modulated his no's so that I would understand that he'd meant something else. He looked toward the bedroom, so toward the bedroom we went, then to the closet.

"Do you want me to open the closet?" I asked. With satisfaction edging his no's, he shook his head from side to side. It looked as though he meant no, but I knew he meant yes. When I opened the closet door, he laughed out loud, the strangled sort of guffaw that had replaced his laughter after the stroke. Sure enough, under the bottom shelf in the right-hand corner, pushed toward the back of the closet, was an entire box of envelopes.

Our successful exchange and his laughter were a breakthrough— Daddy and I could communicate. But there was more to this success than communication. For the first time since his stroke Daddy had been able to help.

My father's eyes had always spoken, laughing when he was pleased, stern when concerned. Alone with him during my mother's absence, I discovered that his eyes still talked. With those eyes he could ask me for a cookie fresh from the oven, could signal that he was thirsty, or that he wanted to go to the bathroom. Once he even indicated that he'd like a real drink, pointing to the bottle of Don Q Rum Mom kept in the kitchen cabinet. His no's softened when we were together—actually developed inflections: rising slightly in an effort to signal acquiescence—Yes, I'd like to go for a walk; dropping to signify a negative—No, I don't need anything.

We went out often. I pushed the wheelchair along Ashford Avenue to the park, where the children were building sandcastles or whizzing down the slides. Their bright little shouts made him smile. The younger ones reached out to touch his brace, offered him their plastic shovels or a lick from their ice-cream cones. His no's became softer in reply to the children's babble. They seemed to share a common language.

Our days without Mom passed quickly. Then, just as suddenly, the travelers were back. No sooner had my mother walked in the door than my father took up his old refrain, banging his left arm and saying "No."

And, as usual, my mother rushed to his side. The immediate resumption of their old patterns of behavior—my father's demands and my mother's response—irritated me. "How did everything go?" she asked.

"Wonderful. We had a great time together. It doesn't have to be hard!"

As I spoke, I felt a terrible exhaustion sweep over me. I excused myself and went to take a nap. I slept for thirteen hours.

I watched all that my mother did for my father, the way he relied on her, how her response to his demands drained her. I was suddenly frightened of my ongoing involvement in their need. Going back to the monastery would be even harder this time. I'd entered the monastery to seek freedom from worldly demands, but the freedom the world offered was now more welcoming. I wasn't sure I would have the strength to keep choosing the monastery. If I was to stay faithful, we'd need to look at other options besides my help.

One night, after putting Daddy to bed, I confronted Mom. Had she considered putting Daddy into a nursing home? Her answer was instantaneous. Daddy needed her. She'd never again abandon him.

Daddy had been late coming home the night of his stroke. Mom was certain he'd been out drinking. How many times had he promised to stop drinking, and she'd believed him, trotting off to Alcoholics Anonymous meetings with him, hopeful that this time his sobriety would last. And had it? No. He still loved the damn bottle more than he loved her.

That night, when Daddy finally showed up, his speech was slurred. He insisted he'd had only one drink, an excuse she'd heard so often that it drove her wild with anger. She stormed off to the bedroom and locked the door behind her. No goodnight, no embrace. He could sleep where he damn well pleased. Hours later, she was awakened by a loud crash and found Daddy crumpled on the floor, Churchill's *World at War* spilling from his hand. Mom replayed this image over and over, along with another image: that of Daddy's head smacking against the ambulance door as the attendants lifted the stretcher. She'd thought he was drunk. She'd abandoned him when he needed her the most.

# 21

*A Drive in the Country*

When I returned to Puerto Rico for my second sojourn, Vittorio was still in Italy for the summer. I looked forward to seeing him again, an expectation he did not seem to share, for when he returned in late August I saw him only rarely, primarily at Mass and when he brought Communion to Daddy. Disappointed, I began taking numerous not-really-necessary trips to the drugstore and the supermarket, hoping to bump into him. Any excuse for a meeting would do. I attended his Masses, rather than those offered by Monsignor Maissonet, to remind him I was back. Then, one Friday after Mass, Vittorio stopped me as I left the church.

"Sister, would you like to accompany me to the bedside of a woman who is dying? She is grandmother to one of my students and the family would find honor to have a contemplative to join them in prayer. I will drive you home to let your mother know you are with me."

It was such a reasonable excuse to be together that of course my mother allowed me to go. The day mirrored my joy: the morning exceptionally bright, the light sharp enough to etch every leaf against the blue of the sky and the roadside foliage shimmering and luminous. It was the first time I'd been alone with Vittorio without my parents around listening or a parlor grate separating us. And there we were, sitting next to each other in his car, taking a drive into the country. If I wanted to, I could reach out and touch him. The thought made me tremble.

Vittorio drove like a fighter pilot. He maneuvered at breakneck speeds along Avenida Ponce de Leon through a massive rush-hour traffic jam the locals call a *tapón*—a cork. I clung to the edge of my seat, totally amazed by his ability to spot openings into which he deftly inserted his canned-pea-colored Fiat. The car zigzagged in and out of thick cords of vehicles streaming into the countryside.

"Aren't you driving awfully fast?" I asked, as he swerved in front of a truck filled with bags of cement.

"You are nervous of my driving, Sister? Do not fear. My reflexes are very fast. I grew them riding my bicycle down the Spanish Steps in Rome."

I laughed, thinking he was joking. I'd seen pictures of those steps and couldn't imagine anyone riding a bike down them.

"No, really," he said. "We lived one block distant. I was balancing, sometimes using no hands! Imagine? My poor Nona! I laughed at her screaming, 'Vittorio! Vittorio!'

"I was an incorrigible child! I preferred to sail paper boats in the Villa Borghese Gardens to going to school! Do you know how many times I had to repeat grade four because of those hookies?" he asked.

"Playing hooky," I corrected, grinning at his expression. "No, how many times? Two?"

"Four times! I was *biriccino*. How you say? Naughty? I once stole a medal of attendance from my principal's office to make my grandmother, my *Nona*, happy. So proud she was when I brought home that medal. She puts on her best clothes and goes to give thanks to the principal. I was discovered. Nona was *furiosa!*"

"Why were you living with your grandmother?" I asked, puzzled because he hadn't mentioned his mother or father.

"Mama, she died when I was four years, of the Spanish influenza in 1918. My father, he lost all energy when she died. So, my Nona, she raised the children."

I'd thought he was in his early forties, but if his mother had died in 1918 when he was four, then he must be fifty-seven years old, I thought. I actually relaxed a bit. An older priest didn't seem quite so dangerous. Then I saw his eyes crinkle.

"You are surprised that I am so old?" he laughed. I blushed and admitted that I was.

We rode on like this—chatting and learning more about each other—almost comfortable but not quite, until we entered a housing development in Carolina, one of the growing suburbs around San Juan. Neat little stucco houses with arched porticoes and bright gardens filled with flowering shrubs lined the streets. A lovely young woman, her dark curls shining in the late-morning light, was waiting for us. She led us into what had been the living room but had been transformed into a sickroom. Her grandmother lay in a hospital bed near a window surrounded by her children and grandchildren, a hand-embroidered sheet covering her emaciated frame, her hair flowing around her on the pillow. She plucked at the fabric, her breath shallow and rattling. Vittorio began the prayers for the dying. He dipped his finger into the small brass-plated container containing the oils of anointing, making the sign of the Cross on her eyes and ears, her lips and hands and feet. She struggled to lift her head.

"It's all right, daughter," Vittorio whispered. "You rest now. May the sweet Mother of Jesus hold and comfort you on your journey to God."

My mother had begun wearing wigs. She had no time to fuss with hair, especially since the hairdresser forgot to time her permanent and her new curls cracked off by the handful.

She had three wigs, all of them casual, short and sexy, Zsa-Zsa Gabor style. She had a fourth, but my brother's children snatched it from her head during a trip into the mountains and tossed it from the car window. Screaming with laughter, they watched it soar over the hibiscus bushes to drop in a wilted heap by the side of the road somewhere near Cayey.

The children hated her wigs, but I understood why she wore them. I too wore a wig of sorts, the black veil of a nun. Every morning, my mother and I performed a similar ritual. She pulled the remnants of her chestnut-colored hair into a ponytail and tucked it under her wig. I placed a cap over my short hair and onto this I pinned my veil.

My mother wore her wig because she expected visitors. She wanted to look good. I wore my veil because it was symbolic of my commitment as a nun. My mother's wig made me feel sad. As the week slid toward Sunday and no one came to visit, she'd say, "Week-days are difficult. People will come on Sunday."

On Sunday, we dressed my father in his favorite yellow shirt and khaki shorts, buckled his hand into a brace that kept his fingers straight, and put both arm and brace into a supporting sling. His right shoe also had a brace that extended up his shriveled calf. We took pains to keep him clean. At lunch, we wrapped a towel around his neck so he wouldn't spill food onto his shirt, but the spoon jerked as he brought it to his mouth. Rice and calamari spattered onto his towel and over the floor. Mom shook out the towel over the terrace. Pellets of rice floated seven stories down to land on the pavement, some making a detour onto other terraces. While Mom was on the terrace, I tossed some of my calamari onto her plate. I hate calamari. Daddy's eyes crinkled. He tossed an asparagus at me. I flung this, too, onto Mom's plate. Daddy started shaking. Since the stroke, he hadn't been able to really laugh; instead his body jerked with laughter.

"What's so funny?" Mom asked as she tied the towel back around my father's neck. Mom's fork held a loop of calamari. Daddy could hardly bear it. He tried to take a sip of milk but it spewed across the table. My veil was spattered with white droplets. I tried not to look at him as I wiped off the milk. My chest hurt from the laughter bottled there. Mom shook her head. She took a bite of asparagus. Daddy rocked in his chair, and I covered my mouth with my napkin, laughing aloud. I felt so good. The haunted look had left my father's eyes.

After the meal, my father sat in his big yellow armchair and gazed at the beach. He watched the joggers and the tiny figures riding the waves. I sat across from him and wrote to Sister Mary. Mom read the Sunday paper. We waited until two, when my father got restless. He banged his left hand up and down on the armrest of his chair, pushed himself up, tottered, and fell back into the chair. Mom looked at me, and we both looked at Daddy.

*"Should we wait any longer?"* Mom asked silently. I answered by asking Daddy if he'd like to take a walk. Though he said no, I knew he meant yes. If visitors didn't come to Daddy, we'd take him to them. I settled him into the wheelchair, lifting his right leg onto the metal footrest. Daddy's eyes held a request.

"Do you want a pillow?" I asked. He shook his head.

"The bathroom?" My father was trying hard to frame some words. His eyes rolled up then down again. He bent his head slightly and showed me his bald spot.

"A hat?" His eyes said yes.

I brought him the gold and beige tweed golfer's cap he bought in England. He sighed as I put it on him and he tried to adjust it with his left hand. Instead he pulled it down too far. Only his right eye showed. I adjusted the angle. He looked at me expectantly.

"How do I look?" he seemed to ask, a crooked smile flitting across his face and aching into my heart. We pushed Daddy out the door to the elevator. Just going for a walk.

Mom wore her wig, Daddy sported his hat, and I wore a veil that proclaimed God's care of the three of us.

# 22

❧

# *The Flowering*

On my desk, spread around me like seeds scattered from a milkweed, are a series of photos taken during my various trips to Puerto Rico. One, taken the day I left the monastery for the first time, shows me sitting with my brothers, Steve and Greg, in front of the fireplace in Greg's home. The three of us are grinning like Cheshire cats—so happy to be together after twelve years of separation. In the photo I wear the heavy woolen habit and black veil that Poor Clares had worn for centuries. Although they can't be seen in this photo, Greg and Steve's children are bouncing around just outside its borders. They shout and giggle and show off. They've been tumbling in and out of my arms all afternoon. They no longer need to poke their tiny hands through the monastery grates to try to touch my fingers. We can hug.

A photo taken on my second trip to Puerto Rico shows me wearing a lightweight wool-blend habit instead of the heavy woolen one. In this picture I'm sitting on the rattan couch in my parents' living room and strumming a guitar. That's another of the changes that has taken place in the monastery. Some of us nuns have learned to play the guitar. We sing "Michael Row Your Boat Ashore," and "Kum-ba-ya, M'Lord," and other new liturgical songs in the folk style of the early sixties. We think we're Bordentown's version of the Singing Nun, the Belgian sister who became famous by writing a song about Saint Dominic that hit the top of the pop charts. "Dominique-nique-nique" was such a catchy little tune that even teenagers loved twirling around to its snappy beat. We entertain visitors in the parlor and spend our free time composing songs about Saints Francis and Clare and other religious themes. We practice together in any secluded place we can find: the crypt among our deceased sisters, where it's cool on hot summer days; the empty room under the Mass chapel; the far reaches of the cloister garden.

A third photo, taken in the monastery yard two years after my father's stroke, shows Judi and me wearing short gray jumpers with white blouses. We are in the yard with a German shepherd, the latest addition to our monastic family. Our veils are a very light fabric and are tucked behind cute little headbands. It's obvious that we've only begun to grow hair because the bangs that rim these veils are short and scraggly. As the monastic garb continued to change, I became freer in adapting the habit for use in Puerto Rico.

On my next trip to Puerto Rico, in the spring of 1971, I decided to create my own religious garb for use on the island: a simple brown skirt, white blouse, and veil. Admiring the ribbed cotton shirt I saw one of the nuns in Puerto Rico wearing, I found a similar style in K-mart and bought two of them. Then they began to shrink. With each washing they grew tighter. When I wore them, men whistled openly at me on the streets, despite my veil. Mrs. Fuentes, who lived several floors beneath us, came to visit one day bearing the gift of a new blouse.

"I noticed you needed a new one," she said tactfully, handing me a white cotton blouse with a Peter Pan collar, one that would not shrink.

Though I was in my early thirties, I was seventeen in experience. I see myself as others must have: a pretty, tanned young nun with smiling hazel eyes and a buoyant, expectant smile.

When one of the two brassieres I'd brought with me fell apart in the wash, my mother sent me to K-mart to buy a new one. I looked for bras similar to the serviceable ones we wore in the monastery, but the closest I could find were the sturdy Playtex brand. Though they promised to "lift and separate," they were simple and made of cotton. I bought two and brought them home to try on. That night as I got ready for bed, I noticed several nickel-sized circles on my breasts. I showed my mother, who thought I might have gotten them from the bra. "You never know who might have tried them on before you." She thought the circles looked like ringworm and suggested I make an appointment with a skin specialist. By the next day the circles covered my back, breasts, buttocks, and belly. The doctor said it looked like syphilis.

"Syphilis?" I gasped. "But that's impossible. I'm a virgin. How could I get syphilis when I've never had sex?" The doctor shook his head and said that he was required to check anything that resembled a venereal disease. He told me to go to the lab across the street for a blood test. My face burning with embarrassment, I scooted past the receptionist, wondering what the technician would think of a nun who came to be tested for syphilis. I removed my veil before entering the lab so that the technician would not know I was a nun.

My mother wasn't worried; she knew how naïve I was about sex. On my first trip to Puerto Rico we had tried to attach a Texas catheter—a condom-like appliance used as an alternative to an inserted catheter—to my father's limp penis. I'd asked how a man got inside a woman when the penis was so soft.

"He gets hard, of course," Mom retorted. "You know that."

She was right. I did. When I was eleven a car had squealed to a stop next to Judi and me as we walked down Oratam Road in Saddle River to get the mail. Thinking the man needed directions, I trotted toward the car. "Ever see a man without his pants on, honey?" he asked, rolling down the window. There, waving from a hairy knoll, was the first fully erect penis I'd ever seen. Judi screamed, "Run, Beryl, run!"

She'd been warned at school that a man had tried to abduct one of her classmates at Airmont Elementary. I'd received no such message at Holy Child.

While awaiting the results of the blood test, I wondered whether God was sending me a warning, a "he who looks on a woman to lust after her has already committed adultery with her in his heart" kind of warning. If wanting to be held in a man's arms met the lust criterion, I had sinned. Ever since Papi had wrapped me in his welcoming embrace, I'd found myself enjoying this Puerto Rican gesture with untoward delight—especially when a man was doing the embracing. My body had not forgotten the warmth of Fernando's arms; it remembered and ached. For years I'd been free of such longings, but on arriving back on the island my menses had returned after an absence of twelve years (finishing what the thyroid medication had begun while still in the monastery), and with it came a fully restored sexuality.

A phone call from the doctor assured me that I had contracted not syphilis but a tropical fungus that he had seen only once before. Sunlight or ultraviolet radiation would destroy it. "You've probably noticed," he said, "that you only have the rash where your skin has not been exposed to the sun. I can treat you with ultraviolet light, or you can sunbathe in the nude until it clears up."

I laughed at the idea of sunbathing in the nude and went that very afternoon for my first, and what was to be my last, ultraviolet treatment.

"You'll have to remove your bra and panties," the doctor told me.

"Of course," I said, blushing. "I forgot." I tried to sound nonchalant, as if removing my underwear did not bother me. I wanted to show a healthy attitude toward my body, but I was uncomfortable. *He's a doctor*, I told myself. *You shouldn't feel embarrassed in front of a doctor;* yet as I lay down on the table I felt very vulnerable. The doctor covered my eyes with a thick pad and turned on the ultraviolet lamp. The emanating rays felt warm and sheltering. They felt like a protective shield from the air-conditioned room and the doctor's eyes. The treatment lasted only a few minutes front and back. When it was over, the doctor reached out to help me slide off the table.

What happened next is a blur, a timed-release photo of a speeding train. I feel the doctor press my hand against his penis. I hear him say, "Look what you do to me!" I say the first words that come to mind: something about him being a married man—as if what happened was wrong because he was married. Did I really think being *un*married would make such an act tolerable? The doctor mumbled something about not meaning anything, and hurried from the room.

I don't remember my mother's reaction when I told her what had happened in the doctor's office. I want to give my mother the benefit of the doubt, to believe she was outraged and told me that what happened wasn't my fault. But she might also have excused the doctor, saying, "He's a man. Why didn't you insist that a nurse stay with you?" Had she been indignant, would I have believed it was *my* body that caused the doctor to respond physically? Wouldn't I have realized that any young woman's body can arouse a man? Instead, I began to fantasize about what I mistakenly thought was *my* seductiveness, even though I'd been the one violated. I wondered whether other men responded to me in the same way. Vittorio, perhaps?

"Look what *you* do to me," the doctor had said. And I assumed responsibility for his actions.

# 23

## Keeping the Faith

$I$ grew up thinking that getting sick was your own fault. My mother implied as much when we children got ill; her voice would assume a panicked timbre and her face would grow taut with irritation. She took our sicknesses personally, as if they were evidence that she had somehow failed to be the perfect mother. I saw her get so distressed with Steve's chronic earaches that, rather than tell her, he'd take his pain outdoors and lean his head against a tree. Steve, especially, had health issues: boils on his knees, nearsightedness, skin on his hands that would "crack right down to the bone." Despite her efforts to keep us healthy—feeding us yogurt and wheat germ, and juicing vegetables long before such foods were in vogue—we fell prey to whatever cold or childhood disease was making the rounds. Deep down I knew people were not responsible for getting sick, but when my father had his stroke I silently blamed him for his illness.

My father's illness had first manifested itself in the early sixties, seven years before his stroke, in the form of intense and crippling leg pain. At the time Mom and Dad were on a cruise to various pilgrimage sites throughout Europe—one of the first real vacations my father had ever taken. It was the pilgrimage aspect of this cruise that appealed to my parents and lured Daddy away for a holiday that was not a bankers' convention, which until then had been "enough of a vacation." Unable to walk because of the severe pain, Daddy waited on the boat for the other pilgrims as they jumped on and off tour buses visiting various shrines. He spent his evenings banging his legs with his fists, trying to get the circulation into his feet, which had turned a bruised purple. As soon as they arrived in England, a doctor told Daddy that his aorta was clogged and to get back to the States immediately. Days later, Daddy lay on an operating table in a Boston hospital while a team of surgeons performed then-revolutionary bypass surgery. When the replacement artery became blocked, he was rushed back to the operating room for more surgery. Despite this brush with death, my father was not one to lie around a hospital recuperating. As soon as he could walk, he signed himself out of the hospital and returned home.

Daddy made a halfhearted attempt to follow the doctor's orders. He tried to give up smoking, watch his diet, and get more exercise—take long walks. Eventually, however, he found walking too painful, and he also returned to his old habit of smoking several packs of cigarettes a day—often having two cigarettes burning at the same time, one in the ashtray and one in his hand. During a visit to the monastery, he laughed when he told me how a doctor friend had seized the cigarette he was smoking and put it out on his arm, exclaiming, "Each puff is another nail in your coffin, Ferd!" My father's nonchalant attitude offended me.

"What will you do if you become a basket case, Daddy?" I asked, not really knowing what I meant by such a statement except that I'd heard the expression used of leg amputees and knew that a stroke would cripple him in much the same way.

"I'll handle that when the time comes," he replied, his eyes twinkling, implying that not for a minute did he believe he'd become a basket case. In Puerto Rico, where Mom and I were the ones dealing with my father's debilities, his words were to take on special meaning.

After I entered the monastery, my parents became involved with the Blue Army, a worldwide organization of lay people, founded in 1947, dedicated to spreading the message of Our Lady of Fatima: the promise she made to three peasant children in Portugal in 1917 that if people prayed the rosary and lived lives of grace, an era of peace would be granted to the world.

During my third trip to Puerto Rico in the summer of 1971, my mother received a personal invitation from John Haffert, a Blue Army cofounder, to join him in bringing a miraculous statue of the Virgin Mary behind the Iron Curtain. My parents had met Haffert while on the cruise where Daddy began having trouble with his legs. Haffert had offered them the use of his stateroom so that they would be more comfortable and they soon became the best of friends, my parents finding in this young man the same dedication to God that they saw reflected in their daughters' lives. If Mom was going to take a break from her duties with Daddy, a Blue Army cruise was the way to do it.

"Go, Mom," I encouraged her. "Look. You're exhausted. You need a rest. You can't even hold a cup of tea without it practically jumping out of the saucer. Besides, you haven't had a full night's sleep since Daddy got ill."

Mom didn't need much encouragement. She knew I was capable of caring for Daddy alone. What she didn't know was that while she was gone Vittorio would come to visit more frequently and that while he was there my father would walk back and forth, banging his cane and looking fiercely at us while saying "No, no, no."

One night Daddy was already in bed when Vittorio came to visit. That night we were able to sit at the dining-room table without Daddy's distracting presence. When the conversation turned to the theology emerging from Vatican II, Vittorio took issue with a term then being bandied about in theological circles: the *dynamic* presence of Christ in the Eucharist.

"Dynamic presence? Dynamic presence?" he asked, raising his hands in exasperation. "It means nothing. For centuries the *real* presence has defined the reality of transubstantiation: Jesus really, truly, and substantially contained in the Eucharist. These theologians are full of themselves. They don't know what they are talking about."

"What's wrong with 'dynamic presence'?" I asked, distressed to see him adhering with such firmness to a theological term. In those days I used words with greater abandon and less precision than I do now. I considered the issue a simple matter of semantics. "Why do you think 'real presence' is a better term? Doesn't 'dynamic' mean living? Isn't God a living God?"

To support his argument, Vittorio began quoting the writings of Saint Ignatius of Antioch and Saint John Chrysostom—some of the earliest fathers of the Church who had spoken of the real presence. He reminded me that as far back as the thirteenth century the fourth Lateran Council and the councils of Lyon had adopted this expression, and that the Council of Trent had authoritatively confirmed its use. I listened with half an ear and ran to get the dictionary. I was gung-ho for the windows of the church to be thrown open, as Pope John XXIII had wished, and was not unduly troubled by changes in terminology or dogma. I was already nourishing doubts about the necessity of baptizing children to ensure their place in heaven, and the concept of a God that would condemn people to hell. But to argue about terms used to express the miracle of transubstantiation seemed trite. One either believed or did not believe. Faith wasn't belief in dogma. Faith was belief in God.

"Look, here it says: 'dynamic: of or relating to physical force or energy. Marked by continuous productive activity or change.' As far as I'm concerned, what doesn't change is static, dead. 'Dynamic presence of Christ' means the living presence of Christ within the Church, within you, within me. What's the problem with that?"

The argument went on like this for close to twenty minutes. My mind was closed to Vittorio's point of view, and he was immensely frustrated with my unwillingness to listen. It was time to end the discussion. Vittorio stood up and moved toward the door. Contrary to custom, I didn't kneel to ask his blessing.

"Well, Sister," he said, raising an eyebrow, "keep the faith." And with that he closed the door and disappeared.

While I was arguing with Vittorio, my father messed himself. We were so engaged in battle that I didn't hear him calling. He'd not only wet the bed, he'd also had a bowel movement. The catheter, the bars of the bed, the sheets, and even his face were covered with excrement and urine. I had no idea where to begin cleaning him up. I realized he must have been lying there for some time as the stuff had begun to dry. *How could you have been so selfish, so neglectful?* I chided myself. *So busy arguing with Vittorio you pushed your father out of your mind, dismissed him as less important.* As I tried to scrub the mess off his face, I grew more distressed and upset by the minute. Shame never brought forth the best in me and my father's no's grated on my nerves. Wasn't I doing my best to clean him up?

Daddy's no's grew louder. He began to bang his hand on the bars of the bed. Normally slow to express anger because I'd seen the devastation it had wrought in my parents' lives, and because good nuns and good women weren't supposed to get angry, I tried to ignore his yelling, but as I worked to clean him up I could feel my jaw tightening. Soon I was clenching my teeth, and as they grated together my hands grew stiffer.

*What a mess!* I began rubbing harder at the dried shit. I wanted to scour away this mess—the one my father had gotten me into by not taking care of himself. If he hadn't gotten ill, I wouldn't have had to return to Puerto Rico and I wouldn't now be struggling with my vocation. I wouldn't feel more heartsick and disoriented each time I returned to the monastery. He needed to know how his behavior had affected me.

"Stop it," I said, my voice shaking. "Stop it! You think you have it bad? Well you asked for this, you brought this on yourself. You just had to have another cigarette, another drink, didn't you? You knew how serious your condition was, yet you continued to destroy yourself. 'I'll take care of it,' you said. Well look at you. You're not taking care of a thing, are you? We are!"

I paused to get control of myself but the venom I bottled up for the last two years hissed into the gap and spewed forth without constraint. "Damn you. Why don't you just die and get it over with!" I shoved him onto his side and yanked the sheets out from under him. He lay on top of his filthy catheter.

My father had too much inner dignity to allow this. He began ramming his head against the bars of his bed in protest, whacking it with all his might and shouting at me, his mouth wide open. The sight of his pain and fury sobered me.

My God! I was abusing my father. I, his daughter, was abusing my helpless father. Horrified, I dropped the sheets and put my filthy hands to my face. I had done to my father what I'd wanted to do to Sister Mary Jacoba.

"Oh, Daddy, I'm sorry," I whispered, the words catching in my throat. "I'm so sorry." I reached out to roll him back into a reclining position, but he tried to push me away.

"I won't hurt you, Daddy," I pleaded. "Please, let me help you."

As I recall my father's illness, the nights we spent responding to his cries, the days consumed by his needs, I am stricken with the pain of his wordlessness. It is this suffering that I still dread thinking about because I made so little attempt to understand it. Even the old nuns in the monastery could tell me what they needed: Sister Mary Brigidae could ask for a cup of tea to warm her bones; Sister Mary Jacoba could refuse to take a bath. But my father could not tell us what he needed. He could not tell us how terrible he felt about being dependent, about having nothing to give except the need to receive.

In a letter he wrote before I made my final vows he asked whether I'd entered the monastery to make reparation for his sins, and reminded me of the "vast array of saints who were beloved of God *because* of their weaknesses." I think he wanted me to know that reparation wasn't necessary. He'd made such an effort to connect then, and I'd missed it. We could no longer connect with words. My father's words were locked inside him. They bounced against the edges of his mind and railed against the cords that tied his tongue. Only one word, "No," could pierce the wall the stroke had wrapped around him.

"No" challenged, demanded, defied, and acquiesced. With "No" his only word, it was all too easy to forget he was a man.

## 24

## *Staggered Time*

"Absence makes the heart grow fonder" goes the old adage, and so it was with Vittorio. Early in 1971, my sister Judi began taking turns with me helping at home. Alternating trips would shorten the time we were away and would ensure that Mom had someone with her all the time to help with Daddy. When I next returned to the island, Vittorio was in Rome for the summer. From then on, as I traveled back and forth, my trips did not always coincide with his presence on the island. Even when we were both on the island at the same time, we did not have many opportunities to see one another. Vittorio taught at the university during the week, and traveled to Ponce, on the other side of the island, every weekend to visit his friends the Roviras and say Mass.

So, how *did* we fall in love?

I have difficulty recreating the exact moments in our progression toward love. I'd like to believe that my knowledge is vague because I met Vittorio in Puerto Rico, where I was already drunk with life, where everything vibrated—from the chirruping of the tiny *coquís* in the cooling evening to the clanging of construction sites. I'd like to believe that I fell in love with the island first and then, because Vittorio was there, wrapped him within that passionate embrace. I'd like to believe this, but Puerto Rico was simply the setting in which we moved in love toward one another, deliberately, one step at a time.

I knew that Vittorio loved me though he'd never overtly done or said anything to let me know this. I, in turn, thought of him constantly, especially when Mom and I took Daddy on trips through the beautiful Puerto Rican countryside. As we dined on the shaded poolside terrace at Dorado Beach Hotel, I fantasized about having lunch there with him, walking hand in hand on the beach afterward. I imagined traveling with him to Barranquitas, where we'd drive past dark groves of bamboo and mountainsides aflame with color to picnic in a secluded spot; of riding the ferry from San Juan to Cataño, the evening breeze caressing our bodies while we looked into each other's eyes. In these dreams I nourished our love.

My mother saw the ad first. Berlitz was offering a crash course in Spanish for a minimal fee. The classrooms were within walking distance of the condominium and Mom encouraged me to go. I was grateful for the suggestion. I needed something to divert my attention from my growing preoccupation with Vittorio. The concentrated effort to learn Spanish would be a good distraction. Vittorio had his life. I needed a life of my own as well. Thus it was that for two months, five nights a week, I tried to empty my mind of Vittorio as I struggled with seven other adult students to conduct entire conversations in Spanish under the tutelage of a vivacious young blonde. In Spanish class I grew lighthearted and silly as we coaxed, cheered, and stumbled our way through trips to the *colmado* to buy groceries or imagined traveling to Mexico as *viajeros a Mexico*. Afterward I'd hurry home to share my latest adventures with my mother, who appeared to take vicarious pleasure in my efforts.

"You don't have to rush home after class," she told me when I mentioned that the group often stayed after class to chat. "It would do you good to get to know more people. I can handle Daddy."

One night I decided to take her at her word and joined the others as they headed off to a charity concert at the local high school, having gathered up their books and sprinted down the stairs toward their cars. If we hurried we could get there before it began. A spasm of misgiving jolted through me. I wanted to call my mother but didn't want to delay the group. I'd call her from the concert. It was a bad decision. I couldn't find a phone at the high school. Instead I worried about my mother worrying. I was so concerned that I considered asking a married couple in my class if they would take me home, then changed my mind. I couldn't ask them to leave in the middle of a concert. When I finally did get home, I didn't wait for the elevator but ran up the eight flights and rushed into the apartment to apologize.

Mom was in Daddy's room when I got there. Before I had a chance to speak Mom turned on me in a fury.

"How dare you do this to me? I've been worried sick. I almost called the police to report you missing." Salted liberally throughout her rant were words I hadn't heard her use since I was a teen and accidentally tracked dog poop onto her freshly washed kitchen floor.

"I'm really sorry I didn't call, Mom. I couldn't find a phone," I said. It was useless to try to reason with her when she was so angry, so I didn't try to tell her how worried I'd been about not being able to call her, how I'd regretted accepting the invitation. Instead, I left the room and went to bed. The next day Mom would not speak to me, not even when I tried to initiate a conversation. We lived in silence for days after that. We even took care of Daddy in silence—not that we needed to talk much. We had our routine: I would get up during the night to care for Daddy; Mom would take care of him in the morning when I went to Mass. She bathed him; I washed his bedding. She dressed him; I took him out for walks. I made the meals, and she fed him. Any attempt I made to start a conversation was ignored. I finally lost my temper.

"What's the matter with you, woman?" I challenged. Calling her woman was the perfect word to express my frustration. "Woman" was sure to cut through her silence. She'd gone weeping to Vittorio when I stopped calling her Mommy. He encouraged me to return to the diminutive form, saying, "It's such a little thing." He was Italian. To him "Mommy" probably seemed to be the equivalent of "Mama." I refused. I was thirty years old, and I was not Italian. It was about time my mother became Mom.

"I've already told you. I'm sorry about what happened the other night. I made a mistake; I didn't mean to worry you. What more do you want? How long are you going to punish me for coming home late?"

Mom turned in disbelief and amazement. "Is that what you think?"

"Of course. What else could it be?"

"You didn't kiss me goodnight," she said, her voice trembling.

She looked so small and vulnerable as she said this that I was quite taken aback. Her statement continues to surprise me. Could it be that through all the years we'd suffered from Mom's shunning, a simple expression of ongoing affection was all that was necessary? Was it our forgiveness she'd needed but hadn't asked for; our understanding she'd wanted but hadn't received?

# None

You are tired and reflective as you recite the hour of None. You have been working all morning and it is time for the noon meal. The return to choir for the recitation of the hours reminds you of your purpose in choosing this life. Did you remain conscious of the presence of God? Did you perform each task with full attention? You are reminded of your shortcomings, of your humanity. In the monastery, you have every opportunity to live in the presence of the Divine, yet you have been distracted. Your focus of attention has swung like the pendulum on a clock from eternal to present realities. The day is only half through, but None reminds you of the coming night. "Grant to life's day a calm unclouded ending, an eve untouched by shadows of decay."

Around you in the choir are your sisters: each of them aware as you are of sin and failure, hope and forgiveness. "Mercy and truth shall go before you, O Lord . . . " Forgiveness shines through the hour of None, as does perseverance. Buoyed by these gifts you resolve to begin again—ever again—the work of living in God's presence.

You close your breviary and kneel to await the bells of the Angelus, those joyful bells that ring from the outside bell tower at noon, celebrating the gift of salvation to the world.

## 25

*Teaching Vittorio Yoga*

Whije cleaning the hall closets, filled, as they were with all those things once considered important—handmade tablecloths, porcelain vases, souvenirs, mismatched dishes—I discovered a small pile of Mom's old books.

*The Sensuous Woman*, by "J," commanded my immediate attention. I took it to my room and opened it for a look. "J" suggested that a woman run a feather up and down her body to enliven her sensations. The image of my mother stimulating herself this way popped into my head and I fell onto the bed laughing until I cried. For years, I believed the book had been written in jest.

The second book was *The Godfather*. Such an interesting title, I thought, but it was far from the book I expected. Besides using words differently (I'd never heard women called broads before or lovemaking called screwing) it appeared to be about little but sex and violence. I was interested in sex, but the world portrayed in *The Godfather* was not one I wanted to get acquainted with.

The third book turned out to be a keeper. I think it was called *Sonia Richmond's Beginning Yoga*. This book interested me because it combined stretching and breathing exercises with techniques for quieting the spirit. I thought that perhaps, especially as interest in Eastern methods of spirituality had begun to penetrate the Church, this little book might help me regain the sense of tranquillity I had once possessed.

I began practicing yoga on my own and became so proficient in breathing and in achieving the various positions that when I returned to the monastery I started to teach the younger nuns what I'd learned. We'd meet in the altar-bread room in our pajamas—so many of us that we spilled into the hall—to breathe and stretch for an hour before going to bed.

Vittorio and I had been corresponding via tape recorder for almost year, a method Vittorio initiated to facilitate communication and to improve his English. Although he spoke several languages fluently, English was not one of them. When Vittorio preached in English, his American parishioners groaned.

These tapes were probably one of the strongest forces in our growing intimacy. On tape we could share what we could not risk sharing in person. I could speak of my increasing sense of alienation from cloistered living, and Vittorio could talk about the loneliness of being a priest. On tape, we did not have to worry about the proximity of our two yearning bodies; we did not have to fear an intimacy we had not yet openly acknowledged. It was on tape that I suggested to Padre Vittorio that he do some yoga as a way for him to regain some of the mobility in his leg, which had been broken in a car accident. I promised to teach him if and when I next returned to Puerto Rico.

I did in fact return to Puerto Rico in the spring of 1972. When I reminded Vittorio of my offer to teach him yoga he laughed and said, "Are you going to try to work a miracle? And where do you propose we do these amazing exercises?"

I didn't expect Vittorio to agree, but this sounded enough like agreement. Now, I had to approach my mother about using the living room in our apartment. She had interfered so often in my relationships with men when I was a teenager that I was certain she'd say no. By this time, she must have been aware of our growing relationship. Vittorio was visiting more often and inviting me on frequent trips to visit sick parishioners. I was stunned when she consented, even though she considered this one of the craziest suggestions I'd ever made. What to wear? Mom's leotard was too risqué, pajamas inappropriate. A jumper over a leotard would have to do.

Vittorio arrived for his first session before seven in the evening, so my father was still up, and he sat and watched as we stretched. When I first began practicing yoga at home in Puerto Rico, Daddy had gotten a bang out of my ability to stand on my head or lower my legs over my head in the position called the plow, but his pleasure doubled when Vittorio's stiff left leg forced him into some ridiculous postures. No matter how I tried, I couldn't get Vittorio's arms and legs into the proper position for the spinal twist. Daddy smacked his hand on his chair and quivered with silent laughter. With my father watching, our session remained a comic lesson in yoga, but when Mom took Daddy down the hall to prepare him for bed, the atmosphere changed. Vittorio and I were still laughing, but we were alone. Our mats were pressed next to each other on the terrazzo floor, our bodies close, face and necks shining with perspiration, arms touching. The air shimmered with expectation—it was such a short distance from there to a kiss.

"Beryl?" Vittorio whispered. Was it a question? His eyes drew mine to his. His eyes, those beautiful dark eyes, told me what he wanted me to hear. In his arms, I laid my head on his chest; he buried his face in my hair. "How long I yearn for you, for this." It was a sob. I heard the thumping of his heart, inhaled the salty dampness of his chest, and lifted my face to his. Our lips met in aching sweetness before they parted.

A tiny lizard scuttled across the entrance to the sacristy, enjoying the bright sun beating down on the pavement. It was only seven o'clock, but already I needed to shade my eyes from the glare. I watched the lizard intently and tried to forget why I waited.

"What you are observing so intently, Sister?" Vittorio stood in the doorway of the church, smiling.

"Oh, just a lizard. He doesn't seem to mind the heat," I answered, striving to sound nonchalant.

"Yes, he has adapted well to this place. Not like me, who must bumble around in dark glasses."

I smiled because it was I who had told him that dark glasses would weaken his eyes, that they'd get stronger if he didn't wear them. I clutched my breviary against my breast and said quickly, "Can I talk with you, Padre?"

"For you, I am always available. Would you like a cup of coffee?"

"No, this won't take long." Tears, unbidden, began to fill my eyes.

"Ah! It is something that makes your eyes greener than grapes."

He was making it difficult to continue—letting me know he noticed the color of my eyes, sounding so solicitous. My voice squeaked its way past my constricted windpipes. I could barely get the words out. Our kiss had taken our relationship to a new level, something I thought I wanted but now regretted.

"I don't think I can see you any more."

"No? Are you leaving again so soon?"

"No, Padre. It's just that . . . well, how can we, after what happened last night?"

Vittorio was silent. I was silent. We waited. Then he spoke.

"And that is a reason not to see me?" Vittorio sounded unreasonably happy.

"I don't trust myself." My voice cracked.

"Then you shall have to trust me," he replied, taking me by the arm and steering me toward the rectory for "coffee."

In offering to teach Vittorio yoga, I had crossed a boundary from which it would be difficult to turn back. His kisses called to the woman within me and my body responded. I wanted his love but I was afraid. I didn't want his love to take me beyond my vows. I wanted to stay a nun. I believed Vittorio wanted to remain a priest as well. I had to talk to my mother.

"I'm going to make some tea. Want some?" I asked Mom.

The first hour after tucking my father in bed was usually the most peaceful. Mom was already in her nightgown when she joined me in the kitchen. She sat on the side of the counter nearest the sink and I, on a stool opposite. It was obvious that she was very tired: her cup and saucer rattled as though she'd been stricken with palsy.

"How much longer are you going to try to keep Daddy at home, Mom?"

"What do you mean?"

"Well, look, Mom. Daddy's not getting any better. And you're so dreadfully tired. He might outlive you at the rate you're going. Besides, I can't keep coming down to help."

My mother put down her cup and tried to settle the shaking in her hands before answering.

"Why can't you?" she said. Her face had taken on a blank look and her eyes gazed unseeingly at me, which meant she really didn't want an answer to her question. She broke her crackers into halves, then quarters. They were down to eighths by the time I responded.

"Because I'm losing my vocation."

Mom didn't answer at first. She sat staring at me, looking bewildered.

"Losing your vocation? . . . Losing your vocation?" Her voice rose querulously. "What kind of a vocation is it if you can lose it so easily?"

I fell silent. I felt trapped between her needs, my desire to remain a nun, and my love for Vittorio. I didn't dare tell her that I was falling in love, that I kissed Padre Vittorio in the rectory after Mass, that I'd never experienced anything like his embraces—the catch in the breath, the intoxicating longing, bodies pressed together and aching for more. Vittorio had told me to trust him and I'd gone along, wanting his kisses, his love. But I didn't want it to go any further. I didn't want to choose between love and religious life. My mother was right: How could I lose a vocation for which I'd once fought so hard? How could I love a man when it was God I really wanted?

When Mom left the kitchen, I stood absentmindedly at the sink washing the cups, my mind churning. I didn't have the courage to make the break myself, yet choosing to stay in Puerto Rico meant risking both of our vocations, just as choosing to leave the island would mean abandoning my parents. I knew I wasn't strong enough to stay on the island and away from Vittorio, but neither did I believe my mother could survive without my help. Show me what you want, God, I prayed. You choose! God, of course, did not answer. God doesn't get involved in matters of free will. It was up to me. God would accept whatever decision I made. God would continue to love me, either way. But would I love myself?

My mother unknowingly pulled one of the last threads attaching me to the monastery and my life as a nun when she suggested Vittorio take me to the university with him so that I could attend a rehearsal of the Casals Festival Orchestra. Every year the celebrated Pablo Casals Festival drew musicians from all over the world. The festival was the great cellist's message of thanks to the island that had provided a home for him when he exiled himself from Franco's Spain in protest against its right-wing regime. Mom thought it a crime to be on the island and not attend a rehearsal, at least. As Vittorio taught at the university, where the festival orchestra practiced, she suggested he drop me off before class and pick me up later.

The Casals Festival had been a high point in my parents' lives for many years, especially when a childhood playmate of mine had been invited to play with the festival orchestra. Allison, who played the viola, filled my parent's home with musicians such as the famed Romero brothers, masters of the classical guitar, who came to celebrate music around our Baldwin grand piano. These musical salons were recompense for the sacrifices my parents had made to purchase the concert grand and to ship it all the way to Puerto Rico, even though I had given up lessons as a child, and Judi stopped playing when she entered the monastery. My mother had never forgotten the thrill of those festival concerts.

"What a wonderful idea!" Vittorio exclaimed, concurring with Mom. Later that morning he called from the campus to say that Casals himself would be conducting the rehearsal the following day.

To get to the university, we had to pass through Hato Rey. Hato Rey had become the island's new center for economic development, and traffic was heavy. As Vittorio chauffeured me past Banco Popular's main headquarters, I tried to imagine my father working there still, tried to will him back into his office. Because he wasn't in that office, because a stroke had changed our lives, I was in a car with a priest whose presence sent my heart skittering.

Pablo Casals was in his late nineties when I attended that practice. Although he tottered onto the stage, and sat often during rehearsals, his pleasure in music was visible. As he hummed the musical scores to illuminate what he wanted the orchestra to do, his arms became exclamation points, his hands whispers. I sat in the rear of the auditorium transported by this experience, my soul quivering with something akin to ecstasy.

"Did you enjoy the music, Beryl?" Vittorio said when I joined him later in his office. He put down his pen and stood up to greet me, his smile so sweet and hopeful. When had he started calling me Beryl? When had he ceased to be Padre?

I didn't know how to respond to his simple question. My soul craved music. Music expanded within my soul until my heart could no longer bear it. There were times when I thought I would die from so much beauty—Albinoni's Adagio, Pachelbel's Canon, Bach's Mass in B Minor—when I would have to lie on the floor to keep from flying.

"Oh, Vittorio. It was beautiful. Thank you! Thank you for this gift."

"But why are you crying? Are you so happy that you must cry?" Vittorio opened his arms, and as naturally as rainwater gathers in pools, I flowed into them.

Kissing Vittorio. The sweetness of it, his mouth tasting of anise, his arms enfolding me as a cupped flower, so light and tentative at first, growing warmer and more forceful until I could feel the full length of him pressed against me, my heart knocking as persistently as the person at the door. We let him knock and did not answer.

## 26

*Ashes of a Vocation*

By the fall of 1972, my life held only the coals of what had once been a burning passion. Caught up in the joys of island living, the needs of my family, and my growing relationship with Vittorio, my commitment to religious life had been tamped down. Despite this, I returned to the monastery hoping that a prolonged stay might restore what I had lost in religious fervor.

With each trip back, I found the monastery a bit more changed to conform to the recommendations made for monastic observance by Vatican II. The election of a new abbess soon after I left for Puerto Rico in 1969, the third since I'd entered fifteen years earlier, had stimulated these changes. Mother Patricia believed that religious life should adapt to modern-day expectations, and she moved swiftly to enforce those beliefs. In the space of a few months she changed much of our religious observance, simplifying ritual and doing away with obsolete customs. Among the most stunning changes was the way the nuns began to flit in and out of cloister to take classes at nearby colleges on psychology and human development, and to friaries, where we discussed theology and prayer and monastic observance with Franciscan priests and brothers. The physical appearance of the monastery changed as well. The community room now held a television set encircled by orange-, avocado-, and gold-colored easy chairs, rather than the tables around which we'd once sat sewing and talking of "spiritual matters." In the refectory, we sat at round tables to encourage conversation, rather than at the long narrow tables where we'd once eaten in silence. Our cells glowed with bright fabric coverlets and curtains. Linoleum covered the wooden floors.

Our customs changed as well. Rather than practicing abstinence, the nuns now ate meat, and fasting was left to the individual to practice. Rising for Matins also became a matter of personal preference. Some rose, some stayed in bed. These changes were intended to create psychologically mature nuns. Imposed as they were with such lightning speed, however, many of us were left reeling in a sea of choices for which we were ill prepared. Having lived much of our lives in obedience, we found that the sudden freedom to choose the direction our religious life would take caused a mini-havoc. Confronted with these changes, I questioned my vocation even more. What was I doing in a contemplative life that was so comfortable?

When I returned to the community late that summer of 1972, Mother Patricia told me that my trips to Puerto Rico were causing conflict in the monastery, creating two factions. She told me that I needed to forget my parents and return to full observance of the rule. I was having a problem with cloister was how she phrased it. I felt an urge to laugh. Cloister? *I* was having a problem with cloister, when under her management nuns were leaving the cloister all the time for activities that seemed frivolous when compared to my parents' needs? I was angered at the comparison.

How easy it was to deceive myself, to be blind when confronted with the truth. I was indeed having a problem with cloister and Mother Patricia had stuck her finger right in the wound. Instead of acknowledging my problem, of admitting that cloister and I no longer agreed, I grew defensive and accusatory. Perhaps if she had spoken to me with understanding, had drawn from me the issues that were tormenting me, had helped me to unravel the complexities of human and divine love, I might have been able to open myself to change. Instead, I was in turmoil when I left her, convinced that I could not abandon my parents, and angry that their need should be causing conflict within the community. This perception was the knife that would eventually sever my ties with religious life.

Every few years, the monastery held what was called a canonical visitation. During these visitations, a representative of the local Franciscan provincial director would conduct one-on-one interviews with each nun to ascertain whether the rule of Saint Clare was being faithfully observed, and to define any problems that needed resolution. We had such a visitation the year Mother Patricia told me to forget my parents and settle back into cloister. After interviewing all the nuns, the friar called a conference during which he issued a warning. Some nuns were causing turmoil within the community, he said. It would be far better for them to leave than to destroy the fabric of contemplative life. After what Mother Patricia had told me, I believed that he was talking about me and I went to her to ask if I had understood him correctly.

"What do you think, Sister?" she asked, tipping her head and smiling archly. I accepted her response as confirmation that the friar had indeed meant me. It was only during a recent visit to my friend Sister Mary, who is still a Poor Clare, that I learned the truth. In the course of our conversation, we discussed the steps that had led to my leaving the monastery and I shared with her, for the first time, my understanding of the friar's comments.

"Oh, Beryl, it wasn't you he meant," she said, her eyes filling with tears. "It was Patricia; Patricia and her little clique of favorites." Within two years of my leaving, Mother Patricia herself had left the monastery to found her own community, taking with her a small group of followers. I still sometimes find myself pondering the direction my life might have taken had Mother Patricia told me, "No, he wasn't speaking of you, Sister." Had she answered my question more directly, would I have found the strength to persevere, to sublimate my love for Vittorio into a renewed commitment to chastity?

In *The Cloister Walk*, Kathleen Norris addresses the difficulties of the celibate who falls in love. She quotes an abbess as saying, "The worst sin against celibacy is to pretend not to have any affections at all." Norris takes pains to point out that the abbess was not giving her nuns license to run out and have affairs, but was making an honest, realistic assessment of human sexuality as celibates experience it. Had I confided in my friend Mary, she might have helped me through the decision that at the time I faced alone. Mary would have clarified the real cause of the conflict that Mother Patricia was blaming on me: her pursuit of her own convictions and beliefs at the expense of the group. But Mary knew only what I chose to share with her, and I hadn't kept her abreast of my struggle. Perhaps she sensed I was holding back and wanted to help me with whatever was going on in my life, because she once drew me aside to say that I didn't know how to "work at friendship." I didn't know what she meant then—that working at friendship meant sharing and supporting each other through whatever trials lay ahead. Though at one time I worried that Mary would lose her joyous spirit in the cloister, she has remained faithful to her calling as a Poor Clare. Our ongoing friendship remains one of the bulwarks of my life, her encouragement and belief in me a tangible reminder of God's enduring love.

The day following the friar's visit I told Mother Patricia that I wanted to leave the order. Dispensation from my solemn vows required receiving permission from Rome. Such negotiations had to be conducted secretly so as not to upset the community, and necessitated several trips to a canon lawyer at the chancery office in Trenton. Benny, the monastery's longtime handyman, drove me there and back. He never inquired into the purpose of my trips. I was grateful for this, as his sister was a nun in our monastery and he could easily have told her about my trips. Although Vatican II had opened enough windows to make the departure of nuns in vows common to other orders, our monastery had not yet suffered such losses.

Meanwhile, I tucked my dispensation process between the folds of religious life, confiding in no one, not even when writing to Judi, who was then in Puerto Rico with our parents. Nonetheless, Mother Patricia worried that the other nuns would suspect the purpose of my ongoing excursions outside the enclosure. I was acting "nervous," she said. She received permission from the bishop for me to leave the monastery before the official procedure was complete. I was to stay with Greg before returning home to Puerto Rico, and planned to meet with a job counselor in New York City. (I did this, and she showed me how to draw up a fairly impressive résumé by recasting my experiences as a nun to match various job requirements.)

Without being allowed to say good-bye to any of the nuns, on October 17, 1972, I walked for a final time through the doors that had witnessed my entry to the monastery fifteen years earlier. I was not afraid. Instead I felt an excitement similar to the joy I'd experienced then. I believed that God would accompany me on this journey back into the world. I was thirty-three years old when, once again, I placed my life in God's hands and moved forward to meet whatever the future held.

# 27

*Falling in Love*

Judi welcomed me to Puerto Rico with joy, accepting my decision to leave the monastery with excitement, but my mother's reaction was just the opposite. I had been home only a few hours and was in the kitchen preparing supper when her hostility became palpable. Her voice assumed a pressed and frozen tone that chilled me.

"What are you singing about?" she said, her voice implying that I had no right to be acting happy at having abandoned religious life. "You've lost your vocation. Are you losing your mind, too?"

The daughter who had caused her such pain by entering a cloistered monastery fifteen years earlier had struck again, this time wounding her more grievously than ever. In one devastating blow, I'd rendered her years of pain and loss worthless. Not only had I become temporarily dependent on her financial support, I'd slashed her status with all who knew her as the mother of two cloistered nuns. Beryl, the one who'd convinced everyone that she was to become a saint, had broken trust with God. Soon her friends and acquaintances would know of my defection. What's more, I'd left too late to do any good. Had I returned earlier, she wouldn't have had to put Daddy into a nursing home.

Caring for Daddy had become too much work for Mom, even with Judi's help. Judi had never been trained to care for the sick nor did she have the patience to spend entire days at home caring for Dad and putting up with Mom. Not one to pretend to be holier than she was, she entered with vigor into the life of the island, making scores of friends among the nuns and priests there and even allowing the archbishop of San Juan to recruit her to write and answer letters in English. As his assistant, she spent several mornings a week at the chancery office answering his correspondence and performing other administrative tasks. She didn't return immediately to the monastery after my return, but remained for several weeks. Her presence helped to ease me through those first difficult days. Though Greg and Steve had bought me a lovely Pendleton outfit to wear while still in the States, I needed lighter clothes for Puerto Rico. Judi helped me pick out a lime-green sheathe for church, and a pair of hip-huggers for everyday wear.

I had applied to Saint Clare's School of Nursing, in New York City, and before leaving for Puerto Rico, I'd taken the entrance exam, met with the director of admissions, and been accepted. Nursing seemed a wise career choice. My experience caring for my father and the old nuns had given me a sense of competence. I wanted to be of service to others. As it was too late to enroll in that year's nursing class, I made arrangements to begin the following fall. In the interim, I started working with the set designer Nina Lejet, one of my mother's closest friends.

Nina had always supported my artistic endeavors and, when I entered the monastery as a teen, framed all the work I'd done under Mother Stella's tutelage at Holy Child. When I first returned to Puerto Rico as a nun, I found the apartment decorated with my paintings, but I no longer felt like an artist. Mother Stella had admonished me to "stay as far away as obedience will allow from the terrible art that comes out of monasteries and stick to murals," but at the monastery I had been asked to paint cherubs and roses on tabernacle cloths and dogs and ducks on ties for monastery benefactors.

Nina, however, still believed in me. I hadn't been home for more than a few days when she proposed that I come and work with her.

While working with Nina, I learned to wield a hammer and saw as well as commercial paints and papier-mâché. I climbed ladders and teetered on scaffolding to build new sets for the Tápia Theater in San Juan and the local television station, WKAQ.

Working with Nina had an added advantage. Vittorio's office at the university campus was only minutes away from her studio. During my lunch break we would race through the farmers' market to buy cheese and peasant bread and fruit to share while sitting on a bench in the town square, and he often drove me to and from work, as I didn't have a car. Mom, still in the dark about our growing romance, thought these rides were simply the generous offers of a kindly priest. But they rapidly became much more than that as my freedom from vows liberated my feelings.

During this time our relationship began to reflect some of the striking contradictions that were to become the norm in our journey toward one another. While we indulged in passionate kissing and touching, Vittorio continued to talk about transforming our love into something more spiritual: a lifelong love affair between a priest and a beautiful woman that would never be consummated. His conversations drove me crazy. How could we continue to kiss like we did and stay chaste? Maybe he could. I couldn't.

"You cannot stay a priest and love me the way you do, Vittorio. We cannot kiss and hold one another and pretend we are being chaste. It's dishonest!"

"But we can. You can, Beryl. We can love each other *and* God. We can have a spiritual friendship. Isn't that what we first decided on?" His words wove knots around my life.

"I'm no longer the person I was. I was Beatrix then. Now I'm Beryl."

Nina's Christmas decorations were famous, especially the trees she constructed from huge coral fans captured from the ocean floor. They resembled white cedars, lacy and almost translucent in their delicate beauty. The month prior to Christmas we traveled the island decorating hotel lobbies with her charming native nativity scenes and those amazing trees, which we strung with yards of thin white lights. I worked with Nina's longtime assistants Pépe and Angel, sometimes staying overnight at the hotels where we worked. Vittorio's angst over these arrangements—at my going off, away from him—delighted me. After all, he took off every weekend to visit his close friends the Roviras, in Ponce. He spent every summer in Rome. I liked this exchange of roles, that it was he who worried about my going off for days without him.

Vittorio knew of my plans to leave the island to attend nursing school, but he had not spoken to me about them. As the days passed and I became more frustrated with his denial of our growing passion, I realized I needed to make my intentions clear. One afternoon, as he was driving me home from work, I told him that I was heading for nursing school the following fall; that although I was in love with him I wanted a future that would not include him. I wanted to forge my own way, perhaps to marry and have children. Vittorio became more agitated as I talked. Suddenly he jerked the car onto a side street and squealed to a stop.

"You will be leaving Puerto Rico, then?" he asked in a voice choked with emotion.

"Yes, of course. Mom and Dad no longer need me."

"Don't go, Beryl." Vittorio's eyes bore into mine. "*I* need you."

His plea shook me, but I didn't waver. I didn't want the kind of relationship Vittorio was offering. I didn't want to experiment with love. We either loved each other or we didn't. His love now felt like a cage, the expectation that our love could flourish within the confines of his priesthood. Vittorio pulled me toward him.

"There's no future for us, Vittorio. I need to get on with my life. It's too hard being near you."

Vittorio summoned up such contradictory feelings in me—both longing and anger. As I tried to pull away from his arms, he turned my face toward his and looked directly into my eyes.

"Beryl, all these years I've been a good priest, but I've never been a happy priest. For the first time in my life, I'm happy. I don't want to lose you. I will do whatever necessary to keep you by my side. I will even leave the priesthood."

My mother's schedule, early to bed and early to rise, made it possible to spend evenings with Vittorio in our apartment. That my mother remained ignorant of these trysts I can attribute only to her unwillingness to notice what was happening. One night as Vittorio and I snuggled together in the darkened living room, Mom walked right past us. We hardly dared breathe as we watched her move to the kitchen for water, then back through the living room to her room. Had she turned the light on, she would have seen us. How did she not see us? Our heads must have been silhouetted against the lights shining into the living room from the building opposite. Did she walk through the apartment with her eyes closed, knowing the way so well that opening them was not necessary? Or did she see us and keep silent?

Rather than take further risks of Mom catching us by meeting at home, Vittorio and I made other plans. I would dial his phone and let it ring once. Vittorio would take this as the signal that Mom had gone to bed. I would quietly leave the apartment and wait for him downstairs in the lobby. We would then drive to Isla Verde to look for secluded places to park, to talk, kiss, and neck. We did not have sex.

Vittorio's apartment was small, one bedroom and a bathroom with a tiny kitchenette off the combination living-dining room. On entering it for the first time, I wondered how his nephew, Carlo, found room to live there with him. Despite its confined quarters, the apartment was tidy and elegantly furnished. While I checked out his books and glanced through his record collection, Vittorio puttered around the kitchen making coffee. He made strong Italian-style coffee in a small espresso pot with a nozzle through which it surged, thick and black, when ready. While it was brewing, he took my hand and, smiling like a happy Santa, led me to his bedroom.

"Come and see," he said, motioning for me to follow. Rather than leading me to his bed, he walked to the closet, which he opened.

"Others have clothes. I have tools!" he said, bowing and smiling jubilantly at me.

There, squeezed between the two narrow sides of his closet, was a wooden jeweler's bench and a wall full of tools. From a metal arm jutting from the wall dangled a jeweler's torch; on the floor sat the small fuel tank that fed it. A small electric drill lay on the bench, along with a leather mallet, cardboard boxes filled with burs and files, a charcoal cube, asbestos coils, soldering solutions, and a heavy stone with concave dents in it. Sweeping his hand toward it all as if he were showing me the treasures of Aladdin's cave, he laughed.

"This is my treasure house. It is here that I play. Look what I make." He twirled an exquisite ring of golden leaves that had been sawed, hammered, and cut from a sheet of gold.

I had never seen him quite so exuberant. This was a Vittorio I hadn't even known existed, a jewelry-making Vittorio. But why was a priest making jewelry?

"Jewelry. Amazing. When did you start making jewelry?" I asked, trying to be diplomatic but needing answers.

"I was trying to help a parishioner, a poor widow, find work. She needed to stay at home. She had small children. As I have many friends in Italy who are jewelers, I think to myself: she can sell jewelry from her home. I grew interested myself and learned how to make jewelry from books. What I needed to learn from an expert, my friends taught me. It is wonderful. You would love it."

I smiled at him, not sure about my loving to make jewelry. I wasn't a jewelry kind of person.

"Now, my love," he said, growing serious, "I want to give you something. Sit down." He patted the bed. Then, looking secretive and delighted simultaneously, he turned toward his bureau and pulled from the top drawer a small ring-sized box.

In it was a beautiful ring, a cone of small diamonds rising to a lovely central diamond and mounted in eighteen-carat white gold.

When I returned home that evening, my mother immediately noticed the ring.

"Where did you get that?" she asked.

"Vittorio gave it to me," I answered, my voice shaking slightly. I had been wondering how to tell her about my engagement. The ring had given me the opening I needed.

"It looks like an engagement ring to me."

"It is," I whispered.

"What?" she gasped.

"It *is* an engagement ring."

"What do you mean engagement ring? Who are you engaged to?"

"To Vittorio. I just told you. He gave me the ring."

My mother blanched. "Padre Vittorio?" she stammered. "But he's a saint. Why would he want to marry *you*?"

As I write this, I have to smile at Mom's remark. Why indeed would a saint want to marry her daughter? Was there no longer anything holy or lovable about me?

Then another realization struck her. Vittorio was much older than her daughter. Good Lord, the man was almost as old as she was.

"Yes. He's fifty-eight, and I love him. I've loved him for a long time and he has loved me. I tried to tell you that I was losing my vocation, but you didn't want to hear it and I didn't have the courage to tell you why. Don't worry. We're not going to run off and get married. Vittorio is going to ask for his dispensation when he goes to Rome in February for his sabbatical."

The doorbell saved me from further explanation. Vittorio had arrived to take me out to dinner. He wanted me to meet his cousin Umberto and his wife, Gabriella, whom he'd just told about our love. Umberto, an engineer, had come to Puerto Rico at Vittorio's invitation and had stayed to build condominiums. When I returned later that night, I found my beautiful mother sitting in the middle of the living room, the remnants of a one-pound Dutch chocolate apple in her hand. Around her on the floor were scattered little heaps of shredded gold wrappers. She had eaten almost the whole thing in one sitting. I didn't remember ever seeing her so desolate.

Two days before he left for Rome, Vittorio took me with him to the university to make final arrangements for his sabbatical. When we arrived, he told me that it might take some time, as he was also going to look into the possibility of teaching at other universities. When I asked him why he couldn't continue to teach at the Rio Piedras campus he told me he didn't want to cause any more scandal than was necessary. Before I could respond, he closed the car door and entered the Humanities Building, leaving me in the car to stew over his statement about causing scandal. I grew more irate with each passing minute. Our love was scandalous? When he returned, he was ashen and was shaking so violently he could barely get the keys into the ignition. I'd never seen him like this before and it frightened me. If he had been angry, he would have slammed his way into the car. Instead he entered it like a shattered man. When I asked what was wrong, he just shook his head. He could barely speak. He put his head down on the steering wheel. He couldn't or wouldn't talk.

"Why can't you tell me?" I pleaded. "What happened in there to make you tremble like this?"

"I don't know, Beryl. It is so hard. Leaving is hard," he whispered.

*Look at me,* I wanted to say. *Didn't I have to do hard things too? Didn't I take a risk in leaving the monastery?* I took his weakness personally, thinking his fear meant he wasn't as happy about our relationship as I was. I thought he should be bursting with confidence and strength because of our love. The mere possibility that he might be wavering again terrified me. I cried all the way home, and nothing Vittorio could say eased my mind. He was trying to be honest and I couldn't accept such confidence. By the time we arrived home, I had gotten myself into such a state that I ripped the ring off my finger and threw it at him.

"Take your ring," I hissed. "If you can't feel good about this marriage, then it's a mistake for you to leave the priesthood." My chest full of rocks, tears caustic as acid pouring down my cheeks, I ran up the eight flights of stairs and burst into the apartment.

"The marriage is off. I never want to see him again," I sobbed. Then I ran to my room, slammed the door, and hurled myself onto the bed.

One can weep only so many tears. My tears that afternoon purged me of all energy. As I calmed, I realized that I'd been so caught up in my own hurt feelings that I'd been blind to Vittorio's efforts on our behalf. He was leaving the priesthood, his vocation for over thirty years, and he was giving up a tenured position at the university. He was risking the respect of the faithful he'd served, of friends who had revered and honored him, of family who'd been so proud of him. It was probably good that he'd seen me in all my rage and selfishness. Perhaps he might be relieved the whole thing was over, that he'd escaped the biggest mistake of his life. Yes, it was best to cut the ties once and for all.

Just then the intercom from the lobby rang, and I heard Carlo's voice respond to Mom's *"Quien es?"*

On hearing her say, "Beryl wants nothing more to do with your uncle," I leaped from the bed, flew from the bedroom, shouted, "Mind your own business," and hurtled down the stairs to meet Carlo.

"Beryl," Carlo said, taking my hands in his. "I arrive home from work to find *Zio* on the floor. He cannot move. He cannot talk. Only one word: 'Beryl, Beryl, Beryl.' You must come! Help him!"

## 28

## *Death of My Father*

Vittorio left for Rome in early January 1973, ostensibly to finish his doctoral thesis in biblical studies, in reality to obtain his dispensation from the priesthood. I have no letters from this time, not because Vittorio didn't write but because, at some point in our rocky courtship, I destroyed every letter he'd ever written. Besides, Vittorio was more likely to phone than to write, especially as we no longer needed to keep our phone calls secret. In late February those calls came to an end when our home telephone died a partial death. We could phone out, but calls could not come in. The timing couldn't have been worse. Daddy was dying and we needed contact with the nursing home, Hogar Carmelitano. The phone company couldn't understand our problem: surely the phone must be working if we could call them.

Run by Catholic nuns in flowing white habits, Hogar Carmelitano had wonderful open verandas that enticed tropical breezes to flow through the building. Unfortunately the rooms were small. My father's room, built for one patient, accommodated two, making visits there almost unbearably claustrophobic when both families showed up at the same time.

In late February, my father was dying. We sat in his room holding his hand, reminiscing in soft voices, and praying the rosary. During one of those visits, Daddy's doctor handed me a small box of morphine vials. I can still see the hallway where we stood, the glint of the sunlight on the small glass vials, the scent of the evening breeze, but I cannot remember why he gave the vials to me instead of to the nun in charge. Morphine is used to ease severe pain. It can also be used to speed dying. Was it for this reason that the nun swept the box of vials from my hand, saying "Mr. Bissell will not need these"?

On the evening of March 8, my mother had one of the presentiments that run so strongly in our family and did not want to leave his side. "Daddy needs me here," she said when I suggested we leave. The other patient's family was packed into the room with us and I didn't know what to do with my body in such close quarters. I found it hard to breathe. I also wanted to go home because Vittorio had written saying he would try to phone that night, and even though our phone wasn't working, I wanted to be there just in case.

"There's no way we can stay in this tiny room with all these people, Mom." I said. "Daddy will be all right. We need to eat and get some rest."

But my mother kept resisting. "I'm afraid of leaving, Beryl. I think Ferd might die tonight."

"But he's been like this so often. He's always made it through. They'll take good care of him here. The nuns can reach us through the Horns' phone if there's an emergency." The Horns were our neighbors.

My mother was too tired to argue and, though still filled with misgivings, followed me from the room. As we walked away, she turned to look at Daddy one last time and grabbed my hand. His eyes were following us, his arm outstretched, the rosary still dangling from his fingers.

At three the following morning the doorbell sounded and I leaped from bed. Dr. Horn, our neighbor, stood at our door in his bathrobe and pajamas. His eyes told me that Daddy had died. I ran to wake my mother.

Mom was awake, and strangely calm. "Ferd is dead, isn't he?" she said as I approached. "He's already been here to let me know."

How does a daughter apologize when she has dragged an unwilling mother from her husband's side and he dies that very night? I was choked with sobs. Daddy's face was so clear, the anguish and longing with which he watched us leave pierced me like a sharp-edged sword. The curse I had uttered on Sister Mary Jacoba—that she would face death alone—had fallen onto one I loved most. Mom reached out and took my hand.

"Don't be so hard on yourself, Beryl. There was no way we could know for certain that Ferd was going to die tonight."

We wandered back into the kitchen, the room in the apartment that had witnessed so many of our most difficult conversations, to make the inevitable cup of tea, my mother's preferred comfort beverage. As we waited for the water to boil she told me what she'd experienced that night. "I heard him walking, Beryl, the clump of his cane, his foot dragging along the hallway. He touched my cheek. Then he left. The nurse said he died at three A.M., but that's when she found him. He died at one-thirty. I checked the clock."

Daddy had died alone and I yearned to turn back the clock, to start that night over, to stay at his bedside despite the claustrophobic atmosphere. How many regrets I was to carry through life, wishing I could undo the results of my mistakes, never quite forgiving myself, never really learning from all that pain.

We didn't go back to bed, but waited until five to call Greg and Steve. Judi's call would have to wait until the monastery's workday began, after 8 A.M. "My God, Mom," Greg said on hearing the news. "There's a huge black horse on our lawn. It's looking straight at me as we talk." The horse remained there looking at Greg during the entire phone call. We took it as a sign. Horses don't appear on lawns in suburban Ho-Ho-Kus. Such a family we are, always looking for signs and finding them in every strange occurrence.

When we arrived at the funeral parlor early that morning, the undertaker was waiting for us in his ornately decorated office. A large black velvet curtain hung behind his desk, making it appear as if he was posing for a photo. We handed him my father's clothes and waited as he gathered his papers and pen and began asking questions, writing our responses on his pad in such a laborious fashion that I thought his fingers must have fallen asleep. Did we have a cemetery plot? Would there be a funeral Mass? Where did we want it held? What did we want printed in the obituary? What memorial card did we prefer? When he finished writing, he put his pen down.

"You'll want to select a coffin." His smile, unexpected and minus a front tooth, made us gasp. Such an ugly man!

"Oh, no," Mom said, suddenly unwilling to proceed any further with funeral arrangements. "We'll do that later."

As if he hadn't heard, the man flung back the curtain behind his desk, and there, neatly aligned throughout a spacious room, were twenty or more coffins from which to choose. It was so theatrical, so dreadful. The little man, the curtain, the coffins lined up like children in a classroom. Years later, whenever Mom and I recalled this event we burst out laughing.

In April, a month after my father's death, Vittorio sent me a check for $1,000. I was to join him in Rome—he wanted to show me "all of Italy." I would see Italy with Vittorio, just as I'd dreamed! But the timing was wrong. Daddy had just died. How could I leave my mother alone so soon after his death?

"You should go," Mom said, "I'll be fine. You might never get another opportunity like this."

She went out and bought me a full set of durable olive-green Samsonite luggage. She also selected several beautiful sets of lingerie— one in bridal white with scalloped lace edging and a gown to match. My mother could be so surprising. The day after learning that Vittorio and I were engaged, the day she ate the entire Dutch chocolate apple in despair, she took me to a small shop to buy linens and towels with our initials embroidered on them and laughed conspiratorially with me when the sales lady wanted to know whom I was marrying. I was amazed that Mom would buy me lingerie, and learned only later that she believed we'd be getting married in Rome—as if I'd get married without my mother at my wedding! I wasn't sure we'd even make love in Italy, knowing how insistently Vittorio protected me from my own passion. To be safe, I asked our doctor for a prescription for birth-control pills. Then I booked a flight to Rome's Fiumicino Airport.

# Dusk

# *Vespers*

Your workday has come to an end, your apron has been set aside, your hands have been washed, your heavy work sandals exchanged for soft ones made of worn pieces of wool. The monastery's hum softens to an almost utter stillness as you wait for the Vespers bell to toll, calling you to chapel for evening prayer.

Perhaps you wait in your cell for the bell, or have already entered the chapel. Or perhaps, if it is summer, you have retreated to the crypt, where it is cooler. There, surrounded by your deceased sisters who lie in bricked niches within the walls, you try to imagine the day you will lie there with them. Your longing, though still strong, bears the marks of time. Life no longer passes slowly; instead it seems to stand still. Several years have passed, yet your spirit has not kept pace with the growth of your young body. You are far from being the saint that you hoped to become. Darkness and distraction have become your companions and days seem to merge, separated not by ecstasy and momentous insights, but by work, prayer, and monotony.

Your day is composed not of hours but of seasons. The liturgy has become the lattice for your prayer, your life climbing year by year toward the sun of God's presence. But where are the flowers? Shouldn't they be cascading from such luxuriant growth, inundating the monastery and the world with their sweet fragrance?

Peace! Believe that your efforts are pleasing to God. You have become a nun not for personal satisfaction but for God's glory.

Light pours in one final burst of glory through the high arched windows as evening falls. *"Magnificat anima mea Dominum"*—My soul glorifies the Lord—intone the nuns; *"Et exsultavit spiritus meus in Deo salvatore meo"*—And my spirit rejoices in God my savior. The Mother of God, still a child when she uttered those soaring words of praise and gratitude—not yet pierced with the sorrows that will follow—shows you how to pray. On to her words you lock your soul.

# 29

⚥

# *Italy at Last*

My longed-for trip to Italy got off to a bad start when Vittorio arrived at the airport dressed in the black suit and roman collar of a priest and carrying in his hands—of all things—his breviary. Not flowers. Not gifts. His breviary!

"Come to me! I want to show you all of Italy," he'd written in letters updating me on the progress of his efforts to leave the priesthood, and so I'd come, bringing my dreams with me. One look at his clothing informed me that Vittorio was still committed to the priesthood. His smile, hopeful yet apologetic, sickened me. Disappointment, frustration, and anger filled me as I confronted the black-robed figure.

"What does this mean? Why are you meeting me dressed as a priest?" I asked.

When Vittorio held out his hand to greet me, my distress turned to disbelief.

"You want to shake my hand? Is this what I've come to Italy for? A handshake?" My voice rose in alarm, angry tears flooding my eyes. How dare he greet me like this?

"Sh-h-h, Beryl. Please. I'll explain everything later," he pleaded, glancing toward the military police armed with machine guns patrolling

191

the airport. It was April 23, 1973. Because of increasing terrorist threats in Italy and elsewhere, the airport was heavily guarded. Several uniformed figures headed in our direction. Nodding to the police and explaining that everything was all right, Vittorio hurried me through immigration toward the baggage claim.

"Why are we bothering with luggage, Vittorio?" I was too upset to be civil. "I want to take the next plane back."

"No, Beryl! Please! You have come all this way. At least let me show you Italy."

"At least, Vittorio? What do you mean? At least, let's have one trip together before we resume our lives?"

I started to cry. I cried all the way into the city. We passed the Coliseum and the Roman Forum—places I'd dreamed of seeing with him—and still I wept. Vittorio made several attempts to engage me in conversation before giving up. We rode in silence, my face turned away from him, eyes focused on the window. Vittorio spoke only to point out the various sights.

"Do you recognize this, Beryl?" he said, pointing to a street sign: Via Gregoriana, the street to which I'd addressed my letters. "Number twenty-three, it's Maria's home"—the house where he had grown up and where his sister and her husband, Gianni, still lived.

Instead of stopping at Maria's, however, we drove past. My heart lurched again. Why weren't we stopping? Where would I be staying, if not at Maria's? As if intuiting my question, Vittorio told me that he had reserved a room for me at Trinità dei Monti. I was incredulous. Vittorio was taking me to stay in a convent? And not just any convent, but one with a direct link to my past—the place where the Bentivoglio sisters, who had brought the Poor Clares to America, had been educated!

"A convent? You're putting me up in a convent? I left the monastery, Vittorio. I don't want to stay in a convent. Why can't I stay at Maria's?"

"Because Maria doesn't know about you yet."

"Maria doesn't know about me? And all those family members you told me about, the ones so willing to welcome me? Do they also not know about me?"

"No, Beryl! Listen to me! It's not a convent in the way you think it is. The nuns run it as a *pensione*. It is beautiful. Historic. You will be here only for a few days. Then we leave on our trip!"

"Oh, spare me, Vittorio. I'm not blind. Your cassock and breviary tell me more than your words do. I thought you were getting your dispensation; if that's incorrect, you need to tell me."

"You are hungry and tired, Beryl. You need something to eat. We can talk while we eat."

Vittorio parked the car in front of the convent and led me down the Spanish Steps to a little English tearoom off the Piazza di Spagna.

"I'm not hungry, Vittorio. I feel sick to my stomach." And I did. I'd cried so hard that I'd developed a blinding headache as well.

He ordered some tea and a small basket of rolls with a plate of ham and cheese and proceeded to lay out his plans. Tomorrow he would take me to meet Maria and Gianni. On Saturday, his niece Lucia's children were making their First Communion and he was to officiate. The Mass would take place at the catacombs of Saint Callistus, on the Via Appia. I would get to meet the entire family. On Sunday we would begin our tour of Rome and on the following Friday we would leave Rome to journey through Italy.

It was late, around 10:30 P.M., when Vittorio walked me back up the Spanish Steps, unloaded my bag from the car, and rang the convent bell. The elderly nun who opened the door scolded us for being so late. Vittorio apologized. She snorted, lifted my bag, and told me to follow her. I left without saying good-bye and hurried down the corridor after the nun.

When we arrived at my room, the nun told me she would fetch me a few minutes before six for the Mass Padre Vittorio would be saying in the Mater Admirabilis chapel in the morning.

A shudder ran through me. The Mater Admirabilis was a miraculous painting for which Constanza, the youngest of the Bentivoglio sisters, had posed while a student at Trinità dei Monti. A copy of that painting hung in the refectory at the monastery. Now, on my first morning in Rome I would attend a Mass offered by Vittorio beneath the original of that very painting.

I put my suitcase on the neat little bed with its crisp white sheets and thin blue quilt. Tucked into a corner of the suitcase were the birth-control pills I'd brought with me. How foolish I'd been. I walked down the hallway, found the bathroom, and flushed the entire lot down the toilet.

The last place I'd expected to see Vittorio in Rome was on an altar. But then, he was still a priest and priests said Mass. And there was I, waiting for Mass to be offered by a priest who claimed he wanted to marry me. In Rome my doubts converged. Two minds were at war within me. One mind knew that Vittorio's presence in my life was a gift. The other mind believed I should reject this gift. One mind reached for his love. The other was appalled and wanted to flee. Only in prayer did I find peace. In prayer, my love for Vittorio was an overflow of God's love. While with God in prayer, I didn't feel guilty about our love. It was only when I left prayer and returned to life in the Church that dogma reminded me of sin, and my yearning for Vittorio became tainted with guilt. Celibacy as imposed by the Church made the love I bore Vittorio grievous. I could not reconcile my two beliefs: that our love was holy and that the Church was holy. Instead I was torn in two, as if the Church inhabited my soul while Vittorio lived in my heart, and it was all I could do to hold the pieces together.

"Make up your mind, Vittorio," I said silently, sighing.

"Give me time," he seemed to reply.

I don't know now whether to laugh or weep at the young woman kneeling in that chapel in Rome. Burdened by dogma and the proscriptions of a Church that did not then, and still does not, give the individual much leeway in finding her own way to truth, she was not capable of making a "right" choice. She only knew that from deep within her a strong and vital spirit was trying to break through the numbing crust of uncertainty, to pursue what was "right" as she saw it, which was to seize this love and give thanks. I am amazed and grateful for that spirit. I have learned much because she lived within me. If she made a mistake in loving Vittorio, then it was ultimately a transforming one.

After Mass, in the sunny dining room reserved for priests and their guests, I broke a crisp roll and drank thick black coffee foaming with hot milk. Vittorio sat across from me. The morning shimmered across the bone-china place settings and illuminated the jewel-colored jellies. It was beautiful at Trinità dei Monti. For the first time since I'd arrived, I felt a surge of happiness. Vittorio's face shone with pleasure. Beryl was finally smiling.

After breakfast we left Trinità dei Monti and walked down an ancient cobbled street toward Via Gregoriana. There we stopped before an iron gate. In response to our buzz, the gate clicked opened to reveal a small courtyard where a lion's-head fountain gurgled and wisteria clambered up the sides of the old stone walls. Maria stood in a doorway wearing a faded apron over a blue silk dress. She was plump and dark-haired. Her husband, Gianni, sat at the kitchen table smiling. He stood as Vittorio introduced me as his student from the university. I stifled a gasp. So, now I was a student!

"Trust me, Beryl," he whispered in English. "I know what I'm doing. I want my family to love you first. Then I will tell them about us."

Vittorio arrived daily at Trinità dei Monti to take me sightseeing. Together we walked through the Forum, climbed the Holy Stairs on our knees, and viewed Rome from the top of the Janiculum Hill. We visited the Sistine Chapel, the Pantheon, and the Coliseum. We attended an opera at the Baths of Diocletian. At the catacombs of Saint Callistus, Vittorio said Mass for his niece and nephew, who received their First Holy Communion from his hands. At the festivities afterward, I met his extended family and began to understand the pressure he was under. Vittorio was their priest. He had performed their wedding services, baptized their babies, given them the Eucharist. They expected him to bury them when they died. That night I wrote in the tiny travel journal Mom had given me to record this trip, "Perhaps Vittorio is right in waiting to tell the family about us. Everyone seems to like me, even his brother Costantino, the poet. He wasn't at all brusque as Vittorio told me he could be. I wonder how he'll feel when he finds out who I really am."

As a young nun, I had promised myself that no one would ever call me fat again. In the years that followed, I held to that promise. I was no longer anorectic, but I carefully watched what I ate. If Vittorio was aware of my stringent eating habits before this, he never made it known. When I arrived in Italy, where food possessed a special magic, he brought up the topic.

One day, after visiting the fountains at Tivoli, east of Rome, we sat down to dine in a garden filled with azaleas, bougainvilleas, and wisteria. I was nibbling at a first course of pasta served in a small white bowl with just a dollop of sauce and a bit of butter, when Vittorio reached for my hand and said gently, "Beryl, *bella*! If you eat what you enjoy, I promise, you will never get fat."

I'm not sure why those simple words affected me so profoundly, but their wisdom erased years of inner programming. Perhaps it was the love with which they were spoken; perhaps I was just tired of dieting. As I look back on it, the healing that Vittorio brought me seems almost miraculous.

From that day on, sightseeing in Italy included sensations of the palate. Vittorio and I prowled the back streets of Rome asking artisans where they ate. In a small restaurant in Trastevere we dined on fresh figs with prosciutto. Outside the Church of Saint John Lateran, we gorged on *tartuffa*—a glorious concoction of frozen chocolate fudge. At a restaurant on the Appian Way, we laughed ourselves silly because we'd filled our plates from a massive buffet, only to be approached later by a waiter asking what we wanted to order for dinner. I ate pasta with olive oil and butter as a first course; savored grilled veal with lemon accompanied by oven-roasted potatoes fragrant with rosemary and garlic; enjoyed dewy apricots and cheese for dessert; and still I stayed thin. I learned to relish the subtle changes in flavors as we moved from region to region, the house wines, the breads, the peppers seething in the food of the south, the more delicate flavors of the north. For years food had been a torment to be avoided. But eating well does not mean eating a lot. When you are satisfied, you stop. Just like that. With Vittorio's love, food had become a gift for enjoyment.

Vittorio had obtained five seats for a papal audience: two for nuns from Trinità dei Monti, two for us, one for Maria. They were good seats, next to the aisle along which Pope Paul VI would be carried on his palanquin. While we waited, Vittorio prayed his breviary and I read a small guidebook. I didn't feel like talking to the nuns or to Maria. I let them chatter together. It was hard work trying to talk in my limited Italian and I was in no mood to talk anyway. The seats might have been good but I was not spiritually ready for a papal audience, no matter how many strings Vittorio had pulled to get us there. The night before, my faith had been shaken.

Vittorio had taken me to the Villa Borghese, to the same gardens he'd played in as a child, to talk. He could no longer conceal from me the difficulties he'd been having getting his dispensation from the priesthood. The most formidable obstacle was the Church's refusal to consider a dispensation for the sole purpose of getting married. He was being advised, instead, to plead a crisis of faith.

"But I have no crisis of faith," Vittorio insisted. "I simply want to marry. Why should it be so difficult for the Church to understand that its priests might want to marry?"

But it *was* hard for the Church to understand. Vittorio's advisers reminded him of the many priests who had fallen in love and had even had children yet who did not leave the priesthood to marry. They held up for examination and emulation the example of a local pastor, *an excellent father who visited his children weekly*. Vittorio threw up his hands as he told me this. "Imagine! This is the example I'm supposed to follow."

I'd heard about priests who had mistresses but I thought this was primarily a problem in mission countries where loneliness and culture could lead to such practices. That this should be suggested as an alternative to leaving the priesthood left me aghast. I felt violated. The Church I'd loved was suggesting that I be loved but not married. The very idea turned priestly celibacy into a sham and Church integrity into abuse. Those priests dishonest enough to remain priests while involved sexually were sheltered. Those choosing the sacrament of matrimony were advised to lie, to claim a crisis of faith rather than admit to wanting a dispensation in order to marry.

A web of emotions fell over me on hearing of this priestly philandering. I was furiously angry—betrayed by the institution I'd thought of as Our Holy Mother the Church. *Cut the "holy" from that endearment*, I thought. *And while you're at it cut "Mother" out as well*. All night I'd wrestled with my emotions. What did I believe? Why did I want to remain in such a Church? What was it that bound me to her? As I struggled, I realized that betrayal did not alter my basic beliefs: There is a God who loves us without limit. This God sent his son to show us how to love, had established a Church to act as nurturer for our journey. That the Church was flawed should not matter. It was, after all, a Church composed of humans, each of us broken, even the saintliest. I loved the Church not as an institution but because it provided us with the sacraments, with worship and liturgy, and because I believed that grace flowed to us through its ministers, no matter how corrupt or unworthy they might be. My belief in the holiness of the Church might be tottering, but not my belief in the Church itself. Nonetheless, I was still angry the next day when Vittorio arrived to pick me up for the papal audience. I was angry as I waited for the Pope. I put the guidebook down, closed my eyes, and took a deep breath. *Open me, Holy Spirit, to the grace of this audience*, I prayed. Help me to believe and forgive.

When the Pope finally entered, carried aloft on a palanquin, we fell to our knees to receive his blessing. Kneeling with my head bowed, making the sign of the Cross in response to his blessing, I was at first moved to be in the presence of the successor to St. Peter—the rock on whom Jesus had built his church—but this emotion was quickly displaced by a wave of desolation. What was I doing, kneeling to a Pope I no longer believed was infallible? I looked up, hoping that the Pope himself would restore my belief. In the glaring lights of the room the Pope's eyes glittered like the eyes in a stuffed bird.

# 30

## Berries at Baiae

On April 30, we left Rome on a five-week tour of Italy, as Vittorio had promised. To all appearances we were just another couple touring that ancient land in search of history and romance, for Vittorio finally had exchanged his priestly garb for comfortable slacks and sport shirts.

We began our trip by heading south toward Pompeii and Herculaneum. We planned to take the trip one day at a time, seeing the sights and staying as long as we wanted wherever we wanted. The Lancia we were driving had other ideas. On our first night away it developed engine trouble outside the town of Capua. The Lancia would continue to break down throughout the five weeks, forcing us to spend extra time in some very beautiful spots, but Capua was not one of them.

We left the car at a repair garage, checked into a nearby motel, and then wandered into the town to try to find a place to eat. It was evening when we arrived and the town looked as if it had been deserted for several years. Lights were dim or nonexistent, and the city was made even more dismal by the cold gray stone of its buildings. The only open restaurant was a miserable little trattoria near the highway. An albino canary swung on its perch in the corner, looking as bedraggled as the town until it started to sing. The canary's singing painted the walls and decorated the tables. Even the food we ordered was transformed. We walked back to the motel arm in arm, singing and laughing.

At my insistence we slept in separate rooms that night. If Vittorio thought we could travel as brother and sister, sharing a bed but not having sex, he was stronger than I was. That night I regretted my request. Unable to sleep, I spent hours writing in my journal, too proud to let him know that I'd changed my mind. We were in Italy. What was I doing sulking in my own room?

Two days later we arrived in Naples. It should have been romantic—our room with a little balcony overlooking the bay; sun, sea, and piles of white clouds in an amazingly blue sky. We'd arrived in Naples the night before but I hadn't slept well. Cradled within Vittorio's arms, I hardly dared move, afraid that my desire would set the bed on fire. We were sleeping in the same bed and loving one another, yet trying to stay chaste. It was an exercise in masochism. Vittorio seemed able to resist my formidable charms and showed no desire, which felt like an insult. He could at least show desire. He could at least let me know how much he wanted me. Saying no to sex while wanting desperately to have it, was infinitely more palatable than stoic resistance.

My behavior had forced an uneasy silence between us that left Vittorio off balance. One moment I'd be breathless with delight, as when we drove through a thick mountain fog and suddenly come upon a herd of goats, bells ringing eerily. The next moment I'd be querulous, complaining about the stench of diesel fuel belching from the truck in front. That morning, when I asked for something "decent" for breakfast, more substantial than the crusty rolls and jam the hotel served, Vittorio was irritated enough to exclaim, "Beryl, we're in Italy. Please. Breakfast *is* bread and coffee!" When the waiter arrived, bearing huge cups of frothy milk and small pots of thick, black espresso, I asked for a pot of hot water. I needed American coffee and lots of it. Plain. Black. Diluted. Hot. The waiter's eyebrows shot up. Vittorio grinned sheepishly and shrugged. "She's an American." He lifted his open palms in a "What can I say" gesture. The waiter smirked, bowed slightly, and left to get the water.

"Beryl, why must you ask for hot water?" Vittorio chided when the waiter had gone. "Italians drink coffee with milk in the morning. It's embarrassing when you ask for water." I frowned and piled a mound of apricot jam on my roll. My eyes smarted.

"I do not mean to hurt you, my love. I only want for you to try the Italian way." He lifted my chin so that he could look into my eyes. I pushed his hand away. "You are upset, Beryl, and I think it is more than just about coffee. Is it the dispensation? You must believe me. I'm doing all I can to make it happen."

It wasn't just the dispensation, I wanted to tell him. It was sleeping in the same bed and having him remain so steadfastly chaste. If he was struggling with chastity, he kept it well hidden. We dressed in silence. I pulled my long hair into a ponytail, and slipped into a comfortable pair of linen slacks and a soft beige sweater. Normally Vittorio would have told me how beautiful I looked, but this morning he busied himself with the luggage and the details of leaving. I loitered in the parking lot while he went to pay the bill. He always handled the desk staff alone, presenting his passport (which showed him with a roman collar) and mine, so that the hotel staff wouldn't smirk in my presence. A priest traveling with a woman!

We left Naples and moved northwest into the hills overlooking the Gulf of Pozzuoli, leaving behind the noise and blare of the city, the thousands of tiny cars that competed for space on the roadways. We were heading for the ancient thermal baths at Baiae. As we drove, Vittorio relaxed. His left arm rested on the open car window, his hand barely touching the wheel. He had picked up a tan. I loved the way the tan accented his features—the chiseled nose, strong chin and cheekbones. Vittorio caught me looking at him. "Are you feeling better, *cara*?"

"Yes," I lied. He was so unfailingly kind, so patient. I sat back and gazed at the passing scenery, lulled by the sound of the tires and the scent of the lemon trees in bloom. I must have dozed off, because I was startled when Vittorio pulled off the highway near a small stand of berries and lemons. A young boy ran toward us, in his hands a small plastic container filled with strawberries. Vittorio asked whether the berries were fresh. Of course his berries were fresh, the boy replied in a voice that sounded like a bell. The berries actually looked rather shriveled—as if they had been sitting in the basket in the hot sun for most of the morning. Dirt and sweat streaked the boy's round brown face. His hair had a faint whitish film from the dust of passing cars, but his small wiry body crackled with determination. His berries were the finest in Baiae; if the gentleman would just buy them for his lady, he would discover this for himself.

We took the strawberries with us when we arrived at Baiae, and washed them in the water running from a spigot near the walkway. As we walked, we popped one fruit at a time into our mouths. They were incredibly sweet. I suggested we save some for later, as they were too delicious to eat all at once.

"Ah, my lovely Beryl has returned." My name on his lips sounded like a caress.

"Yes. I'm back. I think. Oh, Vittorio, my behavior, it's been so awful. I'm so sorry."

"*Cara!* If only you realized how much I love you, how happy I want to make you," he murmured, taking me in his arms, his kisses soft as a rain on my eyes and ears. He slipped his hands under my sweater. My breasts ached to receive them. One hand clinging tenaciously to the berries, I used the other to caress his neck. At that instant, a flock of noisy school children skipped into view, giggling and chattering. We pulled apart and the berries tumbled onto the ground.

The remains of the ancient thermal baths and its surrounding town crept down the hillside toward the blue of the Mediterranean Sea. Such an amazing complex—terraces, arches, stairways, foundations of homes, pools—yet despite all the people moving about, it was strangely tranquil.

Feeling euphoric yet scattered, I told Vittorio to go on without me, that I wanted to sit a bit and enjoy the view. I watched him walk down the hillside, his hands clasped behind him in that way so many thoughtful priests walk. Knowing that he wanted me had eased that thorn from my psyche, but watching him walk alone down the hillside made me ache.

He'd told me that he'd never really wanted to be a priest; that what he wanted was a father, that after his mother's death his father had withdrawn into silence and the priests at his parish became like fathers to him. "I entered the order so young. Only twelve! When I begged to go home, they told me that wanting to leave was a temptation. I was not even allowed to attend my own father's funeral. And then they ordained me early, so I couldn't leave. I hadn't even finished my theology requirements. It was an ancient order, the Minimi—they needed every vocation they could get."

I yearned to believe him, but I couldn't help wondering whether he really wanted to leave the priesthood as he claimed. He had left the Order of the Minimi so that he could work among people as a secular priest. Now I'd seen him in agony because of this decision; he was leaving the priesthood because marrying me was the only way he could keep me with him. Had love for me set him on a journey he did not really want to take? Was it up to me to turn him round? And could I? Would I?

From the bottom of the amphitheater, Vittorio turned toward me and waved. "Come, Beryl," he shouted.

Of course I would come—now, while I was still with him. I hurried down the hill. "You hold my hand so tightly because it is lovely. No?" he said, smiling.

Unable to answer, I let him believe this was so.

Car troubles forced another stop, this one near Positano, along the ravishing Amalfi Drive: thirty miles of hairpin turns and precipitous drops, leading to Sorrento, where we'd planned to take the boat to Capri. While Vittorio talked to the mechanic at a small roadside auto repair shop, I wandered across the highway to look at the view. The vast expanse of the Mediterranean with its sapphire sky and turquoise sea made me feel light and happy. I sat on the cliff-side wall and looked about me, enjoying the light breeze and warm sun, the terraces of blossoming lemon and apricot trees below me.

What a fortuitous stop, I thought, and to think I'd sighed with frustration when the engine started knocking, not wanting more car troubles. When Vittorio joined me to say that we would need to spend a day or two waiting for engine parts, I was delighted. The mechanic had told him there was a hotel down the road a bit, built into the cliff, and we went looking for it. It appeared to float over the sea, everything sun-washed and gleaming white. A young man in a crisp white shirt led us through a breeze-filled open-air gallery toward our room. From our balcony we had a spectacular view of the Bay of Sorrento and a sweet little village that terraced its way in soft pastel colors down the cliff and toward the sea. It was so beautiful that I wondered whether Vittorio had planned it this way.

As soon as we'd deposited our bags and freshened up a bit, we went to town. It was lunch time and we were hungry. Positano was all narrow streets and steep alleyways. Large pots of bright geraniums and trailing aspidistra lined stairways leading to pink- and cream-colored houses, and the cobbled streets glowed with a softly burnished salmon-tinted patina. While I stood entranced, Vittorio disappeared into a small grocery shop and emerged a few moments later with a bag of fresh figs, strawberries, and feathery plumed fennel.

"These will help your bowels," he said, grinning.

I flushed. Vittorio could be so earthy. Crunching the crisp Italian celery as we walked, we wandered through the town and came across a small church bearing a legend telling of the miraculous statue within, a figure of the Madonna that had washed onto the town's beach several hundred years earlier. The church was locked, but something about this story felt familiar. Into my mind drifted the image of the little cell where Sister Mary Philippa had spent her final days. I had loved visiting this old nun, whose cell was right across from the altar-bread room where I worked. She would regale me with stories about the town where she lived as a child—I'd forgotten the name of the town, but not her description of it: the steep little streets, the houses built up the side of the cliff, the statue that washed up on the beach. The legend on the church brought the name of that town back to me, Positano, as if that dear old nun had orchestrated the entire event. I could almost hear her say, "See, didn't I tell you it was beautiful?"

At a small restaurant on the beach we ate freshly caught fish tucked into a bed of roasted peppers, a meal accompanied by the soft lapping of waves, the creaking of the fishing boats, and the sun, that wondrous Italian sun. Euphoric with wine and the surrounding beauty, Vittorio and I climbed the cliff-side steps back to the hotel, passing tiny terraced gardens where peonies and roses and ferns grew together in homey familiarity. Several small children, plump and rosy and dressed in white pinafores, ran past us to disappear through a gate into a peach-hued cottage.

Returning to our room, we placed the bag of produce in a far corner where the sun could not reach it, then tumbled onto the bed for an afternoon nap. Something about the afternoon, the loveliness of our room, and the filmy white drapes blowing in the breeze (or was it the wine?), loosed the temptress within me. I began to undress in front of Vittorio and he did not try to stop me. It was Vittorio, not I, who lifted my sweater over my head, who removed the coral earrings he'd bought for me, kissing each ear as he did so.

Our lovemaking that afternoon was not the leisurely exploring of one another's bodies that I'd once imagined. It was not the tender gentle holding and touching of my dreams, but a wild almost crazed consuming of one another as if we both feared the intrusion of conscience that might have stopped us had we taken our time. Afterward, we lay spent in each other's arms, caressed by the breeze that rose from the sea through the open windows of the terrace, and while we slept, the sun turned from lemony gold to tangerine.

Our sexual encounter was a radiant, if rushed, affair—the only one we would have on this trip. For, in one of those strange decisions made by persons who try to live in faith, making love renewed our efforts to stay chaste. Knowing Vittorio desired me had eased the tension between us. I realized I could no longer tease Vittorio in order to satisfy my need. There were limits to his strength and I knew sex wasn't proof of love. What I wanted was for him to acknowledge our flesh, as I had to do. Vittorio was still a priest sworn to celibacy. As long as he remained a priest we would work together to maintain that commitment.

If we thought chastity was difficult before, it was now a searing struggle. We learned that it was much easier to abstain when one has never tasted sexual pleasure. We both struggled to say no. For the rest of the journey, as we traveled to Capri, down into the boot of Italy and over to Sicily, and then back up to the Italian Alps and through Florence to Venice, we lived as close to the edge as one dared without toppling into the chasm, moving like shuttlecocks between passion and abstinence. But our struggles added an edge of joy to our travels, as if our eyesight had been sharpened and our senses honed. I sometimes felt like those larks that soar over Italy in euphoric, almost drunken spirals. We laughed and cavorted like children, overwhelmed with the sheer wonder of being together in this way, and in such a place.

We stopped in Assisi on our way back from Venice. Assisi, that lovely city where Saint Francis and Saint Clare were born and where they jointly discovered the joy of living in total poverty for love of the "Poor Suffering Jesus." It was in Assisi that Vittorio and I finally revved up the courage to go to confession and receive forgiveness for our night of lovemaking.

"And what will you do if you have a baby?" the priest gently asked when I'd poured out my story. His words pricked my heart with needles of fear and joy. I had already imagined a beautiful dark-haired, dark-eyed baby girl who would look like her daddy and whom I would name Francesca. But having a baby would complicate our already complex situation and so I prayed, "Please God. No baby. Not now."

That night we walked Assisi's cobbled streets from the restaurant back to the hotel past softly splashing fountains, our footsteps sounding almost intrusive in the enveloping darkness. Streetlights cast a feeble glow and sent our shadows wavering across the cobbles. As if a bird had roused suddenly from sleep, the trembling notes of a flute pierced the quiet. I felt my heart leap at that sound, so sudden, melodious, and mystical. Whenever I think of Assisi, I always remember that moment, symbolic as it was of the grace we felt there, of the joy we would continue to find each time we returned.

And so it was that on this, my first trip to Italy, I lost my virginity but learned to travel chastely. When I left Italy, I was not sure that Vittorio's dispensation would ever be granted, and despite the love that we'd shared, I said good-bye knowing that when he returned to Puerto Rico he would most likely return as a priest, and that I would already have left the island. I did not want him to think that I would wait for him forever.

# 31

❧

# *I Join the Blue Army*

Someone once said that synchronicity is "God's way of acting anonymously." This little aphorism expresses what I've often considered to be one of my idiosyncrasies (which I nonetheless like to think of as biblical): the penchant to look for signs in happenstance. My rational spirit quails at this propensity, however common. There are those who seek direction from the movement of the constellations, who read palms to determine life-lines, who attempt to contact the dead for advice about the future. We speak of divine Providence, karma, and serendipity, so perhaps the desire to seek knowledge of the future in signs is not uncommon. More likely, in looking for signs we are simply recognizing confirmation in events of what we already know deep within ourselves to be true.

When I returned home from Italy such a sign was waiting for me. On learning that I'd left the monastery, John Haffert, the Blue Army founder who'd befriended my parents in the sixties, had written asking me "what role Our Lady will now play in your life?" As he saw it, I could do no more important work than to join him and work with the Blue Army to help spread the message of Fatima—to fight the forces of atheistic Communism, not with weapons of steel but with the more powerful weapon of prayer. When I read Haffert's invitation, I saw in this synchronicity a manifestation of God's will. Convinced that God had spoken to me through this letter, I canceled my plans to attend nursing school and made arrangements to begin working with him at the Ave Maria Institute in Washington, New Jersey, national headquarters of the Blue Army in the United States. It was a choice Mom approved of—so much better than marrying a priest.

When Vittorio, who was still in Italy, learned of my new plans, he wrote to congratulate me on my desire to work for such a good cause. He even made arrangements with a Fiat executive to allow me to buy a used Fiat at a good price from a New Jersey distributor. I would need a car, he said, if I was going to work with the Blue Army. Perhaps he was relieved that I would not be going to nursing school, where I might meet a handsome doctor and get married. Through his mediation, and a loan from Banco Popular in New York City, where my brother Steve was vice president, I was able to buy a bright yellow manual-drive Fiat with less than a thousand miles on it for just two thousand dollars.

The Ave Maria Institute was located near the Delaware Water Gap, in western New Jersey. Housed in a renovated barn, the institute was surrounded by miles of wooded hills and acres of grassy pastureland. The exterior serenity of the scene belied the activity that hummed within that building, where printing presses in the center of the barn busily churned out books and magazines, while a small overworked administrative staff worked frantically at either end of the sprawling edifice.

I'd set off to work with the Blue Army in my little car, filled with confidence. I had no idea where I would live, nor even whether I'd be paid a salary. I trusted that God would provide, and arrived to find that no one was even expecting me. Haffert, who'd been out of town, wouldn't arrive until the following day. I spent the night at a motel and ate a hamburger for supper at a local diner.

When Haffert returned the following day, he was apologetic, and asked me to meet with him at 10 A.M. in his office, located in the barn's renovated loft. During that meeting he spoke to me of his hopes for the growth of the Blue Army but did not tell me what I would be doing. Instead he told me I could live in the two-hundred-year-old farmhouse on the property, which had been renovated for a small group of contemplative brothers who would not arrive until later that year. He also told me he could afford to pay me seventy-five dollars a week.

It wasn't until I read the official Blue Army publication, *Soul Magazine*, that I learned I was to be the national coordinator for the Blue Army. "Beryl undertakes this great apostolic opportunity with some trepidation, but with lively faith. Perhaps no single person in our century has been given the opportunity of coordinating an entire nationwide Apostolate that has been waiting, waiting, waiting for someone like [her]!"

Haffert was a man of great vision and creativity, but I did not realize that his preferred mode of operation was to drop someone into a role and expect her to accomplish great things on her own. My new title should have intimidated anyone with as little experience as I had, but I possessed an outsized sense of my abilities and set to work with gusto. As national coordinator I corresponded with the various national Blue Army units, located new leaders, prepared training materials, edited a leadership newsletter, coordinated visits of the Pilgrim Virgin to parishes throughout the nation, and wrote articles for *Soul Magazine*. Other challenges were more difficult, such as dealing with the Blue Army members who stood on the steps of the Cathedral in Cleveland (or was it Cincinnati?) and refused admittance to scantily clad visitors, or the wandering pilgrim from Jamaica who talked out loud to Our Lady and moved into the farmhouse with me.

Aside from an occasional meal with some of the employees and visits with my family, I had no social life. I spent my first paycheck on a turntable and some classical records to keep me company in the farmhouse. Not a radio or television, mind you—a turntable! I'd been living in the farmhouse on the institute's property for several months when the furnace exploded in the middle of the night, sending clouds of black ash throughout the building and covering everything with a fine layer of soot. It was time to find a place of my own.

My first apartment was the converted second story of a small wooden house on one of the town's less desirable back streets. It was accessed via a fire escape and had a bathroom so tiny that my knees hit the sink when I sat on the toilet. But it was mine! I furnished it with a beanbag chair (try getting that into a Fiat), a mattress, and a desk that doubled as a table. Although seventy-five dollars a week had been more than adequate while living rent-free at the farmhouse, living on that *and* paying rent was another matter. I went to Haffert to ask for a raise, but instead of giving me one, he reminded me that I'd made a vow of poverty. No matter how you stretched it, seventy-five dollars—even in the early seventies—did not go very far. Every month I wrote checks to the bank for my car, to the landlord for the rent, and to the dentist for a root canal. This left me with just enough money to buy a tank of gas and a bag of groceries. I found that one chicken, roasted, could provide seven meals, and coffee grounds could be reused three times to brew an ever-weaker cup of coffee. It was the first time I'd ever managed on my own. I was deliciously happy!

Vittorio, meanwhile, wrote "missing-you" letters from Puerto Rico filled with endearments and talking about the day we would "finally be together forever." Although his dispensation appeared to have disappeared into limbo, and nothing, absolutely nothing, was happening in that regard, he still talked about marriage. I gave little credence to his sentiments, having seen how often he vacillated. I had come to acquiescent, if resentful, terms with the fact that we might never marry. Then, in early December, Vittorio wrote a letter that threw me into confusion. He had sold his apartment and tendered his resignation at the university, and was joining me in New Jersey as soon as the fall semester ended.

At one time such news would have thrilled me. Instead it felt as though I'd swallowed a rock. Though I hadn't fallen out of love with Vittorio, I'd resigned myself to life without him. What would I do with him? I couldn't very well live with him. Imagine the headlines.

*Priest moves in with Blue Army leader!* Besides, I was enjoying my independence. I had my own apartment, my own car, my own checking account, my own challenging job.

To avoid scandal, I found him a room at Mrs. Post's Boarding House several blocks away from my apartment, where he could live until his dispensation arrived. Next was to tell Haffert about my secret life. Much to my surprise, he didn't seem shocked when I told him I was in love with a priest, not even when I told him that this priest was coming to live near me. Instead he told me that he didn't see why we both couldn't work for the Blue Army. It was my turn to be stunned. This was not the answer I'd expected. I didn't realize that Haffert and I had very different ideas about what "working together" meant.

Vittorio arrived in early January 1974, convinced that everything was going our way: We would live near each other. We would work together. We would eventually marry. Haffert was traveling when Vittorio arrived, so we spent our free time hiking the hills around the Delaware Water Gap, dining at local restaurants, and necking in scenic places. When Haffert returned, Vittorio borrowed my car and drove off in high spirits to meet with him. It was a Sunday afternoon, so I asked Vittorio to invite Haffert to share dinner with us. While he was gone, I busied myself preparing a roast garnished with fresh mint sauce, to be served with Yorkshire pudding and gravy, a meal that had always been a success when my mother served it. When the phone rang, I expected to hear Vittorio's voice telling me that he and John were on the way. I did not expect to hear my mother's very concerned voice wanting to know if I was all right.

"Sure, I'm fine, Mom. Why do you ask?" What a strange question I thought. Why *wouldn't* everything be all right? Vittorio had moved to the States and we were going to work together for a cause we believed in.

"John just called, Beryl. He's asked Vittorio to take over the apostolate to Spanish-speaking Catholics."

"That's great! But why did he call you?"

"Beryl, Vittorio has decided to remain a priest."

# 32

## Back to the Priesthood

I slammed down the phone, Mom's news reverberating in my head. How dare he make such a decision without me? How dare he get my mother to do his dirty work of telling me? The coward! The wimp! Did he think I was made of Silly Putty? Good reliable bouncing Beryl; pull her this way, pull her that, she'll bounce back. Out into the January wind I ran. Let the roast burn, I raged. I'm not going to be here when he gets back.

The sky was a bitter gray. All it needed was lightning to mirror my emotions. I hated Vittorio all the way into the countryside. I didn't care where I was going, only that I get as far away from him as possible. If I'd had the car, I'd have driven to another state, but he had it—he'd used *my* car! An image flashed into my mind: Vittorio driving back to the apartment, thinking thoughts of divinely inspired love, like Dante for his beautiful Beatrice—blissful in his restored priesthood. How I loathed him! A fine cutting sleet slammed into my face, freezing my tears, but I could not, would not, go back to the apartment with him there. I ran toward a small chapel that I saw next to the road, fled into its simple wooden interior, and collapsed into the silence it offered. Almost as soon as I entered I felt calmer, as if I'd swallowed a painkilling draught.

I've been in some of the most magnificent churches in the world, yet I have consistently found that, no matter what my state of mind, the humble chapels exude the greatest peace. It is so tangible, that atmosphere of prayer and seeking, that I sometimes think even an atheist would feel the presence of God in such a place. Surrounded by the tranquillity of that small chapel, my tears stopped flowing as did the raging of my mind. The pain of betrayal was too huge to dissolve. It remained like a heavy boulder within my chest. Weeks earlier, I might have been happy for Vittorio; I'd been busy shaping a life of my own without him. But with his return I'd allowed myself to dream, and he'd shattered those dreams once more, all in the space of one short morning. I was done playing the victim. I'd pretend I was glad he was remaining a priest, that I'd come to the same conclusion myself. I would not show him my pain; I would not give him the satisfaction of knowing how much I loved him.

Either Vittorio was a master at self-deception, or my performance deserved an Oscar. In the letter he sent Carlo the next day, Vittorio wrote: "Thanks be to God and the Mother Mary, my vocation has been saved . . . Beryl too is happy with my decision to remain a priest and work for Our Blessed Mother."

The following week I drove him to the airport. He was flying to Puerto Rico, then to Spain, and from there to Fatima. His apostolate had begun.

I sat bolt upright and looked at my clock. It was four in the morning. I heard Vittorio calling for me: "Beryl, Beryl, Beryl . . ." My heart pounded. Something terrible was happening to him. But Vittorio was in Fatima. What could happen in Fatima, that city of visions and miracles? Why would he cry for me in a voice so filled with torment that it would wake me from sleep thousands of miles away?

Unable to get back to sleep, I rose and finished packing the suitcase I'd readied for my trip to Detroit, where Haffert was holding an

Apostolic Training Seminar for Blue Army leaders. Arriving at Newark Airport early, I wandered through the gift shops to find a book to keep my mind off Vittorio. I selected *Captains and the Kings* by Taylor Caldwell, an author whose books I'd read while in Puerto Rico, and didn't stop reading until the plane touched down in Detroit.

In Detroit I lived with the Handmaids of Mary Immaculate, who were working with Haffert to train Blue Army leaders. We had just finished supper on the second day of the seminar when Sister Mary Joseph told me that I had a phone call. Vittorio had been trying to reach me for two days via the head office. Terry Cormier, Haffert's secretary had taken pity on his desperation and told him how he could phone me.

"Beryl, you must help me," he said. "Something terrible has happened." His voice was so shaken and heavy that I could hardly understand what he was saying. He told me that he would be leaving Portugal and flying to Rome to be with his family for a while. "I will explain everything when I come to you."

When I returned to the institute four days later, I waited for the phone call that would tell me when Vittorio would be coming back.

Vittorio was carrying a dozen roses and a suitcase when I met him outside the customs area at Newark Airport as he had asked me to do. He tried to present the roses with a flourish, but his attempt at gallantry was almost grotesque because he looked so ill, his face ashen and his back bent, as if he were carrying a load of wood like the peasants we'd seen in the mountains of Italy. On the drive back to Washington, he told me what had happened. The trip had started well. He'd gathered several potential leaders for the Blue Army in Puerto Rico and in Spain. But in Portugal, things had turned bitter. He'd arrived in Fatima to discuss plans with Bishop Venancio, titular head of the Blue Army, only to be told that the Blue Army didn't want him.

"Didn't want you?" I asked, stunned. "What do you mean?" How was it possible that the Blue Army didn't want Vittorio, especially when

Haffert had personally invited him to work for the organization—and, more important, when Vittorio had decided to remain a priest for this very reason?

Vittorio cleared his throat and tried to talk, but his voice trembled. "I am accused of being Communist."

"But who would accuse you of such a thing?"

"Beryl, if I knew, I could make a defense. I begged the bishop, please to tell me who has so accused me, but he would not; he would not tell me who betrays me in this way."

The only rationale Vittorio could think of for such an accusation might have been his friendship with Father Ivan Illich, one of the most radical and controversial political and social thinkers of the twentieth century. Vittorio and Illich had taught together at the Catholic University in Ponce in the late fifties. Both of them had been forced out of that university in the early sixties because of conflicts with the bishop of Ponce. Vittorio found a job at the University of Puerto Rico, and Illich left the island. Soon afterward he founded the Centre for Intercultural Documentation in Cuernavaca, Mexico. Though Vittorio and Illich often disagreed with each other, sometimes vehemently, they remained friends.

Meanwhile, in Puerto Rico, some of Vittorio's loyal friends immediately began a campaign to salvage Vittorio's priesthood from the rubble of events at Fatima. They wrote to Bishop Venancio and to John Haffert, claiming that the accusation that Vittorio was a Communist was slander and asking for an investigation into Vittorio's works, which would proclaim him a loyal son of the Church.

Haffert could not help us. He claimed to know no more than we did, but because of the bishop of Fatima's injunction, he could not allow Vittorio to work for the Blue Army. At a loss of where to turn next, I suggested we contact my former spiritual director Bishop Ahr, who might be able to help us discern God's will in this mess.

Vittorio met privately with the bishop at his residence in Trenton, while I waited in the library.

"What is God trying to tell me?" Vittorio asked the bishop.

"It would appear that God is making His intentions quite clear," the bishop replied. "I will do everything in my power to help you get your dispensation so you and Beryl can marry."

The stress of events had taken its toll. Vittorio was ill. One day I arrived back at the apartment from work to find Vittorio in my bed, trembling violently. For several days he burned with a strange fever that would skyrocket for hours and then plummet back to normal, only to rise alarmingly a short time later. Puzzled by the erratic fever, I went to the local pharmacist to get something to help bring it under control. The pharmacist told me to take Vittorio to the nearest hospital emergency room—immediately.

Vittorio was admitted to the hospital in Easton, Pennsylvania, where we learned that he had an obstruction of some sort. The doctors could not determine exactly what it was. It could be an ulcer. It could be a tumor. They would need to perform exploratory surgery. Not wanting me to "become a living crucifix," Vittorio decided to have the operation in Rome. The next day he once again flew out of my life.

"I am the king of cocktails, intravenous feedings and vitamins being pumped into my arteries. Two bags a day," he wrote in a letter dated April 12, 1974. Because his body was so weakened, exploratory surgery had to be delayed until May.

"I constantly dream with you. Sometimes, painful dreams. Many times I talk to the leaves of the tree outside my window, if one of them is taken away from me, I recommend it to fly to you. . . The birds? They would be more useful, but they are always so busy singing and making acrobatics."

On May 15, the doctors finally operated. I spoke to Vittorio the following day. In a barely audible voice, he told me that the doctors found his pancreas swollen and did a "wonderful restructuring" around it. Everything was fine. An hour later, I received another of my mother's fateful invasive phone calls. Again she asked if I was all right.

Of course I was all right, I told her. I'd just spoken with Vittorio
and he was doing fine. As gently as she could, Mom broke the news
that the doctors had found cancer of the pancreas. Vittorio had a one
percent chance of living six months. "Word is spreading, Beryl."
She'd verified the rumors with Carlo.

I couldn't believe such news. Why had Vittorio told me the doctors had found nothing serious? Wouldn't he be the one with the
best information? As soon as my mother hung up, I made another
call, this time to Vittorio's sister, Maria. I wanted the truth. Maria
spoke no English, but I knew enough Italian to gather that what my
mother said was true. Vittorio was dying, but the family and the
medical team had decided not to tell him. It would be better if he
were allowed to live what was left of his life with as much joy and
confidence as possible.

A week following his surgery, too weak to write himself, Vittorio
dictated a letter asking me to join him in Italy. On June 15, one
month after the surgery, I flew back to Italy for what I thought would
be the last time.

## 33

## *Vittorio's Italy*

*I* no longer had to sleep at Trinità dei Monti, the convent at the top of the Spanish Steps, as I did on my first trip to Rome. On this trip I slept in Maria's house, in the little parlor that was never used, everyone preferring to visit in the kitchen or on the terrace that overlooked this old section of Rome. Every evening, Maria and I fixed the sofa with sheets and pillows, and every morning, we folded them away. Vittorio slept in the hallway, on the fold-up cot where he'd slept as child growing up and as a young priest. I lay in bed, a lump in my throat and tears wetting my pillow, listening to his breathing, the secret of his illness weighing like lead on my heart. But my arrival seemed to have given Vittorio's recovery a jump-start. He was eating with appetite, his red blood cell count rose toward normal with a rapidity that amazed his doctors, his skin lost its deathly pallor, and his step grew more jubilant with every passing day.

"Look, my love." Vittorio beamed at me as I sipped a huge cup of café latte in Maria's kitchen. He pushed a small twig in my direction. "When I was in the hospital, I sneaked outside to take a walk and found this lovely greeting from my tree."

I picked up the small stem. It was slender and opened into a fan of several tiny branches as lacy as those on a cedar. "I am going to make you a pin from this," he said.

What kind of a pin could he make from a twig, I wondered, but, not wanting to hurt his feelings, didn't ask. Later that day, while walking through the nearby back streets and peeking into artisans' workshops to watch them carve wood and sculpt stone, we came across one who worked in fine metals. Vittorio had the twig with him. He asked if a mold could be made from it so that it could be cast in gold. The artisan said this was possible, and suggested adding tiny gemstones to the branches, an idea that appealed to both of us. As I love the combination of varied colors, I selected pale green peridot, amethyst, topaz, and aquamarine for my pin.

"In praise of life," Vittorio said when we picked up the pin later that week, "our tree of life." Tears filled my eyes on hearing those words. Vittorio thought they were tears of joy and smiled at me. "Happy?" he asked.

Day by day Vittorio's body increased in strength and it wasn't long before the doctors said he was well enough to travel. And so we set out on our second Italian sojourn, this one having a different purpose than the last. Vittorio's illness had confirmed his desire to marry. Vittorio wanted to introduce me to all those that he loved. As it turned out, it was they who introduced me to a Vittorio I didn't know.

Nestled on a hill south of Rome, the ancient town of Genazzano resembled a fortified castle with its high stone walls and narrow alleys. Vittorio's mother was born here. Within that city, a cathedral enshrined a tiny chapel with a miraculous image of the Madonna and Child that had appeared on its walls in April 1467. A copy of this image, *Our Lady of Good Counsel*, hung in my parents' apartment. They brought it back with them from their first Blue Army pilgrimage years earlier, to visit Marian shrines. Genazzano is not one of the more popular Marian shrines, yet the fact that my parents had knelt in this church, in the town where Vittorio's mother was born, at a time when my father first suffered the effects of the disease that eventually brought Vittorio into my life, appeared like yet one more sign that God had been with us all this time, accompanying us on our journey through suffering to love.

While in Genazzano, we stopped at an outdoor market to buy fresh tomatoes, strawberries, and apricots. The man at the *salumeria* who prepared our picnic lunch washed the produce for us. We ate lunch on a hillside, sitting on the hood of the car and caressed by sun-filled breezes and filled with joy at the opportunity to travel again together. We bit into the crusty loaf baked that morning in a clay oven outside the city, the juice of spicy olives and fresh mozzarella cheese running over our fingers as we gazed at the valley below. From our lofty perch, we could hear the bleating of the sheep that grazed placidly on the hillside, the pine trees that whispered hushed secrets above us.

Not far from Genazzano, in a lovely old villa at the end of a tunnel of thin black cypresses, lived Vittorio's maternal cousins. Vittorio introduced me as his *vita*, his life. As we dined on a terrace overlooking fields that his mother's family had farmed for generations, I felt separate from this warm family. They were reliving a past I was not part of, and I would never become part of their future. One needs time to blend with a family, years of visits like this, and Vittorio and I did not have that kind of time. From there we turned north toward Umbria. On the way, Vittorio stopped to make a phone call at one of the public telephone stations one finds throughout Italy. He returned to the car looking inordinately pleased.

"Two of the sweetest people in the world are waiting to embrace you," he said, and off we headed for the Stroppolatinis', where Zaira and Marcello practically fell over Vittorio in their joy at seeing him again. As we sat sipping espresso and munching on almond cookies that Zaira had baked that morning, they told me how Vittorio had "saved" them when he was still a young priest. One day he found Zaira sobbing inconsolably in the back of the church. A servant in the house of a wealthy aristocratic family, she had fallen in love with their son, Marcello, and had gotten pregnant. They wanted to marry, but the family threatened to disinherit Marcello if he married her and he had no other means of income.

"And here was this treasure, carrying my child," Marcello smote his breast. Zaira smiled at him tenderly.

I tried to picture portly Marcello as a handsome young aristocrat, and Zaira—front teeth flashing with gold fillings—as a beautiful teen.

The story Marcello told enchanted me: "'God will never abandon you,' Vittorio promised me, coward that I am, so afraid because I had no skills with which to support a family. He marries us, and then, from his meager salary as a professor, proceeds to support us as I try to build my photography business."

Marcello wiped tears from his eyes.

"And you know what he does as he boards the boat for Puerto Rico? He puts into our hands all the money in his pockets. The gifts he's been given for the journey. 'For the child,' he says."

On our way through Umbria, land of rolling hills and cypress, glowing with cream and ochre hillside towns renowned for the saints who had lived there, I asked Vittorio if we could stop at Spoleto. I'd seen billboards advertising the city's renowned music festival, of which I'd heard so much in the States.

"Of course we will, perhaps next year."

I grew silent. There would be no next year. Would Vittorio attend the festival if he knew it would be his last chance? I did not know how to breach the barrier his illness thrust between us; just as on our first trip I had not known how to travel chastely together. And what about the friends we would visit? Were we all holding the same secret? I wanted to share my confusion with someone. Was hiding the news of a loved one's approaching death an Italian thing; or did they know Vittorio better than I did?

Instead of going to Spoleto we headed north toward Florence to meet the Contessa Fidalma Lisio, a descendant of one of the great medieval cloth manufacturing families of Italy and Vittorio's longtime friend. Fidalma was a big woman, perhaps six feet tall, very regal, very elegant. Next to her I felt insignificant and gauche. We dined with her on a hillside overlooking Florence, at a table under a trellis laden with wisteria through which the sun drifted in clouds of pale cream and lavender. In the distance, the city shimmered in a multihued sea of terraced green vineyards and olive orchards. I listened to Vittorio and Fidalma banter about theology and politics and wondered why Vittorio didn't talk to me as he did to her. Although, at my request, he'd given me a list of books to read on the early Sumerian and Babylonian civilizations and I was anxious to learn, I don't remember ever discussing them with him. When Fidalma took us to see the family textile mills, Vittorio purchased several yards of fine brocade for a bedspread for "our home." Our home! Our home did not exist. *Now* was the only home we had, but Vittorio did not know that.

On our first trip through Italy, I was the navigator, the reader of maps, and Vittorio was the pilot. On this trip, however, I sometimes took the wheel, because Vittorio tired easily. I did not like driving in Italy. Italians leapt sidewalks with their little autos, squeezing into any crevice they could find and forcing pedestrians to flee for their lives, all the while shouting, blaring horns, and giving the finger. I could manage on the *autostrada*, even though drivers used it like a race track, but I hated driving in the mountains. All those terrifying narrow, twisty roads with sheer drops on one side or another. We were driving through the mountains on our way to the Italian Riviera when Vittorio asked me to drive. My heart dropped, but seeing how tired he was I pretended to feel confident and set off at a speed that I thought was plenty fast for a mountain road, 90 km. It wasn't fast enough for the Mercedes behind me, which seemed to want to play bumper cars with our rear fender.

"Faster, Beryl," Vittorio urged. "Faster."

The driver in the Mercedes blinked his lights and edged dangerously close as Vittorio exhorted me to speed up. I did, but it wasn't fast enough. The Mercedes roared by, the driver blaring his horn and gesticulating. From the passenger windows several other hands did the same.

"After them," Vittorio shouted. He opened his window and stuck his middle finger into the air. He leaned over and blasted the horn. The driver of the Mercedes started swerving back and forth like a teen with a hula-hoop.

*"Porca miseria, cretino, sanguisuga!"* Vittorio shouted, hanging out the window and banging his arm on the side of the car. The curses flowed fast and furious. He lay on the horn again.

"Pass them, Beryl. Put your foot on the gas. Pass them!"

I'd never seen Vittorio so wild before. He looked like he wanted to pick a fight with the bruisers in the car ahead of us—all three of them.

"Please, Vittorio," I shouted, "calm down. You've just had surgery."

I slammed on the brakes and skidded to the side of the road, letting the drivers behind us whiz past.

"For God's sake, Vittorio. Do you think you can beat those guys up?"

"They meant nothing, my love," he said, laughing at my fury. "It's all show."

At Forte dei Marmi on the Italian Riviera, Dr. Vando D'Angiolo, the president of Campolonghi e Freda, a stone company, treated us like royalty. We were given a room in a beautiful seaside hotel where freshly squeezed orange juice was served for breakfast and thick robes were provided for lounging. Dr. D'Angiolo took us to the factory where granite was polished and custom cut for projects all over the world. With his entrepreneurial spirit, Vittorio had generated a contact that allowed Campolonghi e Freda to supply Puerto Rico with marble and granite for its new buildings and town squares.

"This priest of yours," said Vando, slapping Vittorio on the back, "drives all the way from Rome, without an appointment, and expects to see me! So I think, why not. And, what does Vittorio do? He proceeds to offer *me* a proposal. One I can't turn down: distribution of our product in Puerto Rico, with the perfect representative, his nephew Carlo!"

Vando respected people with ingenuity and *palle*, balls. He told me that Vittorio could have made a fortune in business. "Vittorio, however, doesn't dream of wealth," Dr. D'Angiolo said.

We spent the final two weeks at Maria and Gianni's summer home above the city of Trento, in a mountain village in the Italian Alps where clouds sometimes obscured the view. Vittorio's appetite grew in the mountain air. Every morning at breakfast he'd discuss the next meal, planning our jaunts so we'd be home in time to eat Maria's delicious cooking. His face was filling out and he stood taller.

A mile up a curving mountain road from Maria's chalet-style apartment was a local farmer who raised dairy cows. Every day, Vittorio and I would walk to this farm to purchase cream for Maria's fine cooking, and milk for the morning coffee. We walked slowly, past vineyards where grapes were just beginning to swell, gathering small bouquets of wildflowers, inhaling the rich scent of the pastures and the barns. The farmer, garrulous and witty, loved to take us into the building where he pressed grapes and stored his own wine. Dressed in his grungy white undershirt, droopy blue pants, and small straw hat, he made a comic figure as he winked and offered us grappa, a spirit made from the pits of the grapes. I tried to keep from inhaling the pungent stuff as I sipped, but Vittorio enjoyed it. It put fire into his blood.

The night before we were to leave Trento to return to Rome, the neighbors arrived for a special meal: polenta served with fresh *fungi* gathered that very afternoon by Elena, a very pregnant neighbor who knew her mushrooms. The sauce, made from freshly picked tomatoes and basil, had been simmering for much of the afternoon. Just before we sat down to eat, bitter greens were sautéed with garlic and oil and tossed lightly to wilt the leaves and coat the greens. During desert, Adriano, who was serving coffee and laughing at a ribald joke told in mountain dialect, lost his balance and spilled the scalding liquid over Vittorio's chest. We swathed Vittorio in iced towels right up to his neck. I crushed back an image of Vittorio in a coffin. When I see people in coffins, they die.

There's something about believing one will never return again to a place that imprints it on your mind. It is as if you had never seen it before. In such moments there is no past, no future, only now. Seeing Italy for what I thought was the last time was like getting eyeglasses and seeing what had been a distant blur leap in front of me sharp-edged and detailed. Vittorio wanted me to see Italy from another perspective.

Not far from Trento was a mountain called Paganella; a funicular creaked its way thousands of feet up the mountainside diminishing in size till it could barely be seen. Every time we drove past Paganella, I felt loopy. Vittorio teased me about the funicular, threatening to stop and take me for a ride. "Not on your life," I told him. "You'll never get me into that thing." And he didn't, not until the lovely June afternoon he took me on a picnic to the base of Paganella. Just a picnic, mind you, but one for which he'd already purchased funicular tickets. I had to laugh at his cunning.

"Come, Beryl. The view is breathtaking," he whispered as he guided me toward the line.

Inside the cable car there was only a thin glass wall between the passengers and the abyss, but as more people crowded in, I took comfort from their presence, as if they somehow could protect me from my fear of heights. I was relieved that we were running on a small track, as if a track on the rocky face of the mountain was somehow safer than swinging on a wire. And then it felt as though we were swinging, shuddering and rocking each time we passed a junction. I steeled myself and looked down. If the end of the world occurs while I'm still living, I want to keep my eyes open and watch it happen.

"Beryl, my love, smile for me." Vittorio snapped a picture. I looked happy. I was happy. Below me, growing smaller and more gemlike the higher we rose, were spread the lakes and forests and towns of northern Italy.

Two people in the cable car drew my attention, a tall willowy blonde and a sleek gentleman with silver hair. They looked athletic and tanned. They whispered softly, her laughter tinkling in our glass cage. When we emerged from the car into the blustery cold wind at the top of Paganella, the blonde and her lover whipped off their overcoats. Their taut bodies gleamed gold and shiny. They wore bikinis! They were crazy! I watched them run toward a nearby crater where they spread themselves out upon the rocks.

Outside the crater the wind tore at my hair and tunneled into my ears. Inside the crater it was snug and comfortable. A meteor had fallen on this mountain, leaving a great hole, a hole like the one Vittorio's death was going to leave in my life, but within that crater I was warm.

## 34

## *Together at Last*

While I was in Italy, my sister Judi, having made a painstaking effort to remain committed to religious life, decided to leave the monastery. Monastic life was no longer a life of poverty and penance. It had become a life of comfort, a life that clashed with how others perceived it, and she felt she was living a lie. She saw that living in the world was the real challenge, "not the easy and secure life we had at the monastery since they updated."

Rather than returning home to Puerto Rico, as I'd done, Judi rented a room at a women's residence near Greenwich Village and immediately went job hunting. She began working with Barbizon Lingerie in their main office in New York City and gradually rose from assistant coding supervisor to showroom manager to export sales manager. As soon as she could afford it, she got her own apartment on East Eighty-third Street. When I returned from Italy, Judi's presence "in the world" was a gift. I was in mourning, certain that Vittorio would never make it back to the States as he had promised to do and visited Judi every chance I had. Meanwhile, life went on. The Blue Army was expecting me back at work July 7.

Haffert had a dream. He wanted to build a national shrine to Our Lady of Fatima on the rolling hills above the Ave Maria Institute. This shrine would include, along with an open-air basilica, a convent of cloistered nuns to pray for the spread of the message of Fatima throughout the world. Work on this project had begun only a short time before I left for Italy in June 1974. When I returned a month later, I was surprised to find the convent finished and the nuns already in residence.

I returned to the institute halfheartedly. Vittorio's experience with the Blue Army had been so painful that I had difficulty giving myself to an apostolate that had hurt him so dreadfully. But I saw in Vittorio's terminal cancer a message that I should continue to work within the Church through the Blue Army, so I tried to renew my fervor by attending Mass and praying the rosary with the nuns at the convent chapel—an exact replica of the tiny house in which, it is said, the Holy Family dwelled in Nazareth.

The mother superior of this convent, Sister Miranda, had a reputation for holiness and was believed to have visions of the Blessed Mother. One day, she approached me after Mass and told me she had a message for me from Our Lady.

"Tell Beryl to return to the monastery or she will have much to suffer in this world." It was a tender, loving message from the mother of Jesus, whom we Catholics revere as our mother, the mother of every person who has ever walked the face of this earth.

That message now resonates with me as a mother who has anguished over her children's suffering, but at the time I dismissed it. One would think that with my propensity to look for divine intervention—signs, serendipitous happenings, synchronicity—I would have been awed and touched by that message and would have returned to the monastery. It is not often that one gets a message from the Mother of God. The trouble was that I didn't believe the message. I didn't trust the messenger. Although God has never insisted on holiness in choosing his prophets (Jonah, for instance, did everything possible to try to avoid his role, and complained nonstop about being chosen for the thankless task of being a prophet), I did not see a prophet in Sister Miranda. I saw an ordinary good woman with delusions. Besides, I'd just learned that Vittorio was returning to the States.

I'd been certain that I would never see Vittorio again, that his letters would dwindle until one day I'd receive a phone call telling me he was dying. Instead, his letters were filled with enthusiasm, and his latest gave the date of his return. "Remember, August 8!" he wrote. "When we shall be together forever!" It was a letter filled with exclamation points.

The fact that Vittorio was able to return seemed like a manifestation of God's strange ways of bringing us together. How could I return to the monastery when Vittorio was returning to the States to be with me? Even if our time together was short, suffering was a small price to pay for such a love. Suffering had honed our love into a bright and searing gift. Hadn't Vittorio once told me that to suffer was to live twice?

As with many pre–Vatican II Catholics, my concept of suffering was forged by constant meditation on the passion of a dying Christ, and by reading the lives of the saints. At Holy Child, I'd been deeply affected by the story of Cornelia Connelly, the woman who founded the Society of the Holy Child Jesus in 1846. The story, as I remember it after these many years, takes flight on the afternoon that Cornelia—who'd converted to Catholicism along with her husband, Pierce—offered God her happiness. A short time later, her beloved two-year-old-son, John Henry, was scalded in a terrible accident and died in agony in her arms. And the story gets worse. In October of that same year, when she was pregnant with their fifth child, Pierce told her he wanted to become a priest. Heartbroken, but seeking only to do God's will, Cornelia gave her assent. After giving birth, she left New Orleans, where they lived, and took the children with her to England. There, at the request of Pope Gregory XVI, she founded an order of teaching nuns.

Several years later Pierce (an appropriate name for this two-edged sword) changed his mind and decided he didn't want to be a priest anymore. In an attempt to force Cornelia to return to him, he hired a boat and waited for her to join him on the Thames. Cornelia, torn by grief, prayed for strength to stay steadfast to her vows and refused to go with him. In retaliation, Pierce denied her all future contact with their children.

Impressed by this story, I, too, began to pray, "Oh God, if this happiness is not for your glory, take it from me." Of course, with constant repetition, my child's brain began to think of suffering as more pleasing to God than happiness. I've discovered since then that this belief is a misconception. I cannot believe that God finds pleasure in our suffering. Suffering is simply intrinsic to life, part of the life and death cycle, much of it caused by our own choices, or by the decisions of other humans. But believing that suffering is a blessing is not all bad. It enabled me to survive what might otherwise have destroyed me. In *Life of the Beloved*, the popular spiritual writer Henri Nouwen speaks of this as suffering lived "under the blessing."

Suffering lived "under the blessing" was what the great Saint Teresa of Avila endured. She wanted nothing more than to stay in her monastery and love God. Instead, God sent her hither and yon establishing new monasteries. Just as she'd get comfortable in one, God would send her off on another mission. On one of these journeys her wagon tipped over in the pouring rain, spilling her and the contents of the wagon into the mud.

"Why, Lord?" she cried out.

"Teresa, this is how I treat my friends," God replied.

"Well," Teresa snapped, "It's no wonder you have so few!"

Although thinking of suffering as a sign of God's love can lead to letting oneself be victimized, it can also give rise to a transforming compassion toward others. Certainly this was the case in my life. I had much to learn that only suffering could teach about what it means to be fully human. I also discovered that we do not suffer alone, that God is with us, and within us, as we suffer.

The fourteenth-century mystic Julian of Norwich says that though the world might be a prison and life a penance, God wants us to "rejoice in the remedy . . . that our *Lord is with us, protecting us and leading us into the fullness of joy.*"

# Compline

Darkness has fallen. Your day has circled back to where it began: in darkness. The prayers at Compline exhort you to be vigilant at the coming of night. You understand the need for watchfulness.

You've tried to prepare for the night by living each day in the light, but you have failed. You have neglected what you might have done, committed what you ought to have avoided. Even your good acts are tinged with the dark desires hidden deep within you. Compline provides a gentle place to come to terms with your failures, to ask for and receive forgiveness. Shriven, like the knights of old before entering battle, you prepare to face the night and the death that night might hold.

As children, you were put to bed with the prayer, "Should I die before I wake, I pray the Lord my soul to take." Compline is the Church's bedtime prayer. Like a mother crooning away her child's fears, she murmurs psalms and prayers warm with comfort to assure you that you belong to God, that this universe is his space and you are the child he holds in the palm of his hand. There is nothing he cannot or will not forgive. Enter the night with confidence and rest in peace.

# 35

❧

# *You Have Cancer*

When Vittorio arrived back in the States, on August 8, I had already resigned from the Blue Army. We stayed with Greg while we looked for a place to live. Griselda, Greg's wife, was in Puerto Rico with the children. She did not approve of Vittorio and my relationship and made it clear that while I was welcome in her home, Vittorio was not. Greg did not follow Grissie's dictates, however, and we could not have stayed at a better place. It was a good plan. Greg's home was a spacious and comfortable place to stay and Greg was a brother who loved to give advice. With two neophytes to guide in their home hunting, Greg played mentor and confidant to the hilt.

Searching for an apartment in New Jersey's Bergen County, where Greg lived, was disheartening. In this posh suburban area close to New York City, the rents there were astronomical. Greg suggested we buy some property in Saddle River, where I'd grown up. Even if the house was a shack, he advised, so much the better. Property with run-down buildings was more affordable and the return on investment would be phenomenal.

"Invest $25,000 now, and you'll be sitting on a $500,000 piece of property in a few years," he told us.

Greg's advice was right on target—property in that area now runs in the millions—but we had no money to spend on real estate, nor did we have jobs that would qualify us to purchase property. Recognizing this, Greg suggested that we look in areas near Paterson, as nice rental apartments could be found in towns near rundown cities. This, too, was good advice, for we soon found a cheerful, remodeled apartment above a realtor's office in the small town of Hawthorne, near Paterson. The apartment, 416 Lafayette Avenue, was close to Steve and Greg and their families, and to Judi in New York City. Having family close by was a blessing for an Italian priest who had followed his heart to a place far from any relatives of his own. In Puerto Rico he'd had family nearby because he had brought them to the island: his niece Lucia, his nephew Carlo, and his cousin Umberto and their families. The apartment had another advantage as well; several college campuses were located nearby, and Vittorio hoped to find a teaching position at one of them.

Worried that Vittorio would tax himself by trying to move heavy items, I undertook the furnishing and decorating of the apartment myself. Coming home one afternoon from several futile visits to colleges, and noticing that I'd moved the couch and bedroom bureau, Vittorio confronted me.

"You must not make yourself a slave, Beryl. You are my queen."

This was a theme I was to hear often from him in the coming years. He told me that it was human nature to accept all that was offered in love and to begin to take it for granted. He did not want this to happen to us.

Looking back on that time, I am amazed at the confidence with which I entered into our precarious future. Vittorio was looking for a job while simultaneously and unknowingly harboring death within his body. Did I expect him to support us or did I plan on filling that role? I didn't know the answer, yet I had no fear. We sent out dozens of résumés to colleges all over the country, but the nation was in the middle of a recession and teaching jobs were hard to find. The responses to his inquiries were always the same: "Your credentials are impressive, but unfortunately, we have no positions open. We will, however, keep your vita on file."

If Vittorio grew discouraged, he did not show me his disappointment. God would provide, he said. His confidence was contagious. Besides, he had balls, just as Vando D'Angiolo had said. Hadn't he obtained a lucrative business opportunity for his nephew Carlo? Hadn't he helped set other people up in the jewelry business? One Friday afternoon his chutzpah played a pivotal role in our future.

We were on our way back from Maine, where we'd gone to rescue Greg's ten-year-old daughter, Griselda Clare, from an unhappy camping experience, when we passed Bergen Community College. Vittorio swung the car off the road and into the parking lot. Minutes later we were inside looking for the dean's office. Several weeks later, Vittorio had a job teaching Italian part-time.

Vittorio and I were living together in all ways save one: though we shared a bed, we didn't make love. Once again, I walked that familiar tightrope of longing and abstinence. Complicating matters was Vittorio's ignorance of his impending death. I was tormented with uncertainty. Was it fair to keep Vittorio's condition secret from him when he needed this information? Would he still want to marry me if he knew he was dying? Would he still want to leave the priesthood?

The delay of his dispensation from the priesthood was a relief in a way because it gave me more time to decide if and how I would tell him that he had cancer. I felt that each time he spoke of "tomorrow" and I said nothing, my silence betrayed him.

I don't know why I carried this burden alone. I had friends I could have turned to for advice in making this decision—Bishop Ahr, who had listened with such compassion to our story, and Sister Mary, my dear friend in the monastery. But I did not confide in Mary, as I had not done so when I was deciding to leave the monastery. My mother must have offered advice; she knew her daughter was planning to marry a dying man, but I didn't talk with her about my dilemma. I didn't want her advice. Did my brothers and sister know? If they did, their usual gregariousness had turned to reticence. Instead of confiding in someone, I grew tense with what I felt to be an impossible burden of secrecy, and this dishonesty made me distant. Too much closeness, too much tenderness might lead me to tell Vittorio what his family did not want him to know. His unfailing hope and humor seemed so futile. Time was running out and I didn't know what to do. One night, I took my pillow and some blankets and started climbing toward the attic guestroom, telling Vittorio I just couldn't continue sharing a bed with him. Vittorio followed me.

"I beg you, Beryl. Tell me what is troubling you. Something is not right."

He opened his hands in supplication. "Since my return you've been so distant, so strange. Tell me, please, what is the matter! Do not keep secrets from me."

How do you tell the person you love that he is dying? I tried to speak, but no words came. I sat down on the steps and opened my arms to him. I touched his face, loving the feel of it, the look of tenderness and concern in his eyes. The tears that burned behind my eyes, burned also in my throat, tightening my jaw so that it could not move. I tried again to speak.

"Vittorio, the surgery, it wasn't good."

"What do you mean, Beryl? Not good?"

"Vittorio, they found cancer. They couldn't remove it. They could only do a bypass."

My words fell like heavy stones from the center of my being into his. I tried to move from my own grief to focus on Vittorio's.

"Cancer? But they said it was benign. I don't understand." He'd turned pale and his eyes pierced mine with accusation.

"Oh, Vittorio, I didn't want to be the one to tell you. Forgive me."

"But why did no one tell me?" He stood up and began pacing. Over and over he said those words. "Had they no confidence in me?"

Moments passed as he beseeched me for answers. I had none to give him.

"I am tired." He said, and sat down heavily beside me on the stairs. I wrapped my blanket around him and rocked him like a child.

"Beryl," he said finally, "remember the afternoon in Baiae, the first time we traveled together? Such a beautiful day, and the strawberries I bought for you from that little boy? Remember how we ate those berries, trying to make them last a long time? Were they less sweet because once we finished eating, they were gone?"

I turned to Vittorio. His eyes bored into mine. He took my hands. "Beryl, if we have only a short time together, you will help me make those days as sweet as possible?"

I knew then that we *would* make our days sweet, that we would never greet a day with nonchalance, that each day would be treasured as a gift. He picked up the phone and dialed his canon lawyer in Rome, enunciating each word so that it could not be misunderstood.

"I know I have cancer. I want my dispensation!"

Then he turned toward me. "Beryl," was all he said and I understood. We moved into one another's arms and allowed love to assuage our fear. If our love would not conquer death, it would at least unite us. When confronted with death, Vittorio chose me.

My timing in telling Vittorio about his cancer had been perfect. Later that same night the phone rang and I answered to hear Carlo inquire as to whether his uncle knew about the cancer. He sighed with relief on learning he did. Carlo wanted to tell us about a form of treatment being performed in the Philippines at the time. Through it, his closest friend had regained the use of a shattered elbow that no doctor had been able to repair despite numerous surgical attempts. Carlo gave Vittorio the name of a Mrs. Doris Almeda at the Christian Travel Center in Manila, who could make arrangements for Vittorio to have a consultation with these healers. Vittorio contacted her immediately, and left for the Philippines on September 2,

1974. While there he received treatment from three Christian healers, a noninvasive type of surgery that they claimed removed the tumor from his pancreas. On September 8, the Feast of the Nativity of the Blessed Virgin Mary and one month after he arrived back in the States from Italy, Vittorio sent me a telegram.

"Thanks to God and the Blessed Mother. I am cured!"

# 36

## Pregnant and Married

First, I noticed that I could smell the carpets. Then the scent of coffee made me ill. Soon, the odor of broiling meat nauseated me. One morning, while at Mass, I felt my legs start to shake and a cold sweat made me want to lie down in the aisle. Vittorio took me outside to get some air and I told him I thought I was pregnant.

"But, Beryl! How can you be pregnant?" Vittorio laughed. "One time we make love and you are pregnant?"

I'd taken Vittorio to a cancer specialist after he returned from the Philippines because I did not believe in psychic surgery. But the specialist could find no signs of the cancer. "Get the hell out of this office and start making babies," he'd roared. It appeared that we had done this on the night I told Vittorio about his cancer.

Vittorio was delighted that he was going to be a father, but thoughts of becoming a mother did not make me quite as happy. Vittorio and I had made so much noise about living together as brother and sister to assuage family scruples that I couldn't bear to think of telling them I was pregnant.

"We must call Bishop Ahr. He will help us," Vittorio said.

"But Vittorio, how can I tell him I'm pregnant? He was my spiritual director?" I wailed. "What will he think?"

"An innocent baby? Bishop Ahr would never reject us because of a child! You underestimate him."

Vittorio was right. When I told the bishop that I was pregnant and that we needed his help in speeding up the dispensation, the bishop started to laugh.

"Beryl, you will never guess what has just transpired." He paused.

I hesitated. Not certain whether he meant me to guess or whether he just wanted to surprise me.

"Beryl, when you called I had just opened today's mail. At this very moment I am holding Vittorio's dispensation in my hand!"

Only now, as I write this, do I see in this amazing coincidence a laughing God. At that time I viewed this happening as yet another "sign" that we were meant to be together; I grasped it as a drowning victim might a life preserver—with gratitude and relief; but only now do I hear divine laughter. And, now that I have heard that laughter, I shall store it at the top of my memory box where I can summon it whenever I am in need of a reminder.

On November 9, 1974, Vittorio and I became husband and wife. Bishop Ahr married us in his private chapel in Trenton. This wise man, whom I had at one time feared, had officiated at all the steps in my religious commitment and now celebrated my marriage with Vittorio. And a celebration it was. My mother finally had her wedding— not the one she had dreamed for me, but definitely one she enjoyed more than my investiture as a Poor Clare. Greg served as best man, Judi as maid of honor, and Steve as official photographer. I wore a simple blue silk sheath with a lace jacket and Vittorio wore a new gray suit. We even had an organist. Only the bishop, Vittorio, and Mom knew that I was pregnant. The nausea that made those first months an ordeal was powerless against the jubilant celebration of our simple wedding ceremony. Such a journey we'd been on, Vittorio and I.

To supplement our meager income (Vittorio's salary as a part-time Italian professor amounted to $8,000 a year), I began making dolls like the ones I'd seen in the Italian Alps—tall figures made of starched burlap and clothed in brightly colored aprons and kerchiefs, their arms bent gracefully around sheaves of dried flowers. I bought burlap by the roll, flour paste by the pound, and fabric samples by the box. For days I experimented, sewing burlap around Styrofoam faces and wire arms, which I laboriously cut and bent. Each doll emerged differently. Some carried flowers, others baskets, while yet others held muffs and wore velvet skating outfits. I sold them to friends and relatives and various gift shops and boutiques. A department store in Puerto Rico ordered five dozen to be delivered to their New York office in two weeks. But the amount the stores were willing to pay did not justify the time and expense of making these dolls. We needed another source of income.

One night as we sat at the kitchen table paying bills, Vittorio looked at me intently and said, "Beryl, I think we can sell jewelry right here in Hawthorne."

"In Hawthorne?" I gasped, incredulous. "Hawthorne already has one jeweler too many."

There was Fiorello's, the neighborhood jeweler, and right up the street from us Arthur Groom, a licensed gemologist, had opened a small shop. Undeterred by my negative reaction, Vittorio continued. "We can sell it from the house. Eighteen-karat gold jewelry! No one sells eighteen-karat-gold jewelry." His face beamed with certainty as he explained how we would create a demand for eighteen-karat gold; it was just a matter of educating customers.

"And where will we find these enlightened customers?" I asked.

"Beryl, everyone is a possible customer. We can start with my students, fellow teachers, your relatives, our friends."

His excitement was contagious. I remembered the time he'd shown me his little workshop in Puerto Rico. Remembering that joy, and seeing the hope in Vittorio's eyes, I—who had little interest in jewelry—became enthusiastic, too.

"You are an artist, Beryl. You could design jewelry for us to sell." As if he'd been waiting for just this moment, Vittorio pulled from his briefcase fliers from the Gemological Institute of America. He placed the brochures on the table in front of me and moved his chair close so that we could review them together.

Soon—when I was not making dolls—I was spending afternoons at the kitchen table with protractors, special pencils, and watercolors. Next to me on the table were two large brown binders that took me step by step through a correspondence course in jewelry design. Two other even fatter binders also sat on the table, containing lessons on colored stones: beryl (emeralds and aquamarines—my name was such a happy coincidence); corundum (ruby and sapphire); garnets in all colors of the rainbow, each gem awaiting identification by those learning to become certified gemologists.

Meanwhile, Vittorio contacted a friend of his, Antonio Dini, a jewelry manufacturer in Valenza Po, Italy, who sent him a small case of handmade ring mountings. Vittorio took these mountings to school with him, and within a few days his adult students started showing up at the apartment wanting to buy these rings. Vittorio held the mountings up and tapped them so that they rang.

"Hear that," he said, cocking his head. "These are not cast. Each piece has been cut and soldered by hand. When Beryl's designs are finished they will be made by Antonio."

The world of radiant color to which I'd been introduced through my gemology course opened up new possibilities for these customers: diamonds in every color and hue from white to tangerine to turquoise. Opals, amethysts, tanzanites, topaz, coral, tsavorites. Precious, semiprecious, clear, opaque, luminescent, shimmering, scintillating. This world was theirs to select and combine as they wished. Our plan was to have the mountings made in Italy, and we would buy stones and have them set in New York.

To learn more about the retail trade and supplement our meager income, I obtained a part-time job in a small jewelry store in a nearby mall. The nation was in the midst of a recession, and the store's customers were few and far between, so I spent most of my time cleaning the counter tops with Windex and rearranging the displays. The scent of glass cleaner still brings back memories of those days when, big with baby, I tried my hand as a salesperson in someone else's jewelry store.

It was 1974. Besides the recession, Watergate had shaken the nation and Nixon was now out of office, a fact that caused the Romanian owner of the store to shake his head.

"America has lost one of its greatest leaders," he said, wagging his finger at me. "You need a leader who is willing to do whatever is necessary to maintain control."

I wondered at this statement. How could he equate dishonesty and trickery with leadership? These weren't signs of strength but abuse of power. Was abuse of power justified in certain cases? Perhaps he knew better than I did. He'd fled his native land because its weak leaders had succumbed to Communism. Not used to expressing myself, I listened, but when I went home, I shared his comments with Vittorio.

Vittorio, who had once proudly worn the brown uniform of Mussolini's youth organization, shook his head. "No, dishonesty is never justified, Beryl." He knew first-hand the danger of charismatic leaders. His attitudes toward the improvements Mussolini had made to Italy's infrastructure—the rail and postal services and huge public works projects—changed drastically when Italy became Hitler's ally. As a young priest in Rome under the Fascist government, Vittorio helped Jewish families by giving them the food tickets and identities of deceased parishioners. He was betrayed by La Lupe, a beautiful Jewish informer, and spent three days hiding in a chimney from the Gestapo. On the third day the American forces arrived in Rome, liberating that city from the Fascists and the Nazis, and Vittorio from his chimney.

When the jeweler I worked for bought one of our mountings, I was thrilled. Several weeks later, I found it prominently displayed among the better rings in the small case to the right of the store.

Small diamonds had been added, and it bore a price tag of several thousand dollars. I was stunned. This price was three or four times more than the mounting and diamonds together. When I asked the owner about the price, he told me with a smile that customers like half-price sales, and this way he could mark it down and still make plenty.

After this experience, Vittorio and I decided that markdown sales would not be part of our business plan. Instead, we would price our merchandise as fairly as possible. We would make jewelry affordable, so that even people with modest incomes could own something of beauty. We kept our prices as close to cost as possible, adding nothing for our time.

I did not give birth quietly. I screamed, and so did my mother, who'd come from Puerto Rico to help me. She began this screaming the night I went into labor. Earlier that evening, she'd gone upstairs to the guestroom to read. Vittorio was puttering around in his workshop—a closet like the one he'd used in Puerto Rico—making a pendant for a customer, and I was putting the finishing touches on my last batch of burlap dolls. It was after midnight when I felt the first pain clutch at my back. I waited until the pains were regular before telling Vittorio that we needed to go to the hospital.

"Really?" Vittorio asked, looking both delighted and afraid. He hurried to the bedroom where the small overnight case I'd packed weeks earlier sat waiting.

"Wait, Vittorio. I should tell Mom first."

"But she's sleeping."

"If she's asleep, I won't wake her."

Taking a flashlight I lumbered up the stairs. I could hear the soft whisper of her breathing, the steady, even-paced sighs of sleep. I was about to turn around when a small whine penetrated the quiet. It grew from a barely audible mewl to a full-fledged crescendo of terror. I'd never heard anything like it. Shocked by her scream, I moved toward her reassuringly, but she only shrieked louder.

"It's me, Beryl," I soothed. I repeated my message and still she screamed. I was now almost shouting. The flashlight caught her in its wavering beam. Her eyes were wide open, staring. Vittorio turned on the light. He'd run up the stairs at her cries of alarm.

"I couldn't see you," she whispered in a small accusing voice. "I thought you were a ghost." Her hand clutched her nightgown tightly at the neck.

"I'm in labor, Mom. I just wanted to let you know. We're going to the hospital."

"In labor? Oh my God, Beryl! I need to get dressed." She pushed herself into a sitting position and tried to swing her legs out from under the covers.

"Mom, go back to sleep. It will be hours yet. You need rest. We'll call you."

My mother had been suffering from vertigo since she'd arrived. Overcome by dizziness, she'd collapse and clutch at the floor, moaning and trying to hang on. At other times she'd cling to the toilet and vomit. The local doctor diagnosed an inner-ear problem and prescribed a medication that helped, but she was still weak. I leaned over to give her a hug and noticed that the little tie on her nightgown had come undone, and that she had a tear in her sleeve. A wave of tenderness passed over me. Mom was still wearing the same raggedy old nightgowns she'd worn when Daddy was ill in Puerto Rico. We waited until she calmed down, and then left for the hospital.

My labor was not notable for its duration—it lasted ten hours. But for volume of noise, the last four hours must have been exceptional. I began to scream almost as soon as the doctor said I should start pushing. If prizes were handed out for the woman with the loudest cry, I'm sure I'd have won. My shrieks hurt even my own ears. I could smell the heat rising from them. But screaming did nothing to help with my baby's delivery. Four hours later I was still pushing and wailing. Perhaps my demented cries frightened the baby, and convinced it to stay where the soft reverberations of amniotic fluids and heartbeats were more soothing than the shattering waves of noise outside.

"We'll need to deliver with forceps." The doctor's soft East Indian accent hovered briefly in my consciousness. "Would you like something to help with the pain?"

Oh yes, I wanted something to help with the pain! My resolve to deliver this child naturally disintegrated with that offer of surcease from pain. How I gloried in the relief the anesthetist's spinal delivered. It washed its way through my lower back and into my legs, so warm and loving, and into that comfort I sank with a sigh. Now that I was no longer screaming, I noticed the quiet in the hospital. Was I the only mother giving birth? No, I was told, there were several other mothers in labor. Babies like to arrive around the Fourth of July. Then was I perhaps the only mother who screamed her way through the process? A soft male voice behind me reassured me that this was not the case, that I was doing a wonderful job. Such an understanding, compassionate voice. Italian, too! It did not judge me for crying out uncontrollably. I loved that voice. I was touched that a doctor should be so caring. Over and over it repeated those gentle words, "You are doing wonderfully, Beryl." How strong and brave I felt then. I didn't know doctors could be so tender.

"Push hard, Beryl," the doctor commanded from her position between my sheet-draped legs. I pushed for all I was worth, but could feel nothing. Did I even know how to push? Had I ever known how?

"You're doing just fine," she soothed.

I'd forgotten there was a mirror on the ceiling through which I could watch the process. I looked up just in time to see our baby pulled toward the glare of the room's fluorescent lights. We had a son.

During my pregnancy, I'd wondered whether I would know how to love this baby. All my love and attention were focused on Vittorio, the miracle man who'd survived a diagnosis of pancreatic cancer and left the priesthood to marry me. I wasn't sure there'd be room in my heart for another love. I worried excessively about not feeling love for the child I carried. I felt guilty. I wondered whether the baby could

sense my ambivalence, whether it would accept me as its mother because of this lack of feeling.

"Do you think the baby will like me, Vittorio?"

Vittorio's laugh filled the kitchen. His voice sounded rich
and creamy, like the color of molasses taffy as it is being pulled and
stretched.

"Of course, the baby will like you. How could it not like you?
You're immensely likable. What's more, you're its mother."

But being the baby's mother didn't reassure me. I didn't feel the
bonding I'd read about. In a strange paradox, I, who spent my life loving a God I couldn't see, felt that I needed to see my baby before I
could love it. I prayed that once the baby was born my empty well of
mother love would fill. When Thomas finally slipped into the space
Vittorio and I shared, my heart expanded to catch him. I reached out,
wanting to pull him to my heart, to kiss his soft warm head. Instead
the nurse snatched him away. My arms were open but she didn't put
the baby there. I saw my rosy, golden-haired baby boy for only a fleet-
ing moment before he disappeared.

And Vittorio, he of the kindly, encouraging voice I'd fallen in love
with during the delivery? My mother told me that he rushed to the
nearest phone to dial her and announced jubilantly, "Violet! I have a
son. I have a son!"

# 37

## Baby and Business

With the passion of an Italian, Vittorio-the-priest became Vittorio-the-daddy. The baby's every cry and gurgle became an event at which to marvel. The priest who'd once awkwardly patted the heads of little children became adept at holding, rocking, crooning. He burped Thomas, changed his diapers, and took him everywhere: into New York City on business, to the homes of our jewelry clients, to Italy to show him off to the family. He recorded on tape the baby's nursing grunts, his early-morning cooing, his first attempts to speak. He composed a little lullaby that we sang over and over again. *Tomassino, Tomassino, biriccino"*—little naughty one—whose verses praised his beautiful mama. Vittorio spoke to Thomas in Italian, I spoke to him in English, and Thomas babbled back in both languages. He was a wonderful, happy, gurgling baby. Even while in the womb, he'd been content.

"Probably a girl," the doctor had joked when I asked him if it was normal for a baby to be so quiet in the womb. "They like to sleep."

The designs that I created on paper in our kitchen returned from the small city of Valenza as eighteen-karat-gold mountings—rings, earrings, bracelets, necklaces. Our customers selected the kinds of stones they wanted in those settings. Every penny we made, we funneled back into the business. Vittorio's customers loved him—the handsome Italian professor with the charming accent. We did no advertising but customers flocked to us. Our early clients brought their friends and relatives, and our little kitchen often overflowed with visitors. Vittorio taught everyone the difference between fourteen- and eighteen-karat gold, how to buy gold by weight, what to look for in a diamond. As he talked, I listened. I made and served coffee. I took care of Thomas, whom Vittorio showed off with even more pride than he did our jewelry. Soon our customers were requesting the gold chains and bracelets that were then becoming so popular. As Vittorio predicted, once they understood and saw the difference, they did not want the less expensive fourteen-karat gold that American manufacturers tended to produce, they wanted eighteen-karat, with its greater percentage of gold and rich color. For this, we needed an Italian manufacturer.

In the future our practice would be to go to Italy in the summer to order our rings, chains, and pendants, made to my designs, from Antonio Dini. But since an international jewelry show was coming soon to New York, we decided to order some stock there. Only registered jewelers with actual stores were allowed entry, so a friend in the business gave us tags that identified us as members of his firm.

We brought Thomas with us, as we did whenever we left home. Vittorio would have nothing to do with the American habit of hiring baby-sitters. Children belong with their parents, he insisted.

"Children are not allowed," said the door attendant, pointing to a sign that read, "No children allowed." Vittorio suggested that I make the purchases, and he would stay with Thomas. "Oh no," I replied. "You go and I'll watch Thomas. You know what our customers want. I only make designs and watch you sell."

"Beryl, believe me. You can do this. You go in and buy the jewelry." As he spoke, he began walking toward the exit, pushing Thomas in his stroller. Angry and scared, but not wanting to create a commotion by arguing with Vittorio, I entered the crowded ballroom where manufacturers from Italy, France, England, Japan, and the United States stood behind booths around which swarmed masses of bargaining, straining jewelry-store owners.

I found the Italian manufacturer Vittorio had told me to look for, and nervously awaited my turn. While waiting, I learned that the minimum order was $10,000. Buying these chains would wipe us out. I hurried back to find Vittorio, who was waiting outside the hotel.

"I can't do this, Vittorio," I said. "The minimum order is ten thousand dollars. You will have to do it."

"You will do wonderfully, Beryl," Vittorio said, putting his hands on my shoulders and smiling encouragingly. "Go back and buy the chains. We need to get home. Tomasso is getting restless." I returned to the ballroom and ordered a variety of eighteen-karat gold chains worth $10,000. Then, weak with relief that the ordering was over, I hurried outside to find Vittorio and the baby.

I tossed and turned at night, agonizing over the purchases I'd made at the jewelry exhibition, as we waited for the chains to arrive. Each chain was different; they were designs that I'd not seen in jewelry stores or magazines. I wondered whether I should have bought the basic serpentine and herringbone styles, which were then in such demand. While I worried, Vittorio slept trustingly through the intervening nights. "Wait till you see what Beryl has purchased," Vittorio was telling our customers. "You will be thrilled. As soon as the shipment arrives we shall let you know." And he was right. His customers knew he had their welfare at heart, and they liked buying gold by weight, as it helped them recognize the value they were getting for their money. We had spent $10,000 on about forty pieces, and ten days after their arrival, every one of those chains had been sold.

I enjoyed watching Vittorio at work, especially as it relieved me of the need to do any of the selling. This was to change one weekend after our annual trip to Italy, when Vittorio, looking to the future, insisted that I do the selling. Knowing me so well, Vittorio did not tell me, as we drove toward Queens to show our jewelry, that this time I would be the salesperson. Had he told me beforehand, I would have refused to go. As we were ushered into the house and introduced, Vittorio announced that Beryl was delighted to show them a line of her very own designs as well as popular styles of Italian chains in eighteen-karat gold. There was no time to argue. I followed the hostess into the dining room and, voice quivering with anxiety, opened the first roll of chains. These women wore heavy makeup and flaunted highly teased hairdos. Gold chains and jeweled rings flashed from every neck and finger. They lit cigarettes and pretended to be interested. I could tell they were bored. I lacked Vittorio's flair. I didn't sell a single piece of jewelry. The afternoon was a disaster.

On the way home, I sat in the back of the car with Thomas, away from Vittorio, with whom I was still angry. As I read to Thomas from his favorite book, *The Little Engine That Could*, I realized that the story played right into Vittorio's expectations for me in the jewelry business.

"You did wonderfully, Beryl," he said, looking at me in the rearview mirror. "They are spoiled women. It was a good experience. Only in selling will you learn to sell. Only in working with customers will you create a loyal clientele of your own."

From that day on, it was I who worked with customers while Vittorio watched. He was preparing me for the day when I would be alone, when I would have to run the business without him.

## 38

# A Gift from Tears

If the doctor's remark about baby girls liking to sleep bore any truth, the baby I gave birth to two years later ought to have been a boy. This baby kicked like a soccer player. There were times when I felt as if the baby was aiming straight at the birth canal. With those thrusts, I'd double up with a pain so sharp I lost my breath. At other times, the baby pressed so heavily on my sciatic nerve that I had to crawl up the stairs to our little apartment.

The doctors and I did not agree on the due date. I was certain Francesca would be born on or around Thomas's second birthday, on July 2, because I'd been having contractions for over two weeks. Although the contractions had prevented the doctors from performing an amniocentesis—which would have helped to pinpoint the date— they assured me that I was experiencing false labor. An ultrasound had indicated that my baby wasn't due for another month.

Mom arrived in time for Thomas's second birthday and planned to stay until after the baby was born. She cooked meals, took Thomas for walks, and put him down for naps. Her presence enabled Vittorio and me to attend daily Mass at the parish church, which was within walking distance of our apartment. I sometimes wondered why Vittorio never mentioned what it was like for him to attend Mass. He didn't speak of feeling deprived, of longing to ascend the altar and celebrate the Mass himself. Perhaps he did not speak of this to spare my feelings; perhaps he knew that I might think he was expressing regret at leaving the priesthood. When the local pastor asked for volunteers to teach catechism, however, his eyes filled with tears. In leaving the priesthood, he had had to promise never to teach religion to children. I do not know if this was common practice at that time, or if it was related to the accusation leveled at him in Fatima: "You are a Communist."

Vittorio's fidelity to the Church was much stronger than mine. I was still angry with the way the Church had treated him, and, though I never considered leaving the Church, I found my loyalty faltering. Did the Church really assist us in our journey to God, or did it hinder that journey by its abuse of power? One day while we were walking to Mass I asked Vittorio why his Catholicism remained so strong.

"Beryl, the Church is not the hierarchy. The Church is the community of the faithful, the people you see walking with us *into God*."

On the morning of Friday, July 8, we were at Mass when the "false" contractions became more rhythmical. I told Vittorio about the timing and frequency and he insisted we go right to the hospital.

"But what if it's another false alarm?"

"If it is a false alarm, they will tell us, and we will return home."

In the examining room it became clear that I was, indeed, in labor and dilating nicely. As the nurse began to prep me for delivery I had a contraction that didn't want to stop. I told the nurse. She took one look and gasped. The baby's head was crowning. And once again I started screaming, this time not from pain but from fear. I wanted my husband with me. As they rushed me toward the delivery room, I kept shrieking Vittorio's name.

"Don't push! Don't push!" the orderlies yelled as they raced with the gurney toward the delivery room. When we hurtled through the door, I could no longer wait.

"I have to push," I said, as my little girl shot from my belly into this world. Rather than whisking Francesca away as the nurse had done with Thomas, they laid her in a little bassinet next to my stretcher where I could gaze at her all I wanted.

"A baby in distress," the doctor said. "Old—perhaps two weeks overdue."

Francesca was so brown and wrinkled that my heart lurched with pity and tenderness. I wanted to pull her toward me, to press her little body next to mine, to fill her with my warmth and love. Such a homely baby needed to know she was loved right from the start. Francesca squirmed and her little fists wobbled in the air. I reached toward her in the bassinet.

"Someday, you will be beautiful, my darling," I crooned, my voice wavering toward her in the empty room, this child that I had dreamt of five years earlier. She opened her eyes and seemed to smile. Yes, I will be beautiful, Mama. Oh, yes.

Thomas associated Francesca's birth with the beginning of woe, for when she was born his daddy began to die. Several days after his sister's birth, the daddy who had trotted with him through New York City crowds, who raced with him across Hawthorne's town parks, who got down on the living room carpet with him and parked toy trucks under a sofa garage, was himself in the hospital.

Vittorio's sickness had begun almost imperceptibly several months earlier, when I was newly pregnant with Francesca. It started with minor indigestion. Soon the queasiness became constant. On a trip home from Long Island a week before Francesca was born, Vittorio could not stop vomiting.

"I cannot eat this terrible American food," he said in anguish.

I took his place at the wheel and pulled back into the traffic where we were soon surrounded by other vehicles. When the vomiting began again, I could not work my way out of the traffic to the side of the road. With Vittorio vomiting next to me and little Thomas strapped in the backseat crying, I inched our way home.

Vittorio's doctor recommended Mylanta, but it didn't help. He next prescribed digestive enzymes, suggesting Vittorio try them for two weeks and get back to him if he didn't improve.

"Doctor, I'll be dead in two weeks. You must help me now!" Desperation cut holes in Vittorio's usual calm.

The following week, a specialist performed an endoscopy on Vittorio's pancreas to try to get a reliable diagnosis. I held Thomas tightly by the hand as we watched the nurse wheel Vittorio through the swinging doors and out of sight. When they brought Vittorio to the waiting room two hours later, his face was pasty gray and he was dazed. He leaned heavily on my arm as we walked toward the car.

"Daddy, Daddy! We go bye-bye car?" Thomas trotted next to Vittorio, hanging on to his hand.

"Yes, Tomasso! We go bye-bye car." Vittorio replied, but his voice was scratchy and weak.

Throughout our life together, Vittorio's every fever and stomachache had triggered in me a responding panic. The possible return of the pancreatic cancer diagnosed in Italy slunk through my imagination like a mythical beast waiting to pounce. I'd wanted to trust in the success of the psychic surgery in the Philippines, but to believe this demanded that I set reason aside. Miracles from God I could accept. I could not accept psychic miracles. Even the cancer specialist's reassurance that the Italian doctors had misdiagnosed cancer didn't assuage my fears. I awaited the result of the endoscopy with trepidation.

Vittorio was teaching when the doctor called with the results of the tests. "The tests revealed nothing unusual," he told me. I don't know why I didn't ask the doctor what he meant by "nothing unusual." Did he mean nothing unusual considering the diagnosis of pancreatic cancer three years earlier? It wasn't until after Vittorio's death that I saw the actual results of that endoscopy: pancreatic cancer. I asked a doctor friend why he thought we hadn't been told, and he replied that it might have been what he termed "medical compassion." Why add more stress to an already difficult pregnancy? I was an older mother with a nonfunctioning thyroid, and nothing could be done for Vittorio.

Vittorio claimed he was there when Francesca was born, but I didn't believe him. Nor did I believe my mother when she said that Francesca was looking better. She was three days old when we returned to the hospital because her eyes were filled with pus. "Conjunctivitis," the doctor said, recommending a weak solution of boric acid on a cotton pad to loosen the crust on her eyes, and drops to be administered twice daily. The following morning, Vittorio and I left the house to make arrangements for Francesca's baptism the following weekend. When we returned, I looked at my little girl and knew something was terribly wrong. Francesca's eyes were sealed with pus, and the skin on her face was more wrinkled than ever. It was sloughing off in patches. Frightened, I called the clinic and described her condition. The doctor in charge of the clinic called back. "Bring her in immediately," he said. "There is an infection circulating throughout the hospital."

Francesca had acquired a deadly staph infection, especially serious for a newborn the doctor warned, possibly resulting in meningitis, blindness, or death. Taking her in his arms, he rushed our newborn off for a spinal tap. Vittorio and I held each other as we listened to Francesca's screams. Vittorio laid his head on my lap. I stroked his face. His skin felt clammy. His complexion had turned yellow. When he threw up, the vomit was black.

## 39

⁑

# Into the Valley of Death

$B$ecause Vittorio's doctor was so nonchalant about his condition, I called a doctor that my brother Greg recommended. After running a barrage of tests on Vittorio, this doctor was reassuring but concerned.

"We're not sure what the problem is," he said, "but we don't think it could be pancreatic cancer"—as the doctors in Italy had diagnosed. "He'd never have lived this long if it were. We will have to perform surgery, though, to determine why he's so ill."

On the afternoon of July 13, five days after Francesca's birth, Vittorio was admitted to Valley Hospital in Ridgewood. Twenty miles away in an isolation ward in St. Joseph's Hospital in Paterson his newborn was strapped into a baby's crib with intravenous needles and tubes projecting from her tiny head. I curled in the rocking chair next to her bed and waited for the doctor to call me about Vittorio's condition. I tried to pray. I was in agony. My baby was dreadfully ill, and my husband was dying.

Milk leaked from my swollen breasts. I was not allowed to nurse Francesca in case the infection came from my milk. From my milk? When the infection was in the hospital when she was born? The staff brought me an electric breast pump instead, an angry monster

261

that bore no resemblance to my baby's sweet mouth. It sucked and tore at my aching breasts without mercy.

I had difficulty sleeping the night before Vittorio's surgery. I had no bed, though the nurse had promised to bring one, so I sat in the hard-backed rocking chair next to my baby's bed. I didn't dare complain, fearing the hospital staff might send me home, and I could not bear to leave my tiny girl. When morning came, I pushed myself from the chair and moved clumsily toward Francesca's crib. Her skin had plumped up and a rosy color suffused her cheeks. Thank you, God, thank you, thank you, thank you I cried. Then laying my face on my baby's tummy I kissed her and ran from the room. Vittorio's surgery was scheduled for eight o'clock. I wanted to be with him until then, but when I arrived they had already taken him to the operating room.

I waited in the Valley Hospital lounge. Outside, the hot summer sun beat against the black asphalt parking lot, contrasting vividly with the green lawns and trees. I yearned to leave the waiting room and walk on that lawn, but was fearful that the doctor might come while I was gone. Periodically I'd get up from one of the soft chairs that clustered in small groups around thick area rugs to check with the woman at the information desk. Why was it taking so long? Surgery should have been over two hours ago.

"Your husband is in the recovery room," she told me. But still the doctor did not come. Waiting anxiously, my breasts leaking, every passing baby triggering a release of milk, I tried to still my growing sense of fear. Something must be wrong.

The doctor did not come to see me. Instead he phoned the receptionist desk and asked to speak with me. His voice wavered over the phone.

"The doctors in Italy were right, Beryl," he began, but as he spoke his words separated and broke. I felt a wave of confusion sweep over me. I could hear the doctor but could not understand what he was saying. Only an occasional word made sense: *specimen, lab, diagnosis, verification, cancer.* The cancer had already metastasized, invading the lymph nodes and liver. They'd rerouted the intestines to relieve the pressure, but little else could be done.

"How long does he have?" I managed to ask. The receptionist looked up from her papers.

"No time, Beryl."

When we first returned home with Francesca, Thomas ran expectantly to the door looking for the surprise I'd promised him. He was disgusted to find a baby. What could he do with a baby? Why didn't I bring him something better—a truck, a toy car? He was relieved when, several days after the baby's arrival, she disappeared again. But, then, so too did his daddy. Francesca recovered within a week. Six weeks later, Vittorio was still in the hospital. Thomas would look at the baby and ask me where his daddy was, and, when I wasn't looking, he bopped her on the head.

Vittorio walked the hospital corridors for hours at a time, pushing with his right hand the rolling stainless steel pole to which his i.v. was attached, carrying in his left hand the urinal bag. From his nose hung the tubes they used to feed him and to suck the liquids back out when they didn't get digested. Daily, the doctor put his head against Vittorio's abdomen, listening for nonexistent signs of peristalsis. I'd not realized till then what a miracle passing gas was, what a gift, the gurgling of our stomachs. Each time they removed the tubes to see if his body would resume normal functioning, he filled with fluids and the tubes had to be reinserted.

Although I had no real hope that Vittorio would leave the hospital alive, I began weaving a dream: when Francesca is baptized, I told him, you will get better. Vittorio's veins were collapsing, making intravenous tubes a torture, but I needed hope, and so did he. I arranged to have the baby baptized in the hospital so that Vittorio could be present for the ceremony.

At home Francesca screamed continuously. "It's your milk," my mother told me. "She's picking up on your fear." As with the staph infection, my milk was once again being blamed for my baby's distress. I needed my little girl. Her sweet body pressed against mine eased my grief, and she needed me. When I brought Francesca home from the hospital she would push away from me when I tried to pick her up. It was only gradually, through the nursing process, that she learned to relax into my arms. And then, such a comfort her little body became. She'd been born in a time of stress and I clung to her as to a lifeline.

"Francesca Maria, Francesca Maria, Francesca Maria, the bells sing your name," I crooned, a little tune I'd made up that soothed her. Vittorio was too ill to compose a song, as he'd done for Thomas, so Francesca had to make do with my poor attempts at composition. She nursed, not like her brother with long periods of sucking and unblinking gazing into my eyes, but in short bursts interrupted by sleep. I'd gently wake her and she'd begin to nurse again. When she wasn't in my arms, she cried, a high-pitched wail that set my teeth on edge.

On the day of her baptism, Francesca's piercing screams rang from the hospital parlor where the family gathered to wait for Vittorio. The priest smiled awkwardly and squatted next to Thomas, attempting to talk, but Thomas didn't respond. Leaving the baby with my mother, I took Thomas into the sunny, window-filled hallway. Thomas, who was wearing a little white sailor suit with crocheted Italian socks and little black Italian shoes, climbed onto a window ledge in the hallway and looked sadly into the hospital courtyard. He'd become a pensive little boy since his father's illness. The chatter that once personified his presence had all but disappeared.

"I want my daddy," he whispered. As I sat there with him the busy hospital corridor faded away; so, too, did the family and priest waiting in the parlor. I sank into a silence as heavy as the water at the bottom of a lake, in my arms a little boy with blond curls who drifted down with me. We hovered there awhile, until we were pulled back to the surface by Vittorio's voice.

"Tomasso! My Tomasso." Vittorio's voice broke with yearning. So, too, did my image of that moment. Pieces of it fell around me, mirror images that scattered like reflective confetti. A wheelchair, outstretched arms, a flash of white, and Thomas's sturdy black shoes running toward his daddy.

Two weeks later we were in Italy and Vittorio was driving.

# 40

## Living with Cancer

*I* used to claim that Vittorio defied the odds and lived as long as he did because we were so happy. I still believe this rationale. How else explain the fact that he lived almost five years from the first diagnosis of a type of cancer considered one of the most virulent and deadly? Vittorio's happiness spilled onto his family, great buckets of joy that sickness could not quench. After years of celibacy he'd found a human love that filled the aching expanse of his heart, just as it had mine. In our too-short life together, we woke every morning grateful for the blessing of yet one more day, our bodies bending like grass to the winds that blew around us, pressing us closer together, lifting our children into our arms. Our children! Our lives grew luminous around them. We were poor, but we were happy.

Our apartment, the second story of a small house, left much to be desired, but it was inexpensive, and it was sunny. One bedroom served as our living room while the other became a communal bedroom, where the four of us slept in crowded comfort. The walls were decorated in typical 1970s style: bright gold and orange foil wallpaper in the kitchen, brown foil wallpaper in the hallway, yellow foil wallpaper on the stairway. The room in the attic was so confined you had to duck your head around the edges.

We ate lots of minestrone and pasta, which Vittorio always prepared. His pastas would vary from night to night: pasta with grated carrots and walnuts, pasta with onions and tuna, pasta with parmesan and zucchini. Because our income was low and we had no insurance, both babies were delivered in the clinic for the poor at St. Joseph's Hospital in Paterson. Unable to afford disposable diapers, we used cloth and washed them ourselves. We gladly accepted hand-me-downs and found garage sales a wonderful source of furnishings for home and body. Though there were times when we weren't sure we'd have enough money to pay the next month's rent, we always had enough to travel to Italy every summer. Our small jewelry business was helpful in this respect because we could write off most of the expense of these trips. While traveling, we stayed with family, showed off our babies, and worked our way from one jewelry manufacturer to another looking for items to bring back with us to sell. But if ever our marriage was tested, it was while on these trips. The first time we took Thomas to Italy, he was not quite one year old and still in diapers.

"What shall I do about diapers, Vittorio?" I asked. "Should I buy disposable ones?"

"No paper stuff on my Tomasso's bottom," he replied.

"But where will I wash the diapers?"

"What do you think? Italy doesn't have laundromats? Don't worry. Laundromats are everywhere."

My thirteen-year-old niece, Griselda Clare, who accompanied us on this trip, used to laugh about Vittorio's "everywhere." Everywhere did not exist. That entire summer, I washed diapers in hotel bathtubs and hung them over hotel balconies to dry. I once even had to wash diapers in a bucket in the town square. Never again, I promised myself. When we next went to Italy, Vittorio was still recuperating from his six weeks in the hospital, and Francesca was a newborn. This time I brought two full cartons of disposable diapers, one for toddlers, one for newborns. Livio, one of Vittorio's nephews, who came to fetch us at the airport, took one look at all those diapers and threw up his hands in a gesture of despair. The car he'd rented for us was a teensy Fiat, smaller than a Volkswagen beetle. We wedged those bags of diapers everywhere and were so well padded that it became an ordeal just to get in and out of the car. And in this way we traveled, tucked between diaper packs, with one toddler and one newborn who screamed her way through Italy.

Vittorio and I grew hoarse singing Francesca's bell and Thomas's *biriccino* songs. "Old MacDonald" got a workout as never before. We filled his farm with pigs, chickens, goats, and ducks until we grew giddy with animals. One day, as we arrived exhausted at a small hotel in Vacenza Po, where our jewelry was made, I put Francesca on the bed and threw myself down next to her, exclaiming that I didn't know what ever possessed me to bring a newborn with a dying man to Italy.

Vittorio's reaction was instantaneous. "Beryl," he pleaded, opening his hands in supplication. "Do not deprive me of my children."

His words shook me. Would I never learn to think before I opened my mouth, to consider the effect my words might have before uttering them? If Vittorio, who had escaped death and was weaker than a newly hatched butterfly, could stay patient with his screaming baby girl, what was the matter with her strapping, healthy mother?

Diapers and screaming babies, however, could not dampen the joy of these trips to Italy. How blessed I was. Spending six weeks every summer traveling through the luminous Italian countryside, boating on alpine lakes, playing in gardens bursting with roses and lilies and lush with basil and artichoke and summer squash, shopping in outdoor farmers' markets, wandering from *panetteria* to *macelleria* to *latteria* to purchase crusty breads and homemade pasta, seafood and meat, cheese and cream. While traveling with my beautiful husband and my precious babes, I thanked the God who had made all this possible. I, who once believed I would never have a family of my own, was indeed beloved.

In March of 1978, Vittorio decided that we needed to buy a house. "How can we buy a house?" I asked. "We have no money."

But buy a house we did, after looking at one dinky place after another, trying to find something decent yet affordable, until the realtors threw up their hands in frustration.

"This house has everything you want," one realtor said irritably when we rejected, yet again, a house she was showing us. That house might have provided a small workshop for Vittorio and a separate bedroom for the children, but it was on a busy street and lacked the sense of home I was looking for. One day, Vittorio told me that I must make up my mind; we couldn't spend any more time looking for a house.

"What do you mean?" I asked. "Make up my mind? I haven't seen the right house yet."

"Beryl, you must choose now." There was urgency in his voice that I hadn't heard before. And so I chose a house, a small yellow Cape Cod cottage at 54 Orchard Street, in Pompton Lakes, a town I had once driven through, thinking, "My God, can you imagine living there?" because it looked so dreary. But that was the view from the highway. The town was actually charming. Our house was on a tree-lined street, only a block away from the lake and public playground. Better yet, this house had a swing and slide and sandbox. The living room had a working fireplace with built-in bookcases on either side as well as a bay window, and the kitchen was large enough to skate in. How happy we were on the day we moved in, settling the furniture this way and that and saying "our house," over and over again.

That summer we added a second-floor bathroom, and Greg planted eighteen hemlock trees along the back fence to give us privacy. Giacomo, Vittorio's great friend and fellow professor at Bergen Community College, who had been instrumental in helping him get a job teaching Italian, planted a marvelous *orto*, a vegetable garden replete with beans, beets, chard, tomatoes, and peppers. A tree in the backyard bore bushels of juicy golden pears.

We celebrated Francesca's first birthday and Thomas's third birthday on the Fourth of July and invited the entire family to a barbecue in our backyard. The children loved the new house and spent entire days playing outside. How proud we were of our lovely little home, of the precious children who filled that house with laughter and love.

In August, we invited the family over again, this time to celebrate the blessing of our new home. Father Rip Collins, a close friend of the family, came from his rectory in New York City to officiate. The evening before, I stood like a sunflower in our little house, turning first one way to look at the children playing with blocks on the deck, then the other way to gaze on Vittorio working at his jeweler's bench. I was filled with a soaring, light-filled sense of God's loving presence. Our joy had a touch of the miraculous. Vittorio had been resurrected; he was alive and well and we had a home of our own.

The children and I are in a high tower. Around us surges music so beautiful I think my soul will shatter with its loveliness—voices, angelic voices, searing the heart and piercing the spirit. I look from the window and see that angels are leading a man across a courtyard toward a scaffold. That man is my Vittorio and I know he is going to die.

I scream in anguish and fall on my knees, the agony of loss rending my soul with grief. "Why?" I cry.

"So you might live." The words are so clear they must have been spoken.

Grief like a fist slams into my belly. I curl in pain and wake in torment. And there, right by my side, is my love, sleeping. I curl my aching body around his warmth and try to calm my heart. He is alive. It was just a dream.

That afternoon, as Father Rip sprinkled holy water throughout the house and in the yard, blessing every room and tree and blade of grass, inviting God to dwell in a house filled with love, Vittorio pressed his hands into the small of his back and bent forward.

# 41

❦

# *Last Rites*

$P$ain drove us back to Italy that October of 1978. Vittorio wanted to say good-bye to his family while there was still time. We booked an inexpensive flight to Luxembourg. From there we planned to drive through France on our way to Italy. Vittorio wanted to pray at the grotto of Massabielle in Lourdes where a healing stream of water has flowed ever since the blessed Virgin Mary appeared to Bernadette Soubirous in 1858.

I had imagined Massabielle as a lovely blue grotto framed by ferns and laden with moss, the fountain of clear water at its center flowing into large outdoor pools bathed in sunshine. Instead the baths were dark and chill, surrounded by tentlike curtains behind which we stripped and wrapped ourselves in thin towels to cover ourselves. With my baby girl trembling in my arms, I lowered myself into the pool under the compassionate eyes of an elderly volunteer. In the men's section, Vittorio was doing the same, Thomas clutched tightly in his arms, our prayers united with the screaming of our children in those icy waters—*O sweet Mother of God, you who know how it is to lose both a spouse and a child, give us the grace of healing. Above all, strengthen us for our journey through life and comfort us as we die.*

My mother joined us in Italy to help with the children, and we needed more room, so we rented a farmhouse near Maria's summer home in the Italian Alps. In that farmhouse, consumed by pain, Vittorio spent his nights taking hot showers and praying aloud for strength.

"Jesu, have mercy. Blessed Mother, sweet Mary, help me."

With daylight, the pain appeared to dissolve as Vittorio drove us to various locations: the shoemaker to order for the children the sturdy Italian shoes I loved; the town square in Trento, where we bought gelato and sat admiring the geranium-festooned fountains that sprayed diamonds into the air. He took us to Lago di Garda, where we piled into a small rowboat and skimmed into the center of the lake to admire the surrounding mountains. We visited a castle where we ate a seven-course meal and dreamed of returning to spend a week. We spent the evenings with Maria and her family. During these excursions, Vittorio did not complain about the pain. But as soon as we returned to the farmhouse, the nightly siege of pain and prayer would begin again as Vittorio pleaded for the return of morning.

"I'm not convinced that Vittorio is as ill as his nights would lead us to believe," Mom said to me one day. "How can he drive like he does if he is in such pain?"

Although Vittorio was unfailingly kind and loving toward my mother, her influence could be unsettling. On more than one occasion her opinions affected my own.

Our kitchen in Pompton Lakes had a heavy brown ceramic sink. For some reason, I'd decided that stainless steel was the way to go and Vittorio encouraged me. I would have the sink that I wanted as soon as we could afford it, he promised. Mom, however, polished the old brown one until it looked fairly decent. "You don't need a new sink," she said jubilantly, pleased with the results of her efforts. "Ceramic sinks are much better than stainless." It made sense. The old sink looked almost new. "You're right," I told Mom. Vittorio, noting how easily I acquiesced, took me aside to ask how I really felt.

"Don't let your mother make your decisions for you, Beryl," he said. "You are entitled to do things your own way."

If Mom saw me hauling the garbage to the sidewalk, she'd get indignant. For Mom, it wasn't enough that Vittorio taught, made jewelry, and cooked most of the meals; it was also his job to take the garbage out.

On the way back to Luxembourg for the flight home we stopped for the night at a small inn in the mountains of Bavaria. While I struggled up the stairs with the luggage and the children, Vittorio stood at the reception desk talking with the proprietor. I began to unpack clean clothes for the children and to settle them onto the fluffy bed—a huge white eiderdown that swallowed them up. They laughed and jumped around, squealing with delight in the plump bedding, but my mother was strangely silent. When I asked her what troubled her, she told me that Vittorio should be helping me. "You should not have had to carry the luggage upstairs by yourself." At first I made excuses, saying that if Vittorio was delayed there must be good reasons for it. But when more than an hour went by and he still hadn't returned, I began to think that, yes, he should be helping me. The more time went by, the more irritable I became. What made him think that he could stand at the front desk gabbing when his family needed him? When Vittorio finally did show up, I had worked myself into such a state that I'd become a mirror-image of my mother.

At supper that evening, I devoted myself to caring for the children and ignored Vittorio. I thought we'd finished eating when the waitress appeared, carrying a small cake to our table with a candle burning in the middle.

"Happy Birthday, my beautiful Beryl," Vittorio said, taking my hand in his, with the whole map of his love shining on his face.

I hadn't even remembered it was my birthday.

"Make a wish," he encouraged me. For the children's sake I closed my eyes as if I were making a wish, opened them, and blew out the candle. Baby Francesca screamed with delight. I began cutting the cake but it was dry and the apples inside were not thoroughly cooked.

"What kind of a cake is this, anyway?" I complained.

"It's a torte," Vittorio responded. "I'm sorry I couldn't find a better one. The bakeries were closed. It was all I could find." The joy in Vittorio's eyes had dulled.

I felt sick. My husband, though consumed by pain, had remembered my birthday and gone looking for a little cake with which to celebrate. Ashamed, I dined on my guilt. I swallowed it whole and let it sit, undigested, in my belly. I said nothing, not even when we climbed into our downy bed, and the children's soft breathing fluttered around us asking me to reconsider.

*November 30—Feast of Saint Andrew the Apostle.*

Vittorio's mouth is full of sores. When I try to comfort him, he cries out because even my gentlest touch hurts. I sleep as far away from him as possible to ease his pain. Loneliness sears my being. I cannot bear what is happening. That night Vittorio reaches toward me and tries to kiss my distant face.

"Tell me that you love me," he says softly.

"I love you, Vittorio," I whisper. Tears, hot and salty, burn through my eyes and course down my cheeks. I am so lonely. So hurt by this process of dying.

"I worry that after I die, you will marry again. I dream about the man you will marry. He will not love you as I have. He will not love our children. Promise me you will not marry again."

I do not want to make this promise to Vittorio. I am young. I am afraid of a future without him. He cannot die and expect me to make such a promise. Yet I have known no other love than Vittorio's. He loves even the way I walk.

"Look, Violet. Look at how my Beryl walks," he tells my mother. "She dances."

*December 8—Feast of the Immaculate Conception.*

We are on our way to the doctor's office, a "For Sale" sign in Vittorio's Fiat. Vittorio, his belly swollen like that of a pregnant woman, sits next to me moaning softly.

I stop for gas and the sales clerk asks about the car. "Does it run good?" he asks.

I say yes and give him our phone number. Then I drive off. Several blocks away the car stalls and won't start. It is ten degrees, the roads are icy, and a freezing wind bears down on us. As I get out of the car to walk back to the station to ask for help, I feel like a fool. I've just told the clerk that the car is working fine and now I must return to admit we are having engine trouble. I have a dying husband in the car and I must leave him alone to seek help. I am exhausted. I don't need this.

"Thanks a lot, God. You're really on our side, aren't you?" I rage as I get out of the car, conveniently forgetting all the blessing of my life with Vittorio, the years we've been granted that we never thought we'd have.

Vittorio leans toward me, pleading, "No, Beryl!" because he knows that, like Job's wife, I'm going to point my finger at God and curse. I am going to rail against this God whom I so love, who is not afraid of my fury, who loves me even as I rage at him. But raging at God has never been Vittorio's way.

"Thanks for nothing, God." I scream into the wind. "Thanks for not being here when we need you!" And then, impelled by the anguish on Vittorio's face and by his total acceptance of what is happening to him, I add with special vehemence, "Shit on You, God! Shit on You!"

With the force of my anger coursing through me I march off toward the station to get help.

*December 12—Feast of Our Lady of Guadalupe.*

Vittorio tells me we must purchase a cemetery plot. I cringe. I cannot do this by myself. I call Greg's wife, Griselda, who, despite her original opposition to our marriage, has grown to love Vittorio.

"Will you come with me, Grissie? Help me select a place for Vittorio?"

Mom is helping during Vittorio's final days, but she must stay with the children. Vittorio, however, wants to come. He waits in the car while Griselda and I go into the cemetery office at George Washington Memorial Park in Paramus, New Jersey, to get the map listing available sites. We drive around looking at plots. It is a rolling cemetery unmarked by large tombstones, with only flat marble or bronze memorials marking the spots where loved ones have been buried. Artificial flowers are not allowed. This fact appeals to me. I can't bear the faded plastic things that mark so many grave sites elsewhere.

We find a lovely site near a small tree. I do not know what kind of tree it is because the leaves are gone. I would like Vittorio's grave to have a tree nearby. The gold pin he had made for me from a tree sprig shines on my coat lapel. "To life," Vittorio said when he gave it to me. To life, I think, and start to weep. Vittorio waits in the car as we walk through the snow to inspect the site. Griselda whispers, "How strange it is to have Vittorio with us as we pick out his grave site." I turn to look at my husband. His eyes are wide, trying to see.

*December 13—Feast of Sants Lucia.*

Vittorio enters his workshop to finish some Christmas orders but after a short time comes back out. He heads toward the bedroom. "I have to go to bed," he says. He leans against the wall as he walks; his feet make small shuffling steps.

"You are going to bed in the middle of the morning?"

I know what is happening and I am terrified. He has lived so long, fought such a valiant fight, that I am angry he is letting go. I cannot face his dying. Even though I have been caring for him for the past five months and know how dreadfully ill he is, I refuse to confront the awful reality of his leaving me. Instead of telling him how brave he has been, instead of telling him how wondrously he has fought to stay alive this long, I turn harsh.

"You mean you are giving up? How can you give up when we need you?"

I am too frightened to understand my pain. All I know is anger. It's coming so close. Death.

"I can't see," Vittorio says. "I've lost my sight."

"Oh God, Vittorio," I cry. I'm sobbing. "At least live through Christmas. For the sake of the children."

*December 21—Feast of Saint Thomas.*

A customer comes to the house to pick up the ring she has ordered for her daughter: a small cluster of leaves that holds a tangerine-colored diamond. Such a brilliant caress—the stone shining like a princess's tears cupped in a golden chalice.

"Can I see him?" she asks.

"He is much changed," I tell her. "Are you sure you want to see him like this?"

"I want to say good-bye," she insists.

I walk to the bedroom door. She stands behind me. Vittorio lies on his back. He is sleeping. He has not moved since I put him to bed. The bed covers remain just as I left them hours before. His face is sunken, his skin the color of beeswax.

"Oh, dear God," she gasps, and turns toward me to stifle a sob. She has known Vittorio for five years, followed his battle with the disease. Like me, she believed he would make it. Handsome, laughing, kindly Vittorio. Like me, she now knows he is dying.

*December 22—Friday of the Fourth Week of Advent.*

It is the Friday before Christmas. I have so much to do: orders to get ready for customers, gifts to buy and wrap, meals to fix, children to care for, a husband to wash and bathe and feed.

Vittorio stretches his arms toward me. "Stay with me," he begs.

I want to tell him I'm too busy. I want to hurt him the way he is hurting me by leaving. Can't he see how much I need him? Can't he beat this thing as he has in the past? Just one more time?

Suddenly I understand that I am punishing both of us for something beyond our control. Whence this grace comes I know not, for I have not fostered it, nor have I prayed for it. I want to spend hours and days at his side. To settle into his presence and savor what is left of its sweetness. And there is sweetness, so much of it. I have been loved as I'd always yearned to be loved. And I've loved with all the responsiveness of which I've been capable. What foolishness to allow busy-ness to interfere with our last days together. I open my arms and kneel next to him.

"Of course I'll stay with you, my love," I say.

*December 23—Saturday of the Fourth Week of Advent.*

The children gather with us on the bed. Francesca crawls up and over Vittorio's feet but he no longer cries out. The morphine helps. Just a tiny bit. Brompton's cocktail: morphine and cocaine in an elixir of orange.

That evening, as the sun begins to set, I make a fire and bring him to the living room. He loves to spend the waning hours of the day with his children. I read to the three of them, Thomas next to his daddy, Francesca next to me, my arm around Vittorio. Then, gently, so as not to hurt him, I wrap him in a blanket, as I did that night on the stairs four short years ago, and tell him I will always love him. We repeat this ritual every day.

*December 25—Feast of the Nativity of Christ.*

We have decorated the house, and the lumpy gingerbread men the children helped to bake hang among the lights and tinsel on the tree. I have brought the tape recorder into the living room to catch the children's voices as Mom encourages them to sing carols with her. Vittorio and I have been recording the children's voices since they were babies. Some tapes are full of song: Vittorio singing "La Donna è Mobile" and "O Sole Mio" at a talent show three years earlier, Francesca's odd little baby voice, like velvet air, as she attempts to sing with me, Thomas chanting, "Tomato, tomato, tomato, tomato, tomato" in a descending scale.

The morning sun streams across the couch where he sits propped among pillows, an afghan pulled over his legs. I turn the television on so he can watch Mass being offered at Saint Peter's Basilica in Rome. Carols swell through the room as the choirs praise the new-born son of Mary.

Vittorio can no longer sing but he can still speak.

"Let's ask Daddy to say something for Christmas." Thomas carefully carries the recorder toward Vittorio.

"Happy Christmas to everybody," he says. His voice is weak and husky, as if he were suffering from laryngitis. There is a long pause. I wonder if he will say more. Slowly he frames his words. "In this moment we are listening to the Mass of the Pope." His voice trembles. "So beautiful . . . So beautiful." I wait for him to say something special for the children. Instead he offers, "We thank God for his presence in our midst."

Vittorio is once again the priest. This is the last recording I have of his voice.

Greg has invited us to his house for Christmas dinner. Vittorio is terribly weak, but he insists on going nonetheless. I dress him in his best wool suit and don my favorite white silken skirt and blouse. The baby wears a red velvet dress with a matching bow on her fine brown hair. "She will grow hair, won't she?" Vittorio once asked. Mom has knitted Tom a navy blue sweater that he wears with a red turtleneck. We would look like an ordinary family except that a skeletal Vittorio leans heavily on my arm.

As the family gathers in the living room before dinner to open gifts, an all-day program of classical Christmas music plays on the radio. A Strauss waltz fills the room.

"You should dance," suggests Greg. I'm not certain who gathered who into their arms and it is only two slow turns but Vittorio and I dance as Greg snaps photos.

*January 7, Sunday—Feast of the Epiphany.*

I know Vittorio is going to die because he tries to tell me so this morning. At first, I cannot understand what he says because his voice is so weak, so I give him a piece of paper to try to write, but all he can manage is a tiny little corkscrew circle that pulls in on itself over and over again, much as his precious life spirals inward, depleting its resources one by one.

"Try again to tell me," I beg, until finally I understand that what he wants is an injection to help with dying. Wanting to promise him anything at this moment, I cry, "Yes, my love, my darling. I'll get you whatever you need, don't worry," hoping that what he means is something to help with pain and not a lethal injection. I do not think he means to take his life, because the Church teaches that this is wrong, and because throughout all the ordeals of his life he has loved her faithfully, even when she has made him suffer as she has, so many times.

I did not realize, as I do now, that he was asking for Extreme Unction, the sacrament of the dying. And so I promise him help with dying, but do not know what he means. And now that he is dying, I cannot find him the help I've promised, because his doctor is in the Bahamas with his own wife, who has cancer, and the doctor on call never answers his phone.

It is Sunday, the feast of the Epiphany, and Vittorio has kept his promise to live through Christmas for the children. The entire family has come for a last visit with Vittorio. We gather in the living room. A fire is burning in the hearth and Vittorio is lying on the couch, tucked into blankets and propped among pillows. He can no longer speak. He is so still that Mark, Greg's ten-year-old son asks, "Is he breathing?" Griselda takes him aside to admonish him.

Francesca dances around the living room, stopping continually to kiss Vittorio on the head. "Dadda," she says. She is not frightened by his skeletal appearance, the gaunt face of nightmares. She sees only her daddy. Greg approaches me and suggests they take Thomas home with them. We know Vittorio will not survive the night.

Later that evening, Carlo helps me take Vittorio back to the bedroom. He has come to be with us during these final days. As soon as we lay him on the bed he begins to struggle for breath. I hold him in my arms as he fights to breathe, my own breath keeping staggered company, and I cry aloud as he gasps for air, his arms flailing with an energy he didn't have this morning when he wanted to see his children playing in the snow and I took him to the window, but he couldn't see them, even though they were right there catching snowflakes and blowing him kisses.

I cannot bear to see him suffer like this and beg God to take him, for it isn't fair that he should suffer more. I worry that my baby, Francesca, might hear my wailing and the terrible machine-gun rattle coming from him that fills the bedroom under hers.

Only when the priests arrive, wipe the black foam from his face, and hold his hands, one on either side, does he stop struggling. Such good men, those priests, coming out in a blizzard to help my love depart this world. I want to lie next to Vittorio, to hold him in my arms as he dies. Instead I lay my head down near his legs and place my hands upon his feet and listen to the slowing of his breath until it is so faint I'm no longer sure he's breathing at all. And then I hear my mother gasp and find I've missed his final smile, the one that illuminated his face and made her catch her breath. I see only his grimace and feel his body turn to ice.

"Was he at peace?" I beg the priests.

"He never had a moment's doubt," they tell me. "You made him very happy."

When the ambulance comes to take his body, Carlo calls the family in Italy to tell them that Zio Vittorio has died. Then he reads to me from *Farfalla Bianca—White Butterfly*—Costantino's book, the poems that Vittorio loved best. When he stops, I creep upstairs and crawl into bed with my baby and feel so terribly cold all night.

## 42

A Tree of Diamonds

The morning after Vittorio died, Thomas returned home from Greg's, where we'd sent him when we realized Vittorio might die that night. The first thing he did was to run to see his daddy.

"Where's my daddy?" he cried on confronting the empty bed. "Where's my daddy?"

"Daddy has died," I said, pulling him into my arms. "He left to go to Jesus in heaven because he was suffering too much. Now he won't have to suffer any more."

I looked into Thomas's eyes, so he could see there the truth of my message. My heart was breaking with his loss. My little boy who loved his daddy who is no more.

But Thomas wanted none of it. "You tell Jesus I want my daddy back!" He pummeled my chest and sobbed, then pushed me away and ran back to our room, where he threw himself onto the bed. I lay down with him, trying to soothe him. I wanted to stay there, forever, in bed.

"Did you have breakfast at Tio Greg's?" I asked. "Would you like a cup of milk and a graham cracker? Come, let's go to the kitchen."

"No! I want to stay here. I want my daddy."

"Okay, sweetheart." I kissed him softly.

I was cutting slices of cake for the family when Thomas appeared, holding in his hands the crucifix that was given to me on the day of my solemn vows.

"You tell Jesus to take good care of my daddy," he said, handing the crucifix to me.

I dropped to my knees and pulled Thomas into my arms, holding his sweet little body close to my aching one.

"We can both tell Jesus, together."

I did not bring the children to the funeral but left them with a neighbor. I wanted to protect them from the awful reality of their father's death. Instead, I unwittingly prolonged their grieving. In the weeks that followed Vittorio's death, Thomas developed strange little quirks. He'd sit in Vittorio's easy chair, rocking and grunting as if he were in pain. He cried for spaghetti, "I want pisghetti, I want pisghetti," and wept real tears, until I realized that it was not spaghetti that he wanted but the daddy who used to make it for him.

"When can we visit Daddy?" he asked repeatedly. When I told him we could not visit Daddy because he was in heaven, he suggested taking the car. A train. An airplane. A spaceship. One by one, all available modes of transportation were eliminated, and still, he refused to accept the fact that we could not see his daddy. Francesca stood next to Thomas and nodded her little head, quick little bobs to emphasize that she too wanted to see her daddy.

I found it almost impossible to go about my daily chores, to get out of bed in the morning, to handle the will, to deal with customers. I kept reliving his final days, his dying. I did not know how I would carry on without Vittorio. His love gave me the courage of a lion; without it I became a mole. I wanted to crawl from the bills that piled on the table with no health or life insurance to ease the strain, from the loneliness that replaced his presence. My bed was barren of love, my mornings, empty of hope.

It was a bleak March morning when I left Harrington Park, where I'd gone to fetch the rings with the stones that Tony, the stone setter, had mounted for me. The jewelry business went on despite my loss. Customers wanted their orders. I needed their money.

I turned off the highway, creeping slowly because the roads were slippery, the trees heavy and bowed under their weight of ice. They resembled my soul, bent and close to breaking. I was not prepared for the clouds to tear apart, for the sun to streak across the valley. As I watched, the trees turned to torches, every branch and twig jeweled with radiance—such utter blackness pierced by sudden shimmering glory, as if the sky had been torn open to reveal the glory of God.

As lightning clears the air of oppressive humidity, that sudden vision split my soul and opened it to light and I was glad, gloriously glad, that it was I who had lived. I felt warmth flood my heart with, if not joy, something nearly akin to perfect peace. I knew we were loved and always would be loved. That Vittorio's love would continue to open me to life in much the same way the sun had just dispelled the darkness and revealed the beauty in the ice.

"Do you see that, my loves? Look at all the diamonds on the trees. They are sending you kisses." I turned and blew my own kisses to the children, whose little faces were rosy with the cold, eyes bright, laughing to see me happy again.

My children! Their births had triggered the most terrible dreams of finding myself once again in the monastery, and my children outside its walls. In those dreams, I clawed the walls with my nails, screamed and pounded against the bricks to get out. I had to get to my children, my children! Even while Vittorio was dying, I thanked God that it was not my children who were dying. I knew that somehow I would survive Vittorio's dying, but I would not survive the loss of one of my children.

I waited until spring arrived, when the apple and cherry trees were sending out their pink and white buds and the dogwoods opened their blushing wounded petals. I waited until the birds were making a wonderful racket with their joyful courting and the tiny purple butterflies emerged from their cocoons. Only then did I take the children to visit Vittorio's grave. As we dressed, I tried to explain how Daddy's body was like the jackets they wore, that he had taken it off when he didn't need it anymore and that we put it in a place where we can go to remember him.

"Like in a closet?" Thomas asked.

"Not in a closet, darling, in a garden, because Daddy's body will turn to dust and dust belongs in gardens."

On the way, we stopped and bought some flowers. Thomas selected tall flaming orange gladioli and Francesca picked delicate baby's breath and tiny pink roses. Not exactly a balanced bouquet, but one Vittorio would have loved. Together, we laid the bouquet on the grave, which was still raw, brown, and ugly—spring had arrived only a week or so earlier and the grass had not yet grown over the soil.

"But where is Daddy?" Thomas asked. So once again I launched into my feeble explanation of what happens to a body when the spirit leaves it.

"Let's say a prayer for Daddy," I suggested and opened a small one-sided conversation with the invisible and loving God who had given us such a precious daddy to love and who would forever fill him with absolute happiness.

Francesca squatted next to the grave and examined it solemnly, then bent over and whispered something indecipherable above the stone marker, as if her daddy had somehow slipped beneath it and was waiting there to gather her words. Thomas waited expectantly for something to happen and when nothing did, asked if we could go home.

On the way, Thomas asked if I would sing the Tomassino song for him. I looked at my children through the rearview mirror and felt my heart stung by shards of joy and tenderness. In each of them I could see my darling's face—in Thomas his eyes, in Francesca his smile. Yet they were both so different, little people who surprised me daily with some new flash of identity. What a gift my life had been, I thought—filled as it was with so much love, and here in the car with me were my children—miracle enough to make any life worthwhile.

"Yes. We shall sing your song, Thomas, and your song, Francesca, and we shall sing so loudly that Daddy will hear us and know how much we love him.

And so we drove all the way home . . . singing.

# *Epilogue*

Next to my front door a pair of elevated clogs waits for the small feet that left them there.

"Don't worry about the shoes, Mama," Francesca said as she kissed me good-bye. "I'll be back next week."

Francesca will never return to claim those shoes. On September 18, one week to the day after the catastrophic events of 9/11, when the World Trade towers went down in flames and she drove five hours to be with me, my beautiful raven-haired daughter was shot and killed. She was twenty-four years old when she died. Her death remains an open case in the homicide files of the Minneapolis Police Department.

Her little boy, Thomas Gregory, lives with his daddy and has Francesca's crazy sense of humor and loving ways. "My daddy and I are not here to take your call. Please leave a message. I love you," his voice announces to all and sundry on their telephone answering machine. He pronounces love you as *"yuv* you" and each time I hear that message, a rush of tenderness and joy fills me. When I hold him, I feel Francesca's presence, even her scent in his hair.

My son, Thomas, has grown into a giant of a man with a radiant smile and stand-up-comic sense of humor. He is married to beautiful

Becky and is the father of two energetic little blondes. "I hope you are missing me," the youngest writes in her e-mails.

We buried Francesca's ashes on a knoll on our property overlooking Lake Superior and marked the spot with a small stone statue of a maiden who gazes out upon the lake. Nearby is the cedar swing where Francesca and I rocked and talked the week before she died, and where I held her hand and thought how like a child's it still was.

A few days after Francesca's death, I sat on that swing with a friend, searching the diamond-shattered surface of the lake and the scudding clouds for answers.

"Was it a mistake to leave the monastery?" my friend asked, giving voice to the question that had, for years, ridden beneath the surface of my life and that I've tried to answer in telling this story: whether the suffering of Vittorio's illness and his death were punishment for our having left religious life. What emerged has surprised and comforted me, for wafting throughout the story—like an elusive but lovely fragrance—is the persistent and unmistakable scent of a loving and infinitely patient God.

"A mistake?" I said. "No. Never! Not a mistake, a gift: an incredible, glorious, miraculous gift."

How clear it is to me now. If I had not left the monastery, I'd never have known the wonder of Vittorio's love or the joy a mother finds in her children. Perhaps I'd have become the compassionate woman I longed to become as a young nun had I stayed in the monastery, but because I left I have memories rich with presence to cherish and a faith in which my loved ones live.

It is true that leaving the monastery brought me suffering that I would not have endured had I stayed, the greatest of which has been the loss of my daughter. It is true that I was warned that if I stayed in the world I would have much to suffer. But I continue to believe—more than that, I know, as I did when I first heard that message before I married Vittorio—that leaving the monastery was worth every anguish, every tear.

A Gregorian hymn that is chanted during the Easter vigil reflects my feelings about leaving the monastery. In this ancient hymn the church rejoices in what it calls the necessary sin of Adam. *"O happy fault that merited such a redeemer,"* sings the priest celebrant. If leaving the monastery was a mistake, then what a blessed mistake it was.

# Readings

Bell, Rudolph M. 1985. *Holy Anorexia*. Chicago: University of Chicago Press.

Flinders, Carol Lee. 1993. *Enduring Grace*. San Francisco: HarperSanFrancisco.

Norris, Kathleen. 1996. *The Cloister Walk*. New York: Riverhead Books. See page 254 for the passage quoted in chapter 26.

Nouwen, Henri J. M. 1992. *Life of the Beloved*. New York: Crossroads.

St. Thérèse of Lisieux, translated by John Beevers. 1989. *The Story of a Soul*. New York: Doubleday.

# Acknowledgments

To all those who helped bring this book from reminiscence to memoir, I offer a heart filled with thanks:

My son, Thomas, whose questions triggered the writing of this book; my deceased daughter, Francesca, who believed in my ability to share our story; my husband, Bill Christ, whose love nourished my writing and prodded me into finishing this book; and my three grandchildren, Thomas, Amber, and Cassandra, whose delight and exuberance keep me young.

My deceased friend Phil De Wolfe, professor extraordinaire, who taught me to love words and inspired me to write; Joan Drury, whose vision and generosity created the writing retreat for women on Lake Superior's north shore where this book took shape; and Emilie Buchwald, whose belief kept me writing when the future looked bleak.

Virginia Reiner, for the wisdom that brought the book's title to life; Christin Lore Webber, Mary Alice Hansen, Kirsten Stasney, Sonjie Johnson, Theresa King, Ranae Hanson, Catherine Watson, and Linda Sharpe, my beloved writing friends, who encouraged and sustained me during the book's many drafts.

Allison McGhee, for her class in memoir writing at Metro State University; Diane Gedymin, whose insights forced me to look deeper; and Sister Lois Eckes, OSB, for her ongoing spiritual guidance.

The New Jersey Poor Clares, especially Sister Mary Flynn, Sister Agnes Valimont, and Sister Natalie Hayes, who shared so generously of their memories; Pat McGowan of the Bordentown Library and George Hartman of the *Bordentown Register*, who helped me find facts that the monastic archives did not yield; Sister Helen Mayer, Holy Child Archivist who delved into her files immediately every time I asked; and the "Ask A Librarian" service offered by the New York Public Library.

Marilyn Carrión and Pedro Misner, for their assistance with Spanish and with Puerto Rican details; Eileen Carrión and Manuel Peredo, for their blessed hospitality; Guillermo A. Baralt, the author of a history of Banco Popular, *Tradition into the Future*, and Carmen Lidin, executive director of the Banco Popular Foundation, who provided me with access to bank archives and a lovely office to work in.

The Loft and the Jerome Foundation, for the Creative Nonfiction Award and for providing Scott Russell Sanders as my mentor and Cheri Register, Barrie Borich, Patrice Koelsch, Judith Neimi, Pamela Fletcher as sister writers; and the Minnesota State Arts Board Grant, which enabled me to receive the editorial assistance of Brigitte Frase when the book was an unwieldy manuscript.

Ann Patchett for the inspiration of her writing and her ongoing kindness; Lisa Bankoff, whose enthusiasm found exactly the right publisher; the entire Counterpoint editorial, design, production, and marketing crew, especially Liz Maguire, who nourished and strengthened the manuscript; Katherine Scott, for her insistent questions and perceptive copyediting; Laura Stine, production midwife par excellence; and Trish Wilkinson and Nicole Caputo, designer and cover artist.

# Discussion Questions for
# The Scent of God

Why do you think the author wanted to tell this story?

What does the title *The Scent of God* mean to you as a reader? Do you think this is an appropriate title for this book?

Were there sections of the story that had special impact on you and, if so, what were they and why did they affect you?

In the book, the author mentions four events as triggering her desire to become a nun: the death of the young boy on the beach, the dream after the school retreat, her mother's intervention in her social life, and the illness that triggered her promise to God. Why do you suppose these episodes affected her as they did? Were there other reasons why she would have chosen such a life? Do you think they were valid indicators of such a choice?

The author reveals the delight with which she entered the monastery and the gradual diminishment of this joy as she became anorexic. Do you think it was religious life that triggered her anorexia or might she have encountered similar compulsions had she stayed in the world?

The author reveals herself as immature both spiritually and emotionally—a seventeen-year-old in a thirty-year-old woman. Did you understand that this was "her" story or did you draw the conclusion that most nuns are immature in this way?

What is your impression of cloistered life as presented by the author? Do you think it is a valid way of life in today's world? Do you relate to her experiences there or did they leave you feeling "outside" the realm of her experience?

Why do you think the author told this story as a memoir rather than taking it into fiction? Do you think it could have been better told as fiction?

What did the author learn about her family from the years she spent going back and forth to Puerto Rico? How did her relationship with her parents change?

What were your reactions to the author's recognition of her sexuality? Of her growing attraction to Padre Vittorio? Do you think she could have or should have made other choices?

Did you have any perceptions about priests and nuns prior to reading this book and, if so, did they change after reading this story? What are your insights into the issue of celibacy and religious life?

Would a reader need to believe in God or to be a Christian to read and enjoy this story?